Sarah Seymore

Close Encounters of the Invasive Kind

Acknowledgements

First and foremost, I would like to thank my advisors Prof. Dr. Rolf Breuer and Prof. Dr. Miriam Strube for their contributions of time and ideas to my research project. I am very grateful for Prof. Dr. Breuer's motivating and inspiring guidance during the past three years. I thank Prof. Dr. Strube for giving me the opportunity to present my thesis in her colloquium and for a stimulating and insightful discussion.

I would also like to thank the third member of my defence committee, Dr. Christina Flotmann, for her time and inspirational questions. Furthermore, I am grateful to all students that discussed science fiction with me in my seminars at the University of Paderborn. Many thanks to Douglas Hallam for proofreading large parts of my thesis and to my wonderful friends for their understanding and interest in my project.

I thank my parents Klaus and Helga Goldmann for their love, for their support in all my pursuits and for their faith in me. Finally, I dedicate this thesis to my husband Wilbur. I greatly appreciate his knowledge in SF films and video games and would like to thank him for his love, encouragement and unlimited patience.

Sarah Seymore

Close Encounters of the Invasive Kind

Imperial History in Selected British Novels of Alien-Encounter Science Fiction after World War II

LIT

This book is printed on acid-free paper.

Dissertation an der Universität Paderborn, Oktober 2012

Bibliographic information published by the Deutsche Nationalbibliothek
The Deutsche Nationalbibliothek lists this publication in the Deutsche Nationalbibliografie; detailed bibliographic data are available in the Internet at http://dnb.d-nb.de.

ISBN 978-3-643-90391-4
Zugl.: Paderborn, Univ., Diss., 2012

A catalogue record for this book is available from the British Library

Klosbachstr. 107
CH-8032 Zürich
Tel. +41 (0) 44-251 75 05
Fax +41 (0) 44-251 75 06
E-Mail: zuerich@lit-verlag.ch
http://www.lit-verlag.ch

LIT VERLAG
Dr. W. Hopf Berlin
2013
Fresnostr. 2
D-48159 Münster
Tel. +49 (0) 2 51-62 03 20
Fax +49 (0) 2 51-23 19 72
E-Mail: lit@lit-verlag.de
http://www.lit-verlag.de

Distribution:
In Germany: LIT Verlag Fresnostr. 2, D-48159 Münster
Tel. +49 (0) 2 51-620 32 22, Fax +49 (0) 2 51-922 60 99,
E-mail: vertrieb@lit-verlag.de
In Austria: Medienlogistik Pichler-ÖBZ,
e-mail: mlo@medien-logistik.at
In Switzerland: B + M Buch- und Medienvertrieb,
e-mail: order@buch-medien.ch
In the UK: Global Book Marketing, e-mail: mo@centralbooks.com
In North America: International Specialized Book Services
e-mail: orders@isbs.com
e-books are available at www.litwebshop.de

Table of Contents

Introduction

> Waldron's mouth was dry. He wanted to shrink away from his eyes, cut the nerves conveying knowledge of such a reality to his brain. Not only the sheer integrated size of the alien city – for from this point one could see a mere fraction of it – but the implication that its builders must be not simply more powerful, not simply more advanced than man, but utterly and inconceivably different, made him cringe [...].[1]

The excerpt from John Brunner's *Age of Miracles* (1973) narrates the human protagonist's first encounter with an unknown alien power on Earth. For the first time, Waldron sees the city he has so often heard about, a city that symbolizes the extraterrestrials' successful conquest and the establishment of colonial rule on the planet. The sight is overwhelming for the human narrator due to the enormous size of the city and its difference from Waldron's base-reality; it seems as if a 'native' is confronted with the Western 'metropolis'. Moreover, the city indirectly characterizes its builders. Waldron immediately understands that the rulers from outer space must be intellectually and technologically superior to man and, simultaneously, they are the ungraspable Others – "utterly and inconceivably different". As a matter of fact, this scene is emblematic of works about alien invasions: it portrays those binary opposites that form the basis of numerous texts of the subgenre: human vs. alien, superior vs. inferior, advanced vs. simple, active vs. passive, Self vs. Other.

The present study discusses selected British science-fiction novels published after World War II. Generally speaking, readers of science-fiction narratives have rather homogenous ideas about what the term 'science fiction' signifies. What come to their minds are *topoi* such as spaceships, extraterrestrial life, cyborgs, *et cetera*. The *Oxford English Dictionary* defines 'science fiction' as "[i]maginative fiction based on postulated scientific discoveries or spectacular environmental changes, freq. set in the future or on

[1] John Brunner, *Age of Miracles* (London: Sidgwick & Jackson, 1973), p. 83.

other planets and involving space or time travel."[2] The earliest source of the terms is William Wilson's enquiry into "The Poetry of Science" (1851) in *A Little Earnest Book upon a Great Old Subject*. Wilson writes:

> [In science fiction,] the revealed truths of Science may be given, interwoven with a pleasing story which may itself be poetical and *true* – thus circulating a knowledge of the Poetry of Science, clothed in a garb of the Poetry of Life.[3]

However, this interpretation does not include any notion of future settings and common science-fiction topics. Various scholars[4] have made attempts to define this rather vague genre which has largely been understood as anything that editors published under the marketing slogan 'science fiction'. The term as we use it today was encorporated in popular imagination by the US-American editor Hugo Gernsback, who published a pulp magazine called *Amazing Stories. A Magazine of Scientifiction* in 1926. The modern term 'science fiction' established itself in the 1930s.[5]

As Brian Aldiss convincingly makes clear in *Billion Years Spree* (1973), the *ur-text* of science fiction is Mary Shelley's *Frankenstein* (1818),[6] although some scholars place the beginnings of the genre earlier (with Homer, Dante and Milton), or later, i.e.

---

[2] *The Oxford English Dictionary*. 2nd ed. 1989. *OED Online*. Oxford University Press. 4 Apr. 2000, http://dictionary.oed.com/cgi (2010/05/01), s.v. 'science fiction'.

[3] *Ibid.*

[4] Cf. Edmund Crispin, *Best Science Fiction Stories* (London: Faber & Faber, 1957); David Norman Samuelson, *Studies in the Contemporary American and British Science Fiction Novel* (Los Angeles, CA: University Microfilms International, 1979); Darko Suvin, *Metamorphoses of Science Fiction. On the Poetics and History of a Literary Genre* (New Haven and London: Yale University Press, 1979). For more information on the definitions of science fiction, see John Clute and Peter Nicholls (eds.), *The Encyclopedia of Science Fiction* (London: Orbit, [2]1999), s.v. 'Definitions of SF'.

[5] Cf. Manfred Nagl, *Science Fiction. Ein Segment populärer Kultur im Medien- und Produktverband* (Tübingen: Narr, 1981), p. 17.

[6] Cf. Brian W. Aldiss, *Billion Years Spree: The True History of Science Fiction* (London: Weidenfeld & Nicolson, 1973), p. 4.

with Poe, Verne, Wells or the pulp of the 1920s.[7] In the original preface of *Frankenstein*, however, Percy Shelley first announces a crucial aspect of any work of science fiction: "The event on which this fiction is founded has been supposed, by Dr. Darwin, and some of the physiological writers of Germany, as not of impossible occurrence."[8] Thus, speculations of science-fiction authors remain within the possibilities of science, albeit the reader realizes that his or her world differs from the setting of the work of fiction (cognitive estrangement).[9] The early history of British science fiction is largely defined by Herbert George Wells (1866-1946). His *œuvre* consists of approximately one hundred titles. Wells' first novel, *The Time Machine* (1895), was immediately a great success. It combines future technology, adventure romance and political reflections on the British class system. Other works that can be classified as science fiction followed, including *The Invisible Man* (1897), *The War of the Worlds* (1898) and *The First Men in the Moon* (1900). Brian Stableford argues that Wells' works – his "scientific romances" – constitute the main influence on the British science-fiction tradition which only later fused with that of the US.[10] Other notable science-fiction authors of the late nineteenth and early twentieth century are Sir Arthur Conan Doyle (1859-1930), Edward Shanks (1892-1953), Sydney Fowler Wright (1874-1965) and Matthew Phipps Shiel (1865-1947).

Already in the first half of the twentieth century, magazines played a major role in the publication of science fiction in Britain. Wells' early stories were published in general magazines, for instance in *Pearson's*, *The Strand* and the *Pall Mall Budget*. His works were then reprinted in specific science-fiction magazines, notably in Hugo Gernsback's *Amazing Stories*. In the following years, British authors such as John Beynon Harris (*alias* John

---

[7] Cf. Carl Freedman, "Hail Mary: On the Author of *Frankenstein* and the Origins of Science Fiction," in: *Science Fiction Studies* 29:2 (2002), 253.

[8] Mary Shelley, *Frankenstein; or, the Modern Prometheus*. Ed. D. L. MacDonald and Kathleen Scherf (Orchard Park, NY: Broadview, ²1999), p. 47.

[9] Darko Suvin discusses cognitive estrangement in *Metamorphoses of Science Fiction. On the Poetics and History of a Literary Genre*. His text still plays a crucial role in science-fiction criticism.

[10] Cf. Brian Stableford, *Scientific Romance in Britain 1890-1950* (New York, NY: St Martin's Press, 1985), p. 4.

Wyndham), William F. Temple and John Russel Fearn sold their stories to American magazines.[11] In the 1950s, sales of magazines rose significantly, and British publishers launched their own science-fiction magazines on the domestic market: *New Worlds* (published by Nova Publications Ltd., a company that was financed by John Wyndham and other science-fiction fans), *Authentic Science Fiction*, *Science Fantasy*, *Science Fiction Adventures* and *Nebula*.[12]

With regard to the British science-fiction novel, among the most important authors of the two decades following World War II are Brian Aldiss, Arthur C. Clarke, John Christopher and John Wyndham, all of which treated different subject matters. Hence, some of their works will be discussed in detail in this thesis. The latter author is best-known for his "middle-class catastrophe"[13] depicted in *The Day of the Triffids* (1951), *The Kraken Wakes* (1953), *The Chrysalids* (1955) and *The Midwich Cuckoos* (1957). These works portray survivors of a catastrophe who try to come to terms with a new world order after a disaster. John Christopher has been considered Wyndham's rival with regard to the disaster novel.[14] In particular Christopher's young adult science fiction is still popular today. His most famous works are the *Tripods* novels (cf. chapter 1.2), which the BBC adapted into a TV series in the 1980s. Arthur C. Clarke's fiction centres around improvements with regard to society and the human condition as such; i.e. there might be something like a higher purpose for the human race. Moreover, Clarke was fascinated with paranormal phenomena. Martin McGrath sums up: "Clarke's work is often associated with a 'sense of wonder' – moments when, through his writing, Clarke appears to open up grand vistas and rearrange our sense of our place in the universe."[15]

[11] Cf. Christopher Priest, "British Science Fiction," in: *Science Fiction: A Critical Guide*, edited by Patrick Parrinder (London: Longman, 1979), 191f.
[12] *Ibid.*, 192ff.
[13] *Ibid.*, 194.
[14] Cf. John Clute and Peter Nicholls (eds.), *The Encyclopedia of Science Fiction*, s.v. 'John Christopher'.
[15] Martin McGrath, "Against Utopia: Arthur C. Clarke and the Heterotopian Impulse," in: *Vector* 267 (2011), 11.

Films of the 1950s and 1960s offered little substance: low-budget productions bordering on horror proliferated. Titles such as *Devil Girl from Mars* (1954) and *Fire Maidens from Outer Space* (1956) reflect the pulp character of the films. What is more, the critics consider British science-fiction cinema a cheap imitation of its US-American counterpart. They also find fault with the fact that it lacks any "'organic' relation to the national culture."[16] This illustrates that British science-fiction films could not compete with the series, for instance *Dr Who* (1963-1966), *Thunderbirds* (1965-1966) and *The Tripods* (1984-1985), which have been successful since they combine "an admirably straightfaced seriousness with the British tradition of whimsical fantasy."[17] Those films that are considered worth watching are adaptations of Wyndham's novels (*Village of the Damned*, *Children of the Damned* and *The Day of the Triffids*), and films that weave references to the War into their fabric, for example *The Day the Earth Caught Fire* (1962) and *Dr Who and the Daleks* (1965).[18]

The 1960s also saw the birth of the so-called New Wave in science fiction. British authors felt the urge to liberate themselves from the American school. However difficult to define, New-Wave stories frequently are "imagistic, highly metaphoric [...], inclined more towards psychology and the soft sciences than to hard SF [...]."[19] The main figures of the New Wave are Brian W. Aldiss, J. G. Ballard and Michael Moorcock. Aldiss clearly went beyond the imitation of American authors; his works are famous for their focus on characters and character constellations, as well as for their explorations of 'inner space'. Apart from numerous novels and several collections of short fiction, Aldiss published various works of non-fiction,[20] which demonstrates his extensive expertise in the

---

[16] Cf. I.Q. Hunter (ed.), *British Science Fiction Cinema* (London and New York, NY: Routledge, 1999), p. 6.
[17] *Ibid.*
[18] For more information, see I.Q. Hunter's chapter on *The Day the Earth Caught Fire*, in: *ibid.*, pp. 99ff.
[19] John Clute and Peter Nicholls (eds.), *The Encyclopedia of Science Fiction*, s.v. 'New Wave'.
[20] The most important ones are *Billion Years Spree: The True History of Science Fiction* (1973), a revised and extended version, *Trillion Years Spree: The History of Science Fiction* (1986), *The Detached Retina: Aspects of SF and Fantasy*

field. Ballard's works deal with the near future, a future that is shaped by drugs, breaking taboos, sexual desire and the media. A central text of the New Wave is Ballard's *Crash* (1973), in which teenagers gain sexual pleasure from watching road accidents. The novel can be read as "an allegory for the dark ways in which technology has become wedded to human essence."[21] Ballard's experimental novel *The Atrocity Exhibition* (1970) caused an outright scandal since it gives a 'scientific report' on how Ronald Reagan's face evokes images of a penile erection.[22] Michael Moorcock, who edited *New Worlds* between 1964 and 1971, supported the publication of stories in the spirit of the New Wave. He usually wrote his novels within three days and holds that, due to the New Wave, there has been an increase in quality writing since science-fiction writers have become more conscious of structure and form.[23] The most successful films of the 1960s and 1970s were *2001: A Space Odyssey* (1968), *A Clockwork Orange* (1971) and *The Man Who Fell to Earth* (1976). Subsequently, British science-fiction film has often blended with horror, as in Ridley Scott's masterpiece, *Alien* (1979), Paul W. S. Anderson's *Event Horizon* (1997) and Danny Boyle's *28 Days Later* (2002).[24]

Since the 'British Boom' of the 1990s, science fiction has become more popular than ever before, and it is an impossible task to give a complete overview of contemporary authors within the

---

(1995) and his autobiography, *Bury My Heart at W.H. Smith's: A Writing Life* (1990).

[21] Tom Sykes, "Ideascape: How the British New Wave of Science Fiction Addressed the Social, Political, and Intellectual Themes of the 1960s and 1970s," in: *Foundation* 39:110 (2010), 74.

[22] Cf. *ibid.*

[23] Cf. "Science Fiction Now and Tomorrow," the *Guardian* books podcast of 2012-01-06, available on http://www.guardian.co.uk/books/audio/2012/jan/06/books-podcast-science-fiction-now-tomorrow (2012-06-27). For more information on the New Wave, see Colin Greenland, *The Entropy Exhibition: Michael Moorcock and the UK "New Wave" in Science Fiction* (London: Routledge & Kegan Paul, 1983). Noteworthy New-Wave anthologies are Langdon Jones (ed.), *The New SF: An Original Anthology of Modern Speculative Fiction* (London: Hutchinson, 1969) and Norman Spinrad (ed.), *The New Tomorrows* (New York, NY: Belmont, 1971).

[24] Cf. "British Science Fiction Cinema," available on http://www.yume.co.uk/british-science-fiction-cinema (2012-06-27).

scope of this thesis. The most celebrated British science-fiction writers are Douglas Adams (1952-2001) and Terry Pratchett (Sir Terence David John Pratchett, OBE, *1984). Adam's satirical sequence of novels, *A Hitchhiker's Guide to the Galaxy* (1979-1992), earned him global fame. His narratives depict strange and absurd worlds which indirectly criticize today's society. Adams also wrote fourteen screenplays for the BBC series *Dr Who*. Terry Pratchett is the author of about forty *Discworld* novels that feature a flat disc-shaped world supported on the backs of four elephants that stand on a giant turtle. Much like Adams, Pratchett uses his fiction to parody political and social issues. One of them, *Snuff* (published in October 2011), was the fastest-selling adult hardback novel by a British author since records began.[25] Outstanding British authors of hard science fiction are Alastair Preston Reynolds (*1966), whose far-future scenarios recall the space operas of the twentieth century, and Stephen Baxter (*1957). Baxter's works deal primarily with time travel (cf. chapter 1.3), alternate history and evolutionary biology. In the field of military science fiction, the *Warhammer* and *Warhammer 40,000* authors Dan Abnett (*1965), Ian Watson (*1943) and Alex Steward (*alias* Sandy Mitchell) reach a wide readership.

With regard to soft science fiction, Ian M. Banks' (*1954) novels featuring far-future settings enjoy considerable popularity. In contrast to Banks, Chris Beckett's (*1955) and Jeff Noon's (*1957) fictions are concerned with the near future in domestic urban settings, and it seems that these authors try to anticipate social rather than technological changes. In the UK, science-fiction associations such as the British Science Fiction Association (BSFA, founded in 1958) and the Science Fiction Foundation (SFF, founded in 1970) give awards, for example the Arthur C. Clarke Award, to remarkable authors, organize conventions, provide research facilities and publish peer-reviewed journals. Consequently, they increase the popularity of British authors and enhance the marketability of their books.

Noteworthy UK writers of short science fiction are – among others – Stephen Baxter (*1957), Mary Gentle (*1956), Nicola

[25] Cf. "Science Fiction Now and Tomorrow," the *Guardian* books podcast of 2012-01-06.

Griffith (*1960), Kim Newman (*1959), Paul McAuley (*1955) and Christopher McKenzie Priest (John Luther Novak, *1943). There are, of course, also female science-fiction novelists in Britain, although few of them are under contract with a UK publisher: Gwyneth Jones (*1952, cf. chapter 3.3), Tanith Lee (*1947), Justina Robson (*1968) and Liz Williams (*1965), for instance. It seems that many of the female writers challenge the definitions of the genre; they produce works that merge science fiction and fantasy or science fiction and steampunk.[26] This might be a reason why their books are rather rare in the science-fiction sections of bookstores. In fact, their way of stretching the fringes of science fiction can be called emblematic of the twenty-first century: more than ever before, science fiction mixes with other genres, so that the categories of genres and sub-genres eventually soften. Or, as Lauren Beukes, whose novel *Zoo City* (2010) won the Arthur C. Clarke Award in 2011, puts it: "[It's] not a bad idea [that] everything gets a sub-genre and reinvents itself all the time."[27] Another important development in the science-fiction community is the use of social media. Authors regularly post news and little stories on Twitter or Facebook, which enables them to advertise their works and establish a closer relationship with their readers.

Discussing narratives of alien-encounter science fiction against the background of British history and viewing them through the lens of colonial and postcolonial debates require some preliminary remarks. Colonial discourse analysis emerged in the 1950s, with Aimé Céaire's *Discourse on Colonialism* (1950) and Frantz Fanon's *Black Skins, White Masks* (1952). In 1978, the publication of Edward W. Said's *Orientalism* was a huge step forward for colonial discourse analysis. The field of studies examines the nature of the colonial subject as represented in works of literature, anthropology and history. In this respect, the subject matters of colonial

---

[26] For more information on female science-fiction authors, see Cheryl Morgan, "Women SF Writers: An Endangered Species?" in: *Vector* 269 (2012), 4-6. Steampunk is a subgenre of science fiction in which events take place against the social and technological background of the Victorian era. Cf. John Clute and Peter Nicholls (eds.), *The Encyclopedia of Science Fiction*, s.v. 'steampunk'.

[27] Cf. "Science Fiction Now and Tomorrow," the *Guardian* books podcast of 2012-01-06.

discourse analysis and postcolonial studies overlap. 'Postcolonialism'[28] does not necessarily signify the period of time that follows colonialism. Instead, the prefix 'post-' implies going beyond the subsequent term. Hence, postcolonialism conceptually exceeds colonialism. Stephen Slemon sums up the different usages of 'postcolonialism':

> It has been used as a way of ordering a critique of totalizing forms of Western historicism; as a portmanteau term for a retooled notion of 'class', as a subset of both postmodernism and post-structuralism (and conversely, as the condition from which those two structures of cultural logic and cultural critique themselves are seen to emerge); as the name for a condition of nativist longing in post-independence national groupings; as a cultural marker of non-residency for a Third-World intellectual cadre; as the inevitable underside of a fractured and ambivalent discourse of colonialist power; as an oppositional for of 'reading practice'; and [...] as the name for a category of 'literary' activity which sprang from a new and welcome political energy going on within what used to be called 'Commonwealth' literary studies.[29]

Thus, postcolonialism is highly heterogeneous (the various colonial encounters differed tremendously), and the key concepts of the field are just as manifold. They include the depiction of indigenous peoples, primitivism, dislocation, exile, race, whiteness, ethnicity, nativism, hybridity and many more. Postcolonial writing contains texts that have been produced in the former colonies of Europe,

---

[28] Postcolonialism is occasionally spelt with a hyphen in order to distinguish between post-colonialism as a field of studies and postcolonialism in general. However, the distinction seems to have lost its importance since scholars use the two terms interchangeably. The body of literature on postcolonialism is enormous. For a comprehensive bibliography, see http://www.postcolonialweb.org/poldiscourse/bibl.html (2012-07-05).

[29] Stephen Slemon, "The Scramble for Postcolonialism," *De-Scribing Empire. Post-Colonialism and Textuality*, ed. by Chris Tiffin and Alan Lawson (London: Routledge, 1994), pp. 16f.

and scholars discuss whether the works of authors from Australia, Canada and the USA should be included. Nowadays, various issues of postcolonialism centre around globalization, i.e. around the question in what way world-wide economic and cultural developments influence individuals. Postcolonialism might raise awareness of and strengthen our solidarity with peoples that used to be termed 'Other', such as the population of Third-World countries.

While the connections between empire and science fiction have been discussed in numerous books and articles (especially with regard to H.G. Wells), it is only recently that scholars have started to employ the term 'postcolonial science fiction'.[30] Publications on postcolonial science fiction deal primarily with the works of authors from formerly colonized countries; the postcolonial nature of the text is thus established by an extradiegetic element. The first collection of "postcolonial science fiction and fantasy" is *So Long Been Dreaming* (2004), edited by Nalo Hopkinson and Uppinder Mehan.[31] It contains nineteen short stories that were all written by people of non-Western origin, for example from India, Mexico and the Caribbean. Moreover, in her recently published study *Postcolonialism and Science Fiction* (2012),[32] Jessica Langer discusses works by Canadian and Japanese authors as well as the online game *World of Warcraft*, and Eric D. Smith analyses works of

---

[30] Cf. for example Gerald Gaylard, "Postcolonial Science Fiction: *The Desert Planet*," in: Ericka Hoagland and Reema Sarwal (eds.), *Science Fiction, Imperialism and the Third World: Essays on Postcolonial Literature and Film* (Jefferson, NC: McFarland, 2010), pp. 21-36; James H. Thrall, "Postcolonial Science Fiction? Science, Religion and the Transformation of Genre in Amitav Ghosh's *The Calcutta Chromosome*," in: *Literature & Theology: An International Journal of Religion, Theory, and Culture* 23.3 (2009): 289-302; Grace L. Dillon, "Miindiwag and Indigenous Diaspora: Eden Robinson's and Celu Amberstone's Forays into 'Postcolonial' Science Fiction and Fantasy," in: *Extrapolation: A Journal of Science Fiction and Fantasy* 48.2 (2007): 219-243; Claire Chambers, "Postcolonial Science Fiction: Amitav Ghosh's *The Calcutta Chromosome*," in: *Journal of Commonwealth Literature* 38.1 (2003): 57-72; Michelle Reid, "Postcolonial Science Fiction," available on http://www.sffoundation.org/publications/essays/reid.html (2012-04-06).

[31] Nalo Hopkinson and Uppinder Mehan (eds.), *So Long Been Dreaming: Postcolonial Science Fiction and Fantasy* (Vancouver, B.C.: Arsenal Pulp Press, 2004).

[32] Jessica Langer, *Postcolonialism and Science Fiction* (Basingstoke: Palgrave Macmillan, 2012).

science fiction that deal with the Third World in *Globalization, Utopia and Postcolonial Science Fiction: New Maps of Hope* (2012).[33] Naturally, analysing postcolonial science fiction on the basis of authors from those countries that were colonized by Europe is a legitimate and fruitful approach. Nevertheless, I have selected works by British authors that depict colonial and postcolonial concepts in the texts themselves. In fact, in the 1950s and 1960s, when few scholars were engaged in postcolonial discourse, science fiction author such as Arthur C. Clarke, John Wyndham and Brian W. Aldiss already wove their nation's imperial history into the fabrics of their fictions.

With regard to terminology, I argue that science fiction becomes postcolonial science fiction when it deals with the effects of colonialism on a species or culture. Generic tropes of postcolonial science fiction are territorial conquests, the establishment and institutionalisation of imperial rule, misuse of power and social change, representation of the subjects by the imperial ruler,[34] resistance and various residues from colonial encounter such as displacement (which is primarily temporal – not spatial – in science fiction, i.e. individuals or entire species become anachronisms) and new identities (through hybridity and mimicry, for example). Furthermore, the postcolonial element manifest itself in the language of the texts since the authors take up the language of imperial politics and, simultaneously, reveal the hollowness of designations such as "overlords", "masters" and "halfcastes".[35]

---

[33] Eric D. Smith, *Globalization, Utopia and Postcolonial Science Fiction: New Maps of Hope* (Basingstoke: Palgrave Macmillan, 2012).

[34] Those who used to be oppressed in times of Empire (the indigenous peoples of Africa or India, for example) are not represented any more in the selected novels, but the reader immediately understands that their role is projected on humans. Mankind as a whole finds itself in the position of the subject race and, thereby, the novels talk back to former imperialist nations.

[35] Nowadays, this process works conversely: journalists take up science fiction tropes as stylistic devices when they report about politics. For numerous examples, see Marleen S. Barr, "Fantastic Language/Political Reporting: The Postcolonial Science Fiction Illocutionary Force Is with Us," in: Masood Ashraf Raja, Jason W. Ellis and Swaralipi Nandi (eds.), *The Postnational Fantasy: Essays on Postcolonialism, Cosmopolitics and Science Fiction* (Jefferson, NC: McFarland, 2011): 188-210.

For my analysis, I have chosen thirteen novels which were all written by British authors. This selection is a reaction to the widespread belief that works about invasions from outer space are first and foremost Hollywood productions. In the selected texts, aliens come to Earth and dominate over mankind. Earth becomes an invaded planet and the extraterrestrials exercise power over the natives and frequently alter their subjects' spaces, bodies and cultures. Naturally, a human colony on another planet could just as well be invaded by aliens, or humans might conquer alien planets and exploit them. However, the focus of my study does not allow for an in-depth analysis of these themes.

In addition, the novels discussed were published after World War II, i.e. after the collapse of the British Empire. Nonetheless, the common foundation of all texts is the history of the British Empire – perhaps the most typical or exemplary of all European colonial empires – which still serves as a crucial background for British authors of the genre.[36] The main areas of interest are five themes: (1) the form of rule the extraterrestrials establish on Earth, (2) the depiction of the alien Other, (3) technology as an agent of power, (4) human resistance and (5) the portrayal of decolonization and postcolonial guilt. In the following, I will introduce the interfaces between alien-encounter science fiction and colonial and postcolonial discourse on the basis of these themes.

With regard to imperial rule, the events depicted in the novels I have chosen for my analysis bear parallels to Britain's imperial past and narratives of Empire. Generally speaking, British imperialism began with the colonies in North America in the sixteenth century, i.e. even before the 'kingdom of Great Britain' was established (following the Acts of Union, 1706-1707), and well before the concept of 'empire' as we understand it today emerged. British imperialism was at its height in the second half of the nineteenth and the beginning of the twentieth century. In 1922, the British Empire had a population of 458 million and covered an area of 33.67 million square kilometres. Thus, approximately one in four people fell under the rule of the Empire. Colonial administration and policy were controlled from the Colonial Office (initially

[36] Cf. Paul Kincaid and Niall Harrison, *British Science Fiction & Fantasy: Twenty Years and Two Surveys*, pp. 59ff.

merely a part of the Home Office) and the Board of Trade; the former became a separate institution in 1854. With regard to the form of governance, the British exercised power through trading companies, indirect rule, settler rule and condominium governments. Trading companies run by private businessmen were granted territories to administer and resources to exploit. Perhaps the most famous trading company was the East India Company (founded in 1600) which traded tea, salt, cotton, silk, opium and other goods with the Indian subcontinent. The officers of the company accrued substantial riches, and the company also had a lobby in the English parliament. Company rule in India officially ended with the establishment of the British Raj in 1858. Parallel to this, there were various trading companies on the African continent. For instance, the Imperial British East Africa Company ruled over Kenya and Uganda, and the British South Africa Company operated in what are now Zimbabwe, Zambia and Malawi. Trading companies did business in accordance with a charter from the Crown, which allowed them to cheat indigenous leaders into signing over their sovereignty to the British, to introduce their own system of taxation, and to discriminate against and exploit local labourers. The British government finally decided to take over control as the companies in Africa proved unprofitable and unable to administer their vast territories.

Employing indigenous leaders to rule a colony on behalf of a European imperial power is referred to as indirect rule. Notably in Africa, the British appointed chiefs that were to exercise power over their fellow countrymen, a strategy that was intended to save costs and increase profits. However, indirect rule was bound to fail for several reasons: the indigenous peoples did not respect leaders that had been appointed by the British, many of the chiefs were corrupt, and the creation of new areas of governance fuelled ethnic tensions. As to the latter, tribal wars actually served the purpose of the Crown since they hampered struggles for independence. Indirect rule also affected large parts of Asia, for example India and Burma. Those territories that were inhabited by a significant number of European settlers fell under settler rule. For instance in southern and eastern Africa, settlers from the Netherlands, Britain, Portugal and Germany claimed arable land ("Crown property") and the right to rule the natives. Around 1900, the settler colonies in Africa fought for their independence and set up their own administrative and political institutions. A condominium is a colonized territory governed by two imperial powers. From 1899 to 1956, the Sudan was an Anglo-Egyptian condominium. However, after the outbreak of a civil war, Britain and Egypt withdrew from the country in 1956. In addition, from 1906 to 1980 the British and the French shared sovereignty over the New Hebrides, which led to a subdivision into Anglophone and Francophone territories. Whenever the British were reluctant to spend money on colonizing territories, they formed protectorates, i.e. they guaranteed diplomatic and military support and, in return, had their say in foreign affairs. British protectorates were spread all over the globe: Barbados in the Atlantic, Bahrain, Kuwait and Qatar in the Middle East, Afghanistan, Brunei, Malaya and the Maldives in Asia, Kenya, Sierra Leone and Uganda in Africa, and Tonga, the Solomon Islands and the Cook Islands in Oceania. Similar to protectorates, dominions enjoyed complete legislative authority and the recognition as separate states. Prior to 1939, Canada, Australia, New Zealand, South Africa, Eire and Newfoundland had the status of dominions. The term 'dominion' was, however, later replaced by 'member of the Commonwealth'.[37]

Literary production of the period of imperialism is interspersed with facts of the Empire. As Edward Said points out in *Culture and Imperialism*: "[W]hen we come to Kipling, Conrad, Arthur Conan Doyle, Rider Haggard, R. L. Stevenson, George Orwell, Joyce Cary, E. M. Forster, and T. E. Lawrence, the empire is everywhere a crucial setting."[38] In the narratives, the colonies are associated with exotic territories and peoples, unknown riches and sexual adventure. In addition, the romances of Empire also illustrate that a colony might serve as a *locus* where Europeans can regain those values that they have apparently lost, for instance masculinity and chivalry.

---

[37] Cf. *Encyclopædia Britannica. Encyclopædia Britannica Online.* Encyclopædia Britannica Inc., 2012, http://www.britannica.com (2012-03-25), s.v. 'colonialism, Western'.

[38] Edward W. Said, *Culture and Imperialism* (London: Vintage, 1994).

Science fiction is likewise characterized by ideals of adventure, expansion and wealth. As to its historical background, John Rieder explains:

> Scholars largely (though not universally) agree that the period of the most fervid imperialist expansion in the late nineteenth century is also the crucial period for the emergence of the genre [...]. Science fiction comes into visibility first in those countries most heavily involved in imperialist projects – France and England – and then gains popularity in the United States, Germany, and Russia as those countries also enter into more and more serious imperial competition."[39]

This is due to the fact that colonialism and science fiction share various paradigms such as the conquest of territories and encounters with other cultures. Rieder's argument does not seem entirely convincing, though: the main reason for the emergence of science fiction must certainly be the development of science and technology, which then advances colonialism. Moreover, Rieder describes the connection of science fiction and colonialism in a way that the latter "is part of the genre's texture, a persistent, important component of its displaced references to history, its engagement in ideological production, and its construction of the possible and imaginable."[40] Hence, according to Rieder science fiction makes use of the past in order to develop fictive future scenarios. In fact, early works of alien-encounter science fiction do reflect the past by imagining future worlds in which structures of hierarchy and power are distorted or reversed. The most famous example is perhaps Herbert G. Wells' *The War of the Worlds* (1898), in which an imperialist nation – England – becomes invaded by extraterrestrials that intend to colonize Earth and destroy large areas in the South.[41]

---

[39] John Rieder, *Colonialism and the Emergence of Science Fiction* (Middleton, CT: Wesleyan University Press, 2008), pp. 2f.
[40] *Ibid*, p. 15.
[41] Cf. Herbert G. Wells, *The War of the Worlds* (New York, NY: Barnes and Noble Classics, 2004).

The second *sujet* I am going to discuss within the framework of both colonial and postcolonial discourse is the Other, i.e. the antagonist that either the invaded or the invader is confronted with. Numerous philosophers[42] have deliberated this phenomenon, which is referred to as 'alterity'. Alterity (from Latin *alter*, which means 'other') explores the reciprocal relationship between two identities. Generally speaking, it signifies that we construct our own identity as distinguished from somebody else. Delimitation criteria are uncountable: the body (sex, skin colour, *et cetera*), origin and nationality, education and profession, age, taste, wealth, political orientation, lifestyle and many more. In colonial and postcolonial discourse, the Other is defined as an inhabitant of those countries that were formerly colonized by European nations (and Homi Bhabha adds immigrants from those colonies).[43] Yet, when we reverse the point of view, the imperial invaders can also be classified as the Other. This perspective seems to dominate in alien-encounter science fiction: the natives of Earth are confronted with an unknown and powerful enemy, the alien Other. The alien Other naturally plays a central role in the subgenre, a theory that can be deduced from Carl D. Malmgren's definition of alien-encounter science fiction:

> Alien-encounter SF involves the introduction of sentient alien beings into the actantial system of the fictional universe; one or more of these actants are nonhuman or subhuman or superhuman. Like SF in general, this type of fiction may feature a number of dif-

[42] Cf. Martin Heidegger, *Sein und Zeit* (*Being and Time*, 1927); Edmund Husserl, *Cartesianische Meditationen. Eine Einleitung in die Phänomenologie* (*Cartesian Meditations: An Introduction to Phenomenology*, 1931); Jean-Paul Sartre, *L'être et le néant. Essai d'ontologie phénoménologique* (*Being and Nothingness: An Essay on Phenomenological Ontology*, 1943); Emmanuel Levinas, *Totalité et infini* (*Totality and Infinity*, 1961); Jacques Derrida, "Violence et métaphysique. Essai sur la pensée d'Emmanuel Lévinas" ("Violence and Metaphysics: An Essay on the Thought of Emmanuel Levinas," 1964).

[43] Cf. Homi Bhabha, *The Location of Culture* (London: Routledge, 1994), p. 5

> ferent novums, but in it the actantial system predominates.[44]

By referring to the alien as an "actant", Malmgren makes clear that it is not only a character in the narrative but a crucial element within it, an element upon which the narrative is constructed. He also holds that the depiction of the alien and its juxtaposition to man lies at the core of the genre: "The alien actant and its human counterpart occupy the story's center stage, and an exploration of their respective qualities is the *sine qua non* of the fiction."[45] Moreover, Malmgren gives a typology of the alien: it is a "technologically transformed version of the Self" such as a cyborg, a mutant, a "monstrous alter ego", an artificially created being, or an extraterrestrial, which is perhaps the most common type of the alien Other.[46] My selection of novels deals primarily with the latter form; however, in Brian Aldiss' *Non-Stop* (cf. chapter 3.2), the aliens are remote descendents of human beings that have evolved away from man, and in Fred Hoyle's and John Eliot's *Andromeda* novels (cf. chapter 2.2), scientists create an enhanced human female from a blueprint from another galaxy. What all these types of aliens eventually have in common is that they are viewed in comparison to human beings. They define what is human and, especially in a colonial context, hold a mirror up to mankind.

A central issue for this work is that the representation of the Other is used to establish hierarchy: much like Western conquerors in colonial history, the alien invaders in science fiction are represented as superior to their human colonial subjects. Interestingly, the depictions of humans in alien-encounter science fiction and the image the so-called 'Orientalists' have produced of the Arab world bear striking parallels: especially in texts from the nineteenth century, the Orientals are said to be technologically and mentally inferior to Europeans, they are rather dumb, and they are considered either passive or fatalistic in the fights for what they consider a good course. Briefly, the Orient is entirely different from the West.

---

[44] Carl D. Malmgren, "Self and Other in SF: Alien Encounters," in: *Science Fiction Studies* 20:1 (1993), 15.
[45] *Ibid.*, 16.
[46] Cf. *ibid.*, 15f.

However, the resources of the area are precious, and exploiting them would be economically beneficial for any potential invader. Perhaps the most famous work on the West's representation is Edward W. Said's *Orientalism* (1978).[47] *Orientalism* is generally dedicated to the study of representation of the Other, and it illustrates how representation is (mis)used to consolidate European supremacy. Said explains that the Orient does not represent itself but is represented by the West, for instance by eighteenth- and nineteenth-century writers such as Silvestre de Sacy, Ernest Renan, Caussin de Perceval, Karl Marx, Edward William Lane, François René de Chateaubriand, Gustave Flaubert and Richard Francis Burton. He comes to the conclusion that our perception of the Orient is "filtered", i.e. unreal, fragmented and untrue. He also claims that the legacy of those writers was taken up in the twentieth century, and that their image of the Orient still controls knowledge about the Other today. Thereby, the author demonstrates how contemporary cultural discussions are inevitably linked to notions of former imperialism and hegemony.[48] The antithesis of Orientalism is Occidentalism, i.e. the portrayal of the West by the East. Radical political leaders such as Mao Zedong in China, Kemal Atatürk in Turkey, or Peter the Great in Russia paint negative pictures of Europe and the US in order to support their anti-Western policies. They generally set themselves apart from the West and try to estab-

---

[47] Before Said, Frantz Fanon and Aimé Césaire studied the nature of the inferior and exotic Other. Said mentions these scholars, who partly pre-empt his theses, in *Orientalism*. However, it was only after the publication of Said's work that scholars became interested in colonial discourse in the Orient as well as in general.

[48] Cf. Edward W. Said, *Orientalism* (New York, NY: Vintage, 1979). As to criticism, the figure Edward W. Said has polarized academia and public as much as his works; critical responses ranged from eulogies on his books to scholarly criticism and even to death threats. Yet, a long list of reviews on Said's work would be out of place here. For more information, see Bill Ashcroft and Pal Ahluwalia, *Edward Said* (London and New York, NY: Routledge, ²2001), pp. 69-77; Conor McCarthy, *The Cambridge Introduction to Edward Said*, pp. 123-138; Peter Childs, Jean Jacques Weber and Patrick William, *Post-Colonial Theory and Literatures. African, Caribbean and South Asian* (Trier: WVT, 2006), pp. 69f. Articles by and about Edward Said and his works are also collected in an online archive on http://www.edwardsaid.org/?q=node/1 (2012-03-11).

lish a superior position by stressing Western 'sins', notably materialism and infidelity.[49]

In alien-encounter science fiction, the juxtaposition of the Self and the Other happens on the basis of a whole range of paradigms that characterize the extraterrestrial and that simultaneously allow conclusions regarding the definition of the Self, i.e. of what is human. As exemplified in the excerpt from Brunner's *Age of Miracles*, the depictions of aliens and humans fall back on those dichotomies that were employed in colonial discourses and that served as a 'measure' to evaluate and to differentiate oneself from the 'natives': civilized vs. savage, rational vs. superstitious, intelligent vs. ignorant, mature vs. childlike and familiar vs. alien. Additionally, after the takeover of a territory, its indigenous population might either be actively planning and executing resistance or they could be passive. In science fiction, passivity and subjugation are frequently caused by fear, by admiration of the alien beings, or by brainwashing. In this context, I would like to point out that labels such as 'savage' and 'civilized' or 'active' and 'passive' are to be understood as historical categories in my analysis; they are by no means social assessments.

The binary opposites employed to describe the Other are generated by what John Rieder refers to as "the colonial gaze". Rieder's term "colonial gaze" is borrowed from Laura Mulvey's "cinematic gaze" in her essay "Visual Pleasure and Narrative Cinema" (1975), and it constitutes a cognitive framework to describe the position of two parties within a colonial context. Mainly, the "colonial gaze distributes knowledge and power to the subject who looks, while denying or minimizing access to power for its object, the one looked at."[50] Thus, invader and invaded are strictly separated by colonial politics and, as soon as the invader observes the invaded, he or she exercises power over the Other. According to Rieder, this

---

[49] For more information on Occidentalism, see James G. Carrier (ed.), *Occidentalism: Images of the West* (Oxford *et al.*: Oxford University Press, 1995); Couze Venn, *Occidentalism: Modernity and Subjectivity* (London *et al.*: SAGE Publications, 2000); Ian Buruma and Avishai Margalit, *Occidentalism: The West in the Eyes of its Enemies* (New York, NY: Penguin, 2004); Ian Buruma and Avishai Margalit, *Occidentalism: A Short History of Anti-Westernism* (London: Atlantic Books, 2004).

[50] John Rieder, *Colonialism and the Emergence of Science Fiction*, p. 7.

phenomenon is one of the ideological prerequisites of imperialism, and it reoccurs in emergent science fiction. By giving several examples of the colonial gaze in early works of the genre, Rieder explains its various effects. For instance in *The War of the Worlds*, the perspectives of colonizer and colonized are reversed:

> Wells switches the position of his white Western narrator from its accustomed, dominant, colonizing one to that of the dominated indigenous inhabitant of the colonized land. This strategy makes not only the political, but also the cognitive effects of the framework of colonial relations visible in a tellingly distorted way. The narrator no longer occupies the position usually accorded to the scientific observer, but instead finds himself in that role historically occupied by those who are looked at and theorized about rather than those who look, analyze, and theorize.[51]

Hence, narratives of science fiction reverse the perspectives of observer and the one observed: the human narrator becomes the subject of the alien invaders. What is more, the idea that the Martian invaders are superior to the natives on Earth makes them appear anachronistic. Likewise, human beings seem to be 'behind' or 'primitive' in comparison to the aliens, which is a parallel to the Victorian anthropologists' depiction of indigenous peoples from the colonies. The 'savage' was considered a "remnant of the past"[52] that could be observed, studied and classified by the 'civilized'. Simultaneously, it confronts the latter with his or her own savage past, an idea that is developed in Joseph Conrad's *Heart of Darkness* (1899),[53] Henry Rieder Haggard's works, and in several novels by H. G. Wells and Jules Verne that deal with journeys in time, in space, under the sea or to the centre of Earth.

Throughout his work, Rieder exemplifies the critical potential of the colonial gaze. In science fiction, it can question concepts

---

[51] *Ibid.*
[52] *Ibid.*
[53] Joseph Conrad, *Heart of Darkness & Other Stories* (Ware: Wordsworth Classics, 1999).

such as hierarchy, truth and certainty. In addition, it might play with the difference between Self and Other by illustrating that the boundaries are not always clear-cut. For example in Arthur Conan Doyle's *The Lost World* (1912), the English scientist Professor Challenger and his *entourage* undertake a journey to an isolated plateau inhabited by ape-men. Ironically, the professor closely resembles the king of the ape-men, as Rieder points out.[54] Here, Conan Doyle undermines notions of "identity and difference between the observer and the observed that permeat[e] colonial discourse."[55] The same mechanisms occur in contemporary alien-encounter science fiction, i.e. whenever the extraterrestrial invaders imitate man's colonial past or refuse to set themselves apart from human beings. To further this idea, the colonial gaze can (painfully) reveal the nature of the 'civilized' Europeans. In Frank Challice Constable's *The Curse of Intellect* (1895), a scientist from London travels to Africa and brings back an ape "whom he has taught to dress and speak like a human being, and who, in the mode of *Frankenstein*, eventually murders his keeper."[56] Again, this implies a reversal of perspective: the Other looks at and imitates human beings and thereby shows what the latter are really like. Furthermore, according to Rieder, Constable's novel criticizes previous anthropologists' theories of a crucial difference between man and other mammals.[57] To summarize, the colonial gaze deals with "looking and being looked at across the social divide formed by colonial political economy,"[58] and it can be utilized as a powerful means of criticism.

In alien-encounter science fiction, a position of superiority is almost always gained through highly advanced technology; the species with the most powerful weapons and marvellous spaceships usually dominates over others. Therefore, perhaps the most important dichotomy in alien-encounter science fiction is technologically advanced vs. 'simple', or, as Istvan Csicsery-Ronay puts it, "the powers in conflict must test technology as a basis for sover-

[54] Cf. John Rieder, *Colonialism and the Emergence of Science Fiction*, p. 59.
[55] *Ibid.*
[56] *Ibid.*, p. 102.
[57] *Ibid.*
[58] *Ibid.*, p. 152.

eignty."[59] In fact, technology as a prerequisite for imperial expansion is directly taken up in science fiction, especially in works of so-called 'hard science fiction'. Hard science fiction highlights scientific accuracy and details. It creates scenarios that appear realistic because the authors give much background information on physics, biology, astronomy, weapon technology, *et cetera* – information that is supposed to function as "referents" in the creation of a fictive universe. Frederic Jameson explains:

> [Hard science fiction] necessarily involves the construction of something like a 'referent', the outside reality which the reader is called upon to project *out there* somehow, even if the point is to be, as with Lem, that that 'referent' is undecidable and unknowable.[60]

Apart from Stanisław Lem, Stephen Baxter (whose novel *Timelike Infinity* is discussed in chapter 1.3), Isaac Asimov, Greg Bear, Gregory Benford and, to a certain extent, Jules Verne are associated with hard science fiction.[61]

Analogously, achievements in science and technology have defined the hierarchical position of a nation in history. From the 1780s onwards, Britain experienced an enormous increase in innovation. The technological revolution affected communication, extraction of raw materials, manufacturing processes, weaponry, medicine and other fields.[62] With regard to science and empire,

---

[59] Istvan Csicsery-Ronay, "Science Fiction and Empire," in: *Science Fiction Studies* 30:2 (2003), 241.

[60] Frederic Jameson, "Shifting Contexts of Science-Fiction Theory," in: *Science Fiction Studies* 14:2 (1987), 245. Italics by F. Jameson.

[61] For more information on hard science fiction, see for example Kathryn Cramer, "Hard Science Fiction," in: Edward James (ed.) and Farah Mendlesohn (ed. and introd.), *The Cambridge Companion to Science Fiction* (Cambridge *et al.*: Cambridge University Press, 2003): 186-196; David G. Hartwell, "Hard Science Fiction," in: *The New York Review of Science Fiction* 62 (1993): 1, 8-13; David N. Samuelson, "On Hard Science Fiction," in: *Science Fiction Studies* 20:2 (1993): 145-156.

[62] For more information on Victorian science, see for example Bernard Lightman (ed.), *Victorian Science in Context* (Chicago and London: University of Chicago Press, 1997); Peter Allan Dale, *In Pursuit of a Scientific Culture: Science, Art, and Society in the Victorian Age* (Madison, WI: University of Wisconsin Press,

military power as well as the mastering of time and space proved to be key factors for the annexation of territories and the domination of indigenous peoples. Naturally, in times of imperial expansion, conquest and defence against resistance largely depended on military technology. Examples of nineteenth-century innovations are faster loading rifles and more advanced automated machine guns. Cannons became more accurate and powerful, and ammunition with increased ballistic potential was developed. Weapon technology even shaped political consciousness as it was generally considered a crucial indicator of the 'level of civilization' and social development. Likewise, in alien-encounter science fiction military power serves as a tool of domination: extraterrestrial invaders make use of heat rays, singularity cannons, atomic disintegrators, phasers, force fields, plasma weapons, magnetic projectile weapons and so forth. They also employ brainwashing technologies and highly elaborate means of surveillance.[63] The idea that new military technology might alter warfare as we know it particularly influenced works published during the heyday of the British Empire and after the launch of atom bombs against Hiroshima and Nagasaki. This is actually one of many examples of how science fiction weaves historical facts into its fabric.

To come back to British imperialism, an important breakthrough was the communications revolution in the mid-nineteenth century, which had a deep impact on people's perception of space and time. Before, distance had caused significant problems with regard to the administration of colonies in the New World, for example. Settler colonies in the Americas and the West Indies could hardly be monitored and ruled directly from Europe, and there was

---

1989); David Knight, *The Age of Science: The Scientific World-View in the Nineteenth Century* (New York, NY: Blackwell, 1986). The number of books that explore the connections between science and empire continually grows. In "Science and the British Empire", Mark Harrison surveys various works. Cf. Mark Harrison, "Science and the British Empire," in: *Isis* 96:1 (2005), 56-63.

[63] David Langford provides a comprehensive survey on warfare in science fiction. Cf. David Langford, *War in 2080: the Future of Military Technology* (London: Sphere, 1979).

no real sentimental bond between Europe and its emigrants.[64] Then, in 1833 the first steamship, called the Royal William, traversed the Atlantic, and telegraph cables across the English Channel (1851) and the Atlantic (1866) improved communication.[65] These technical advances extended political possibilities as some of the limits posed by space and time could be overcome. Admittedly, new technology was often unreliable and very expensive. In contrast, science fiction frequently depicts future scenarios in which nearly any spatial or temporal limit can be surmounted. In numerous works, space and time travel are indeed prerequisites for the thriving of an interstellar empire. Space and time travel also imply that humanity can be confronted with any form of alien invader: the extraterrestrials might be anthropomorphic, beastlike, an energy or gas life form; they are characterized by various degrees of hostility towards man; and they might either reveal themselves or refuse to do so. Apart from communication technology, the age of imperialism gave rise to 'colonial science' which played a major role in the "location and evaluation of new resources for the purpose of imperial development."[66] For instance, the British built railways, bridges, ports and other infrastructure in India and Africa. Expertise was mainly exported from the Western metropolises to the colonies. Nevertheless, scientific research was carried out in the colonies as well: since science was considered a 'gentlemanly pursuit' in the nineteenth century, some of those Europeans who lived in the colonies occupied themselves with botany, geology, horticulture, irrigation, *et cetera*, and regularly contributed to scientific magazines.[67]

What is more, mobility shaped the image of the native Other. Due to the establishment of overseas colonies and trading posts, the Victorians saw themselves confronted with different indigenous peoples whose existence had barely been known before. The discoverers' attitudes towards these peoples varied: for some, they

---

[64] Cf. Duncan S. A. Bell, "Dissolving Distance: Technology, Space, and Empire in British Political Thought, 1770-1900," in: *The Journal of Modern History* 77:3 (2005), 533.
[65] Cf. *ibid.*, 543f.
[66] Mark Harrison, "Science and the British Empire," 57.
[67] Cf. *ibid.*, 60-62.

were primitive savages or even cannibals; others deemed them the original men in an Eden-like environment. Descriptions of the Other were mainly based on orientalist stereotypes and usually originated in myths and other written or oral records such as travel writings and story-telling; they were in most cases not the result of direct confrontation. For instance, the British public learnt about other cultures from newspaper articles and even works of fiction. Therefore, imagination and expectations rather than experience created the image of the Other. A common orientalist stereotype was the association of indigenous peoples with Nature. In Victorian times, though, the limits of Nature were something to overcome, i.e. Nature had to be 'conquered' and 'subjugated'. For instance, the Scottish writer Thomas Carlyle (1795-1881) announces in *Signs of the Times* (1829): "We can remove mountains, and make seas our smooth highways, nothing can resist us."[68] Accordingly, the fate of the so-called savages was to be subjugated since the 'civilized' colonizers felt a certain right and duty to dominate as well as educate the former, an idea that Rudyard Kipling termed "the white man's burden" in his eponymous poem.[69] In fact, the would-be philanthropic motivation justified the exploitation of countries and peoples.

In addition to narratives and the media, scientific theories generated notions of obligation towards the 'savage' Other. In the aftermath of Charles Darwin's *The Descent of Man, and Selection in Relation to Sex* (1871), in which he argues that all races of man must be classified under the same species,[70] the 'savages' could not be called a different species any more, and people came to believe that indigenous peoples were at a lower stage of social development. This idea justified imperialist tutelage and *la mission civilisatrice*. Futuristic equivalents of the civilizing missions are portrayed in alien-encounter science fiction, especially in those

---

[68] The complete essay *Signs of the Times* is available on http://www.victorianweb.org/authors/carlyle/signs/signs1.html (2012-03-31).

[69] Cf. Rudyard Kipling, "The White Man's Burden" (1899), available on http://public.wsu.edu/~brians/world_civ/worldcivreader/world_civ_reader_2/kipling.html (2012-05-10).

[70] Cf. Charles Darwin, *The Descent of Man, and Selection in Relation to Sex* (London *et al.*: Penguin Classics, 2004), pp. 194-240.

works that feature benevolent aliens, for instance Arthur C. Clarke's *Childhood's End* (cf. chapter 2.1) and Fred Hoyle's and John Elliot's *Andromeda* novels (cf. chapter 2.2). Central questions in this context are: By which means do the aliens achieve their benevolent intentions? In what ways do they alter the living-conditions on Earth? And how does mankind react to the invasion?

Imperialist tutelage and the civilizing mission used to be considered noble endeavours in times of empire. Nowadays, though, the colonizers' means of annexing territories and their intervention into the subject peoples' social and cultural practices are generally regarded as instrumentalist and exploitative, and it is certainly true that millions of natives were enslaved and killed in colonial encounters. For instance, approximately seventy million natives of Mesoamerica died in the aftermath of Spanish conquest, thousands of South Africans were detained in British concentration camps during the Boer Wars, and King Leopold II of Belgium halved the Congolese population. However, the benefits of Western achievements in science and technology cannot be denied. A self-sufficient life, comparable to the one of pre-colonial societies in remote parts of the world, would of course be unimaginable for most of us since we have become used to our high standards of living, housing, mobility and healthcare, and today's life expectancy would be impossible without scientific achievements. Thus, I do not intend to advocate primitivism when I write about superior alien technology that serves as a tool for subjugation; instead, I would like to highlight parallels between works of science fiction and colonial history.

In alien-encounter science fiction, the fighting spirit of mankind almost always wins over the technological advantages of the aliens, and it may be said that human resistance is one of the most crucial elements in all the novels discussed in this thesis. The main question in alien-encounter science fiction is whether alien rule can actually be averted. In most cases, the extraterrestrial rulers are technologically and intellectually further advanced than man. Thus, human beings have to deploy unusual means to liberate their planet. Incidentally, man does not succeed in all novels; the aliens might also threaten the survival of the human species or destroy the planet. In addition, it is debatable if all people on Earth are opposed to alien rule, i.e. there might either be few heroes who fight against the enemy, or resistance can develop into a mass movement. Another interesting element in the novels is how human beings organize resistance. For instance, some authors depict little bands with militaristic structures that infiltrate and sabotage alien strongholds, not unlike guerrilla warfare; others create scenarios in which resistance leaders try to convince the masses to rise against alien domination. This method actually recalls the world-wide demonstrations against the Vietnam War in the 1960s and 1970s, and it might imply fewer casualties than war against the Other. What is crucial for the success of resistance is the creation of a sense of community among former subject peoples. In science fiction, part of this is the rediscovery of long-lost knowledge and technology that used to be suppressed by extraterrestrial rulers, as is the case in John Christopher's *Tripods* trilogy (cf. chapter 1.2). Eventually, the novels discussed in this paper illustrate the significance of liberation in different ways. Liberation might come across as something eternal, something that mankind 'deserves', or as a temporal state in a universe where the struggle for dominance is portrayed as natural.

The final theme to be analyzed in the selected works directly follows resistance since it concerns the end of alien rule on Earth, an end that is either brought about by man's victory over the invaders or their voluntary withdrawal from the occupied area. After an era of alien dominance, the human survivors on Earth form a new society and rebuild their living-space, as is the case in numerous works of post-disaster science fiction.[71] A major issue to be analyzed is to what extent domination by extraterrestrials has changed man. Are there any traces of biological and cultural impe-

---

[71] Post-disaster science fiction is one of the greatest subgenres of science fiction. Works centre around life after a certain (ecological, nuclear or other) catastrophe, depicting the fate of the survivors. Famous examples are Brian Aldiss' *Hothouse* (1961, cf. Brian W. Aldiss, *Hothouse.* With an Introduction by Neil Gaiman and a New Afterword by Brian Aldiss [London *et al.*: Penguin Classics, 2008]), Kurt Vonnegut's *Cat's Cradle* (cf. Kurt Vonnegut, *Cat's Cradle* [New York, NY: Dell, 1963]) and Ursula K. Le Guin's *Always Coming Home* (1985, cf. Ursula K. Le Guin, *Always Coming Home* [Berkeley and Los Angeles, CA: University of California Press, 2001]). John Wyndham's *The Kraken Wakes*, which is discussed in more detail in chapter 3.1, also bears traits of post-disaster science fiction.

rialism, i.e. are there any beliefs and customs formed under alien rule left? Are there hybrid creatures, alien plants, technological gadgets or other new products on Earth? I will also devote some attention to the question of who rules human beings after the departure of the aliens. Does man live 'as one' in a post-national world? Or do the old national resentments re-emerge? Are there power struggles like in Vietnam, India, South Africa and other former colonies? Moreover, mankind might still depend on the former colonizer, comparable to neo-imperialist relations between the so-called First and Third Worlds. An entirely different possibility is that man and aliens establish friendly relations that manifest themselves in space tourism or co-existence. Naturally, the relationship between ex-colonizer and ex-colonized depends on why the aliens give up their colonies on Earth, i.e. whether they are defeated or withdraw voluntarily.

In contrast to these fictive scenarios, the loss of the British colonies was mainly owing to the two world wars. After the Great War, Britain had to cope with severe financial difficulties which rendered the maintenance of the Empire impossible. In 1922, after serious riots, Egypt was the first African colony to regain independence. Simultaneously, the four dominions Canada, Australia, New Zealand and South Africa, which had become increasingly reluctant to accept British rule, claimed political autonomy. This led to the creation of the British Commonwealth of Nations in 1926. In the aftermath of World War II, the British Empire further crumbled for several reasons: again, Britain was weakened by the war, its hegemonic position in the world was taken over by the USA that, at first, followed an anti-imperial policy, and the Charter of the United Nations (signed in 1945) guaranteed the right to self-determination for colonized nations. Britain was prepared to grant independence to those countries that adopted a pro-Western attitude and as compensation for cooperation in the war against Germany and Japan. For instance, two million Indians had fought for Britain in World War II. When Mahatma Gandhi took his toll on the colonizer and declared the independence of India, the British withdrew from the subcontinent in 1947 and Jawarhalal Nehru became the first Indian president. The same year, Pakistan was created. Only one year later, Burma and Sri Lanka followed. Some years after the French had lost their colonies in Northern Africa, the British territories on the 'Dark Continent' also regained independence, starting with Ghana in 1957. In the 1960s, all African and Asian colonies and other dependencies broke away from the Empire. Eventually, after the termination of a 99-year lease, Hong Kong was returned to China in 1997. Today, only fourteen overseas territories have retained British status.

Yet, what might remain after the decolonization process are feelings of postcolonial or postimperial guilt.[72] The *Oxford English Dictionary* offers various definitions of guilt, one of them being "the state (meriting condemnation and reproach of conscience) of having wilfully committed crime or heinous moral offence; criminality, great culpability."[73] Thus, guilt implies some sort of prior deliberate wrongdoing. Postimperial and postcolonial guilt consequently consist of the imperial power's taking responsibility for the crimes and moral offences committed with regard to its subject peoples. Examples might be the appropriation of territories, genocide, slavery, exploitation in the form of theft and indentured labour, and the fact that, eventually, only the imperial ruler benefited from the situation.

Generally speaking, there are two ways of dealing with imperial history: a nation can look back to its past achievements with confidence, or it can acknowledge the evils that accompanied imperial domination. With regard to British notions of guilt, it was only recently (and scantily) that the government officially apologized for some of the crimes committed. One of the few official statements is Tony Blair's apology for the Irish Potato Famine (1845-1849), in which he blamed "those who governed in London" for the disaster.[74] In addition, after the Bishop of York reminded the nation of slave trade in the eighteenth century, Blair expressed

---

[72] While both terms are generally applied loosely, my choice of terminology will depend on whether mankind is subjugated by an alien colonizer (postcolonial guilt) or dominated from another planet (postimperial guilt). For a discussion of postcolonial/postimperial guilt in selected Canadian literature, see Janice Fiamengo, "Postcolonial Guilt in Margaret Atwood's *Surfacing*," in: *American Review of Canadian Studies* 29:1 (1999), 141-163.

[73] *OED Online*, s.v. 'guilt' (2012-04-05).

[74] Cf. http://www.independent.co.uk/news/blair-issues-apology-for-irish-potato-famine-1253790.html (2012-04-05).

deep regret and recorded a video message that was played at a former slave fort in Ghana.[75] In 2009, Gordon Brown issued an apology to the British children that had been taken to Commonwealth countries such as Canada and Australia between the 1920s and 1960s and, during a visit to Pakistan in 2011, the current PM David Cameron refused to get involved in the Kashmir conflict since he claimed that the British "are responsible for the issue in the first place."[76]

However, generally speaking the government and the public seem to look back to the Empire with pride. For instance, Tony Blair expressed in a speech in 1997 that the Empire "should be cause of neither apology nor hand wringing"; instead, it could be used to increase Britain's influence in the world.[77] Likewise, authors such as Niall Ferguson and Depak Lal advocate imperialism by claiming that it increases trade, capital flow and migrations, and that the introduction of Western cultural norms and political values generates order and social welfare. These authors even claim that contemporary grievances in Africa (ethnic tensions, dictatorship, poverty, famines) were brought about by the end of imperial rule.[78] Incidentally, the prerequisites for 'good' imperialism are reflected in Joseph Conrad's *Heart of Darkness* (1899). In the novella, imperialism is judged on the basis of popular social-Darwinist criteria: "efficiency" and "the idea" (the civilizing mission).[79] The narrator, Marlow, explains that colonization is justified and advantageous to

---

[75] Cf. http://news.bbc.co.uk/2/hi/uk_news/6492291.stm (2012-04-05).

[76] Cf. http://www.telegraph.co.uk/news/politics/david-cameron/8430899/David-Cameron-Britain-caused-many-of-the-worlds-problems.html (2012-04-05).

[77] Cf. http://www.guardian.co.uk/books/2011/oct/19/end-myths-britains-imperial-past (2012-04-05).

[78] Cf. Niall Ferguson, *Empire: The Rise and Demise of the British World Order and the Lessons for Global Power* (New York, NY: Basic Books, 2004); Niall Ferguson, *Colossus: The Price of America's Empire* (New York, NY: Penguin Press, 2004); Deepak Lal, *In Praise of Empires: Globalization and Order* (New York, NY: Palgrave Macmillan, 2004); Deepak Lal, *In Defense of Empires* (Washington, DC: American Enterprise Institute for Public Policy Research, 2002).

[79] Cf. Hunt Hawkins, "Conrad's Critique of Imperialism in *Heart of Darkness*," in: *PMLA: Publications of the Modern Language Association of America* 94:2 (1979), 294f.

both parties as long as "efficiency" and "the idea" prevail.[80] Yet, in the course of the novella, we learn that these fundamentals are not fulfilled in the Congo.

Just like Conrad's work, science fiction offers countless possibilities to reflect actual history in fictive scenarios. The question arises in what ways British science fiction authors, especially those who went to the colonies during World War II and published their works during or directly after the decline of the Empire, deal with postimperial or postcolonial guilt. The first step to analyze guilt in the selected novels is to define man's function: does mankind take the role of the native in colonial encounters? Or are human beings subjects and agents of the imperial ruler at the same time, i.e. have they been transformed into assistants by cultural imperialism or brainwashing? Furthermore, the novels illustrate how the human protagonists deal with the wrongdoings of their own nation in the past. Some actually deny guilt by emphasizing the self-destructive potential of humanity (nuclear weapons, wars); others take responsibility and express shame. Finally, some interesting insights can be drawn from the reversal of roles in alien-encounter science fiction (Europeans find themselves in the role of a subject people). Dominance by extraterrestrials serves as a means of 'purification' or 'absolution from sins' since former imperial powers on Earth learn the hard way what it means to be subjugated. However, if imperialism is depicted as something unavoidable (for instance in the context of historical recurrence), redemption is unachievable.

Generally speaking, the thirteen novels that I am going to analyze rank neither among the classics of English literature nor among the most famous narratives of science fiction (albeit Arthur C. Clarke's and Gwyneth Jones' novels have received significant literary criticism). However, I hold that numerous works which might be considered 'pulp' offer more than entertainment. In fact, they provide pointers for the discussion of both historical and contemporary ideas, standards and values. What the novels selected have in common is that they picture British imperial history in a somewhat alienated way. Although there are – inevitably – intersections with regard to themes and motives, the novels will be

[80] Joseph Conrad, *Heart of Darkness & Other Stories*, pp. 34f.

grouped as follows: narratives of exploitative alien invasions, works that depict benevolent invasions from outer space and others (that are, of course, all the more fascinating due to their individuality and originality).

The first group consists of Brian Aldiss' *The Interpreter* (1960), John Christopher's *Tripods* trilogy (1967-1968) and Stephen Baxter's *Timelike Infinity* (1992). These narratives give examples of the most common tropes in alien-encounter science fiction: extraterrestrials conquer Earth with the intention of annexing the planet and exploiting its resources and indigenous population. To a certain extent, the texts directly fall back on British imperial practices as they picture the instrumental use of power, the 'organization' of subjugating the natives and the accumulation of wealth. However, the three authors lay emphasis on different aspects. Aldiss' novel deals with colonial crimes such as abuse of the subject people, corruption, racism and greed. The alien commissioner of Earth manipulates both his subjects and his superiors – his sole aim is personal enrichment. The *Tripods* trilogy focuses on brainwashing and on the struggle of the teenage heroes to liberate themselves from adult authority and ideological straightjackets, a topic that appeals in particular to adolescent readers. As a work of hard science fiction, *Timelike Infinity* illustrates that advanced technology is a crucial prerequisite for interstellar empires. In addition, Baxter's novel is the one that contains the strongest expressions of postcolonial guilt.

Benevolent alien invasions, a topic almost as popular as the first, are portrayed in Arthur C. Clarke's *Childhood's End* (1953) and in the *Andromeda* novels (1962-1964) by Fred Hoyle and John Elliot. In these texts, a more advanced alien species assists in the evolution of man in order to prepare the latter for a higher purpose. In fact, this notion recalls the civilizing mission and European paternalism. What distinguishes *Childhood's End* from the *Andromeda* novels is that, in the former, aliens bring back the Golden Age on Earth and 'nurse' the people, so that humans, who used to be rather self-destructive, eventually have the chance to become part of something greater. In the latter works, the aliens challenge mankind to decide itself on the fate of Earth. A typical invasion never happens: the extraterrestrials control the planet from the Andromeda Galaxy.

The remaining three novels I am going to elaborate on resist clear-cut categories. Aldiss' first novel, *Non-Stop* (1958), demonstrates how tutelage serves the purpose of gaining knowledge from an experiment. It also raises topical questions about Western responsibility for formerly colonized countries. In John Wyndham's *The Kraken Wakes* (1953), the intentions of the alien invaders are as mysterious as their nature: extraterrestrials that nobody ever sees set up colonies in the Deep Sea and occasionally raid coastal towns. The aliens might share some characteristics with those in the first group but, due to the author's narrative techniques, uncertainty prevails. In contrast to all other novels, Gwyneth Jones' *Aleutians* trilogy (1991-1997) presents a somewhat unplanned take-over of Earth: shipwrecked extraterrestrials become spiritual and political leaders of man who, after three hundred years of misrule, eventually abandon their colonial subjects without taking any responsibility for the problems on Earth. Only one character, Catherine, tries to make up for the shortcomings of the rulers by deliberately becoming a rape victim. Thus, each of these novels, in its own way, breaks away from the majority of texts about alien invasions. In the concluding chapter, I am going to sum up and compare the treatment of extraterrestrial rule, the alien Other, technology as an agent of power, human resistance, decolonization and postcolonial guilt in the selected novels of British alien-encounter science fiction.

1. Close Encounters of the First Kind: Exploitative Alien Invasions

1.1 Not Too Alien: Brian W. Aldiss, *The Interpreter*

Due to his literary productivity and his commitment at science fiction conventions, Brian Wilson Aldiss, OBE (*1925 in East Dereham, Norfolk) is undoubtedly one of the most influential individuals in the British science fiction community. Aldiss began his writing career by publishing fictionalized sketches in *The Bookseller*, a trade magazine for bookshops. From 1954 onwards, he published various short stories in relevant science fiction magazines. His early tales are considered resourceful but dark in the atmosphere they create. In 1959, he received the award of the World SF Convention as most promising new author. Aldiss has published more than three hundred short stories and over fifty novels, and many of his works have been awarded the Hugo, the Nebula, the British Science Fiction Award or other prizes. Among his most famous novels are *Hothouse* (1962), *Frankenstein Unbound* (1973) and the *Helliconia* series, i.e. *Helliconia Spring* (1982), *Helliconia Summer* (1983) and *Helliconia Winter* (1985). Steven Spielberg's popular movie *Artificial Intelligence: AI*[81] (2001) is an adaptation of Aldiss' short story "Supertoys Last all Summer Long" (1969). Aldiss' most important non-fiction work is *Trillion Years Spree: The History of Science Fiction* (1986), a comprehensive survey of the genre.

Aldiss is also an anthologist and a critic of science fiction. Among other titles, he edited *Penguin Science Fiction* (1961), *Best Fantasy Stories* (1962), the *Year's Best Science Fiction* series (1967-1976) and a collection of autobiographical essays by science fiction writers, *Hell's Cartographers* (1975). Furthermore, Aldiss reviewed hundreds of science-fiction novels for the *Times Literary*

[81] *Artificial Intelligence: AI* (USA 2001, directed by Steven Spielberg).

Supplement, the *Guardian*, the *Washington Post* and others. From 1982 to 1984, he was president of World Science Fiction, an international association of authors, critics, editors, artists and other professionals of the genre. His memoir, *Bury my Heart at W.H. Smith's: A Writing Life* (1990), depicts his personal experiences with writing and publishing.[82]

My discussion of novels shall start with Brian Aldiss' *The Interpreter* since it is perhaps the one that most clearly parallels British imperialist endeavours. In fact, the extraterrestrial invaders – the so-called "nuls"[83] – are not too alien. A few colonial overlords subjugate millions of natives, as was the case in India between 1858 and 1947, for example. Their rule is based on establishing difference between themselves and their subject peoples. The nuls are more powerful than humans in many respects: they are technologically superior, more active, efficient and industrious (their aim is material gain, i.e. they extract the natural resources of Earth), and they clearly look down on the indigenous population. Moreover, the novel demonstrates the impossibility of ruling an enormous empire through colonial officers. In the note from the author that precedes the novel, Aldiss explains:

> The plot hinges on the notion that the further spread your empire is, the greater are the opportunities for graft therein.
>
> So the villains of the piece are not so much the all-conquering *nuls*, as the size of the galaxy and the eco-

[82] Cf. John Clute and Peter Nicholls (eds.), *The Encyclopedia of Science Fiction*, s.v. 'Brian W. Aldiss'. For bibliographies of Aldiss' works, see for instance Margaret Aldiss and Boden Clarke, *The Work of Brian W. Aldiss: An Annotated Bibliography and Guide. Bibliographies of Modern Authors, No 9* (San Bernardino, CA: Borgo Press, 1992); Phil Stephensen-Payne, *Brian Wilson Aldiss, a Man for All Seasons: A Working Bibliography. Galactic Central Bibliographies for the Avid Reader, Vol. 26* (San Bernardino, CA: Borgo Press, 1992); Michael R. Collings, *Brian W. Aldiss. Starmont Reader's Guide 28* (Mercer Island, WA: Starmont House, 1986).

[83] Throughout the novel, the name of the alien species is not capitalized. Cf. Brian Aldiss, *The Interpreter* (London: Four Square Books, 1967). All subsequent references are in brackets in the text.

> nomics involved in its rule. (*TI*, n. pag., italics by B. Aldiss)

Apart from racism, *The Interpreter* treats colonial crimes such as the oppression and abuse of subjects, corruption and manipulation for personal enrichment. Some brave individuals manage to end the tyrant's rule, but they are unable to liberate Earth from the alien overlords and man remains a colonized species. Yet, despite its obvious references to and criticism of British colonial practices, *The Interpreter* is more than an allegory of imperialism. The merits of the work lie in its entertaining plot and interesting character constellation since the four central characters – two human interpreters and two nul officials – "each have good reason to mistrust the other three [...]" (*ibid.*).

The Interpreter (US title *Bow down to Nul*) is Aldiss' second novel. In 1960, it was serialized in the March, April and May issues of *New Worlds Science Fiction* under the title *X for Exploitation*. The complete novel appeared in 1963. In the note that precedes the novel, the author states:

> Science-fiction stories featuring galactic empires have always intrigued me, partly because I had the chance of seeing at first hand the uneasy relationship existing between 'imperialists' and subject races in India and Indonesia. (*ibid.*)

In fact, Aldiss served in the British Army in India and Burma during World War II. In his autobiography, *The Twinkling of an Eye or My Life as an Englishman* (1998), he dedicates chapters XII to XV to his experiences abroad (altogether, Aldiss spent three and a half years as a soldier overseas). Aldiss writes about his journey from India to Burma and back, the war against the Japanese, the soldiers' living-conditions, the filth and misery he saw in Calcutta, *et cetera*. Aldiss also briefly mentions Gandhi's campaign for self-governance in India. As to the "uneasy relationship" between the British and the Indian population, Aldiss explains:

> A deadening disorder prevailed. India was a different experience from Burma, far more demoralising. The Indians did not want us. They stole from us. We stole from them. Life had deteriorated. The dedication of Burma had evaporated.[84]

Yet, the British still saw India as a source of supplies and troops in times of war.[85] After the end of the war, Aldiss lived in Sumatra for two years. He left East-Asia and started working in a bookshop in Oxford in 1947, the year India became independent.[86]

The novel narrates the story of Earth under the rule of the nuls, ten feet high, three-legged and three-armed aliens from the planet of Partussy. The nuls have controlled Earth – one of four million conquered worlds – for two thousand years in order to exploit the natural resources of the planet. Human cities have been abandoned, and the people, called "bipeds", work as cheap labourers or slaves for the aliens. The hydrogen-breathing nuls build a sealed city on each planet of their vast empire. Inside the city, they have human interpreters at their command as they do not speak any human languages. The ruler of Earth is Chaverlem Par-Chavorlem, a greedy, cruel and corrupt commissioner. After his former nul employee, Wattol Forlie, accuses Par-Chavorlem of corruption and theft, a delegation under Synvoret of the nul Supreme Court is despatched to Earth. Synvoret's personal interpreter is Gary Towler, who senses the opportunity to expose Par-Chavorlem's scheming. However, during Synvoret's investigation, Towler sees himself confronted with various problems: he is shunned by his colleagues as they think he works for Par-Chavorlem, and even his girlfriend, the young interpreter Elizabeth Fallodon, does not always trust him. In addition, Par-Chavorlem bribes him to mistranslate interviews with earthlings. It is nearly impossible for the interpreter to present evidence of Par-Chavorlem's wrongdoings to Synvoret, and his desperate attempt to kill the investigator fails as well. Finally, Towler, Elizabeth and their colleagues escape from the city, kill a band of

---

[84] Brian Aldiss, *The Twinkling of an Eye or My Life as an Englishman* (London, Warner Books, ²1999), p. 193.
[85] Cf. *ibid.*
[86] Cf. *ibid.*, pp. 197ff.

nuls in an ambush, take over their trucks and weapons and destroy the aliens' safe environment. Since Earth is but an insignificant planet in the vast nul empire, the interest of the aliens soon fades, and mankind is liberated from the tyrant.

The Interpreter is a novel about racial inequality. Inequality is generated through representation of the Other, and representation is an essential element in the relationship between nuls and humans, i.e. in the structures of power on Earth. What is interesting is that the omniscient narrator clearly presents both sides: the portrayal of the nuls through human eyes and the image the aliens construct of human beings. This is expressed by shifts in narrative perspective. The nuls are conquerors *par excellence*, and the reader can detect many similarities to imperialist nations in history. Additionally, the depiction of the aliens in Aldiss' novel is complex: certain features appear alien, whereas others are strikingly human. As to the nuls' physical features, they are portrayed as Other, and their traits indicate superiority. Towler makes clear that the enormous size as well as the strange physiognomy of Par-Chavorlem evokes fear:

> Par-Chavorlem stood ten feet high. He was immensely solid. His great bulk was almost cylindrical, except for his arms and legs. A nul was like a canister to which two three-armed starfish were joined, one at the base, forming legs, one midway up, forming arms.
>
> Like the rest of his kind, Par-Chevorlem [*sic*] was almost featureless. At the end of each road-arm were two flexible, opposed fingers, with retractable claws usually concealed. Near the top of his cylindrical body were three regularly spaced eye-stalks, while on top of his "head" was the usual fleshy comb. (*TI*, p. 24)

We can imagine that the first encounter between nuls and humans intimidated or shocked the latter. In the context of human reality, the people on Earth might have perceived the aliens as a giant mixture of various animals, for example an elephant, a slug, a fish and a bird, reminiscent of fabulous creatures such as the sphinx or the griffin.[87] Due to their size, the claws and the comb, the nuls also resemble dinosaurs to a certain extent, which indicates strength and monstrosity.

As in John Christopher's *Tripods* trilogy (cf. chapter 1.2), the number three plays a major role in the depiction of the aliens. On Earth, creatures with an odd number of limbs are rare (starfish, sepia, jellyfish), and procreation in trios as the nuls perform it (cf. *TI*, p. 46) does not exist. Tripods with three different sexes (male, female and neuter) clearly differ from familiar organisms, which emphasizes the nuls' otherness. Incidentally, three is an important number for human beings when we think about many idioms in language, the primary colours, the spatial dimensions, three as a holy number in certain religions, *et cetera*. In addition, the three-parted physiognomy serves as an indicator of superiority as the nuls have more arms, legs and eyes than human beings. With regard to their intellectual faculties, the reader expects advantages as well. In the novel, the structure and function of the nul brain are not mentioned. Nevertheless, the reader assumes that the brain is subdivided into three parts (as opposed to two brain hemispheres in humans), and it might be more powerful than the human brain. The thesis of intellectual superiority is supported by the fact that Partussian technology is highly advanced. For instance, the nuls have developed spaceships and space-ports (cf. *TI*, p. 19), powerful weapon systems (cf. *TI*, p. 123), and an efficient way of categorizing and exploiting their colonies (cf. *TI*, p. 17).

What also appears to be alien is the secretiveness of the nuls. Several physical traits are hidden. With regard to Par-Chavorlem, the human interpreter states that most of the nul's features "[are] concealed under the wide flaps of his arms; his mouth, his olfactory nerves, his aural cavities, his reproductive organs. A nul [is] a secret creature whose exterior betray[s] very little" (*TI*, p. 24). Therefore, human beings are unable to understand non-verbal clues when they communicate with the aliens; the nuls generally appear to be incomprehensible. The only body part that reveals their emotions is the fleshy comb: it "compresse[s] with rage" (*TI*, p. 98) or turns "pallid" when human beings are attacked (cf. *TI*, p. 73). What

[87] In Greek mythology, the griffin is a creature with a lion's body and an eagle's wings and head.

is interesting to note is that alterity is perceived from the side of the nuls, too. For example, they find the sight of a human mouth obscene since it is not hidden from view (cf. *TI*, p. 50). However, in the course of the novel, the nuls rarely express emotions. They are said to be stoic (cf. *TI*, p. 105), and their behaviour is "closely governed by the frigid situation-response selector [...] called conscience" (*TI*, p. 96). Furthermore, love is considered a "whimsy madness" and "weakness" (*TI*, p. 98). The reader receives the impression that the mind of a nul operates like a machine. Of course, callousness serves the purpose of the invasion since the nuls do not feel pity for their subjects; they function like robots that thoroughly fulfil the task of exploitation. Incidentally, the emotionless alien is a frequent theme in science fiction and a paradigm of alterity. For example, the Martians in H.G. Wells' *The War of the Worlds*[88] (1898) or the extraterrestrials in the *Alien* film tetralogy[89] (1979-1997) are monstrous and apparently driven by instincts. The greys in Stephen King's *Dreamcatcher*[90] (2001) or in the Hollywood blockbuster *Signs*[91] (2002) are incomprehensible and mysterious to human beings. Even humanoid aliens such as the protagonist of *The Day the Earth Stood Still*[92] (2008) remain perfectly callous.

Returning to Aldiss' novel, Synvoret and Wattol Forlie seem to be an exception to the emotionless Partussians at first sight. Synvoret is capable of feeling "shame" after having injured an innocent human being with his claw (cf. *TI*, pp. 95f.), and Forlie accuses the nul empire of being "rotten, decadent, through and through" (*TI*, p. 12). Yet, what might be interpreted as pity for the people on Earth is rather an appeal to nul virtues. The same can be said about Synvoret's "honest and perceptive" nature (cf. *TI*, p. 13)

---

88 Cf. Herbert G. Wells, *The War of the Worlds*.
89 Cf. *Alien* (UK 1979, directed by Ridley Scott), *Aliens* (USA and UK 1986, directed by James Cameron), *Alien³* (USA 1992, directed by David Fincher) and *Alien: Resurrection* (USA 1997, directed by Jean-Pierre Jeunet). The latest film by Ridley Scott, *Prometheus*, centres around the species of the "Space Jockeys" or "Pilots" mentioned in the *Alien* movies. Cf. *Prometheus* (USA and UK 2012, directed by Ridley Scott).
90 Cf. Stephen King, *Dreamcatcher* (New York, NY: Scribner, 2001). The novel was adapted into the eponymous film in 2003.
91 Cf. *Signs* (USA 2002, directed by M. Night Shyamalan).
92 Cf. *The Day the Earth Stood Still* (USA 2008, directed by Scott Derrickson).

and about the idea that the investigator is not corrupt (cf. *TI*, p. 10). In fact, none of the nuls feel pity for the human beings; they just do good deeds within their own system of values. This is a parallel to Western conquerors in history that, for instance, abolished practices such as cannibalism or widow burning as they ran counter to Judeo-Christian belief. Just like in Aldiss' novel, the two cultures are unable to understand each other's customs and virtues. Admittedly, it is debatable if a creature – be it a nul, a European, or other – can leave his or her set of values behind and completely grasp the mentality and culture of the Other. In *The Interpreter*, Forlie and Synvoret clearly see humans 'through nul eyes' even though they might feel shame or regret.

Nevertheless, there are certain similarities between the two species. This implies that the nuls are not utterly alien, an antithesis to those extraterrestrials that are beyond our understanding. For example, they can be energetic life-forms, like in Terry Gene Carr's "The Dance of the Changer and the Three"[93] (1976), sentient plants as in John Wyndham's *The Day of the Triffids*[94] (1951), or organisms that can take any form as in the novella *Who goes there?*[95] (1938) by John W. Campbell, Jr. In Wyndham's *The Kraken Wakes* (1953), the nature of the extraterrestrials is never revealed (cf. chapter 3.1). In contrast to the Other in those works, the nuls are not entirely incomprehensible to human beings. Moreover, they speak an articulate language. It differs from human languages since it cannot sound poetic (cf. *TI*, p. 76), but the interpreters on Earth are able to learn it and thereby communicate with the nuls. What is more, the nuls have a religion. They praise Trinity (cf. *TI*, p. 112), which recalls the importance of the number three and which also hints at Christian Trinity (it is not mentioned what Trinity signifies for the nuls, though). A further similarity between humans and Partussians is the city as living-space (cf. *TI*, p. 21). The construction of cities to settle on Earth and control the exploi-

[93] Cf. Terry Gene Carr, "The Dance of the Changer and the Three," in: *The Light at the End of the Universe* (Palm Springs, FL: Pyramid, 1976), 20-38.
[94] Cf. John Wyndham, *The Day of the Triffids* (New York, NY: The Modern Library, 2003).
[95] Cf. John W. Campbell Jr., *Who Goes There?* (Cutchogue, NY: Buccaneer Books, 1991).

tation of the planet recalls the organization of the Masters in John Christopher's works (cf. chapter 1.2). Unfortunately, the cities of the nuls are never described in detail, and the reader receives the impression that they do not serve as a striking symbol of Partussian domination. However, it is assumed that the nuls' home planet and their use of space do not differ considerably from human concepts.

The most striking parallel between humans and the extraterrestrials in *The Interpreter* is probably the desire to expand their empire. In this respect, the novel clearly has a political overtone. We learn that the empire of the nuls is vast and old. It includes four million planets and is approximately two million years old. The home planet of the nuls is "the Queen World of Partussy" (cf. *TI*, p. 17). What is interesting to note is that the organization of the nul empire resembles the one of the British Empire at its height: the size, the inequality in power between the Western metropolis and the colonized territories, the jurisdiction the colonies were ruled under, and the fact that

> [...] in Europe itself at the end of the nineteenth century, scarcely a corner of life was untouched by the facts of empire; the economies were hungry for overseas markets, raw materials, cheap labour, and hugely profitable land, and defence and foreign-policy establishments were more and more committed to the maintenance of vast tracts of distant territory and large numbers of subjugated peoples.[96]

As the all-conquering nuls thoroughly exploit planets, it is assumable that their economy largely depends on the resources of their colonies. Moreover, just like in the British Empire, colonial power is institutionalized. For example, the nuls have established a Foreign Department (cf. *TI*, p. 10), and accusations and complaints are discussed by the Colony Worlds Council on Partussy (cf. *TI*, p. 112). Each planet is controlled by a commissioner (such as Par-Chavorlem on Earth), and Commission City serves as his headquarters (cf. *TI*, p. 18). Incidentally, Par-Chavorlem holds numer-

[96] Edward W. Said, *Culture and Imperialism*, p. 7.

ous titles: he is addressed as "Colony Worlds Commissioner Hiscount Chaverlem Par-Chavorlem, I.L.U.S., L.G.V.S., M.G.C.C., R.O.R. (Smi), […]" (*TI*, p. 17). Naturally, these abbreviations appear exaggerated and incomprehensible, which generates an ironic overtone; the nuls 'over-institutionalize' their policies as well as their civil servants.

In terms of technology, *The Interpreter* treats two topics: the industrialized production system and the communications revolution. The omniscient narrator raises images of an industrialized system by making clear that the woods and forests the nuls exploit are "as neatly organized as factories" (*ibid.*). In the nineteenth century, industrial technology increased significantly and, during the heyday of the Empire, Britain "entered a new phase of industrial development based on steel, electrification, and chemical production […]."[97] Apart from the fact that Britain's wealth largely depended on its industry, the latter also shaped the view of the population on other cultures since "few disputed that machines were the most reliable measure of humankind."[98] Efficiency, industriousness and good organization counted among the values of the Victorian self-made man and, in Aldiss' novel, this image is somewhat projected on the nuls, who deem themselves to be more advanced than the natives of Earth. It can be assumed that the nuls – just like European colonizers – are traders of manufactured and finished goods, whereas their colonies have become suppliers of raw materials. Basically, the aliens have transformed Earth into mere cropland.

Additionally, the novel demonstrates the importance of mastering space in a colonial context. Unlike humans, the nuls are able to travel in outer space, a distinct feature that does not only make an interstellar empire possible but also provides evidence for the aliens' high level of civilization. Their mobility might make the reader think of Britain's maritime fleet in times of empire. The fleet generally guaranteed power and prestige. For instance, the historian, politician and essayist Thomas Babington Macaulay

---

[97] Michael Adas, *Machines as the Measure of Man. Science, Technology, and Ideologies of Western Dominance* (Ithaca and London: Cornell University Press, 1998), p. 134.
[98] *Ibid.*

(1800-1859) considered the English the "greatest and most highly civilized people that ever the world saw."[99] Macaulay argued that the British fleet could "annihilate in a quarter of an hour the [pre-industrial] navies of Tyre, Athens, Carthage, Venice and Genoa together"[100], which implies that conquest of 'lower' civilizations is an easy endeavour. In addition, the nuls in Aldiss' novel extend the infrastructure on and between the conquered planets in order to ensure the transportation of raw materials. It becomes obvious that their roads are one of the pillars of their empire:

> Everywhere ran the roads, good Partussian roads of vacuumized velcan, protected for every mile of their length by force fields. Before all else the Partussians were transporters, circulators. The road was virtually their symbol. Because they had been the first species to establish regular space routes, theirs was the biggest interplanetary empire. (cf. *TI*, pp. 17f.)

Again, this makes the reader think of British colonial history, more precisely of the roads, bridges, railways, harbours and canals they built in the colonies for the purpose of ensuring trade with the rest of the world and of transporting raw materials and troops. As a result, features of the British Empire directly permeate Aldiss' fiction.

With regard to Partussian jurisdiction, a whole catalogue of regulations can be identified in the course of the novel. First, the natives on the conquered planets sign the "standard Protegé Charter" (cf. *TI*, p. 19), which reminds the reader of the charters the British granted individuals or groups in order to establish colonies, or of those charters companies signed as their 'rules' of production and commerce. Some historical examples are the Charter to Sir Walter Raleigh (1584), the Charter of Massachusetts Bay (1629) and the English Royal Charter of the East India Company (1600). Subsequently, various laws regulate colonial infrastructure; others concern the colonial subjects. As to the former, the number of armed forces on a planet is restricted (cf. *TI*, p. 18), the population

---

[99] Quoted in: *ibid.*, p. 136.
[100] *Ibid.*

of Commission City on Earth must not exceed 8,650 (cf. *TI*, p. 48), and the clerks have to keep records of all income and expenditures in the "Recorder" (cf. *TI*, p. 107). Furthermore, the exploitation of subject planets "is rigorously limited" (*TI*, p. 39). Unfortunately, the reader does not receive any information about the legal scope of exploitation on Earth. With regard to the colonial subjects, transferring them to other planets is illegal in order to prevent a mixture of races (cf. *TI*, pp. 27, 33). In addition, "the number of men who might be employed by any one terrestrial boss" is strictly limited (cf. *TI*, p. 20), human beings are subject to paying an "Employee Tax" (*ibid.*), and nul spy-devices that monitor the people in their homes are illegal (cf. *TI*, p. 52). Generally speaking, the rigid organization of the Partussian Empire implies that the extraterrestrials think the same way humans used to. Moreover, the Protegé Charter and the regulations serve as protection against accusations: "If they [the nuls] were unfair it was legally so" (*TI*, p. 19). As a consequence, the Charter that should guarantee justice is *de facto* misused as an instrument of domination. Above all, it is evident throughout the novel that Par-Chavorlem – an outright tyrant – transgresses the laws on Earth.

However, Earth seems to be only one example of many planets in the nul Empire. Due to manipulation and technology, the extraterrestrials are initially welcome on the planets they conquer. They arrived on Earth about two thousand years before the events in *The Interpreter* take place. The first contact between nuls and humans largely shaped the fate of the planet. Despite their repulsive outward appearance, the aliens were perceived as a superior race, and they managed to make the humans feel as if Earth could gain something from the invasion. The reader learns that the people were "delighted to enter the Empire as fledgling member" (*ibid.*). After having signed the Protegé Charter, the humans appreciate the changes the nuls bring to the planet:

> At once, the advantages of Partussy's colossal material and technological superiority had been felt. Fabulous aid programmes sprang up all over the planet. Vast loans were floated. Development schemes were launched daily. Thousands of farsighted tripeds poured

> into Earth via the hastily-built space-ports, bringing with them their ideas, their money and their families.
> Earth hummed with activity. (*ibid.*)

Significantly, the arrival of the nuls on Earth is not immediately perceived as an invasion. Instead, the people are excited about the progress and call it – analogous to imperialist propaganda – a "new renaissance" (*ibid.*). The notion of change for the better is generated through nul technology, for instance roads and space-travel. It seems that technology 'blinds' the terrestrials to the manipulation of the nuls; they appreciate the arrival of the mighty aliens. The inequality in power between the nul metropolis and the natives on Earth bears parallels to British history.

Due to the changes, the people might feel like living in a utopian place. Just like the Overlords in Arthur C. Clarke's *Childhood's End* (cf. chapter 2.1), the nuls introduce new processes and goods, but in contrast to Clarke's novel, the novelties are never described in detail. The reader does not receive any information about the "development schemes" and the "aid programmes", either. It is striking how quickly the narrator in Aldiss' novel destroys the idea of a utopia on Earth. Immediately after having mentioned some 'benefits' of Partussian colonization, the narrator clearly states that "the Partussy-Earth Co-Prosperity Sphere [is] just a mockery, its advantages operating only in one direction" (*ibid.*). Hence, the nuls actually establish development and aid schemes in order to exploit the planet's resources, and the reader assumes that the loans are granted to create financial dependency on the colonizer and to earn interest. With the help of their Charter, the nuls manipulate the people on Earth, and when the latter realize that they are colonial subjects, it is already too late.

Aldiss' novel deals with the nuls' desire for material gain in an ambiguous way. On the one hand, their aspirations do not appear alien at all – they actually stress their 'Victorian' values. On the other hand, they are portrayed as greedy and callous. Evidently, imperialist endeavours have always polarized the public. In the nineteenth century, various influential people advocated imperialism, among them Benjamin Disraeli (1804-1881), who had Queen Victoria proclaimed as Empress of India in 1877, and the writer and art critic John Ruskin (1819-1900), who claimed that imperialism advanced civilization in the colonies. Pro-imperialists believed in the benefits of the Empire: they felt it was Britain's obligation to educate 'savages' or 'heathens' and to assist them on their way to self-governance. Social-Darwinist motives were projected on politics, a concept that deprived 'inferior' or 'barbarous' cultures of their right to self-determination. In addition, trade with the colonies and other dependencies was a considerable source of income for Britain. In contrast, anti-imperialists held that subjugating other peoples was morally reprehensible and far from prestigious. They also feared that Britain overreached its influence so that the vast Empire would inevitably collapse at some point. Last but not least, the costs and political efforts involved in administering the colonies were enormous. Influential individuals who publicly opposed imperialism were, for example, the author and jurist Jeremy Bentham (1748-1832), the poet and diplomat Wilfrid Scawen Blunt (1840-1922) and the philosopher, biologist and socialist Herbert Spencer (1820-1903).[101] Aldiss' work does not seem to favour one side. Even though the reader might sympathize with the subjugated people on Earth, he or she must be aware of the fact that the colonial practices of the nuls cannot be easily stopped since imperialism is highly profitable. Some subject races might liberate their planets, but they cannot shatter the vast nul empire. And there is always the risk that other imperialist species subsequently conquer the planets.

Analogous to the ambivalent depiction of imperialism, the representation of the Other is rather complex since *The Interpreter* illustrates both sides, i.e. the impressions humans receive of the aliens and *vice versa*. Humans have lived under nul rule for thousands of years and the Other is still perceived as an invader. With regard to the image the nuls have of Earth, we learn that the planet is rather unimportant in the nul Empire. One of the aliens calls it "a backward little dump" (*TI*, p. 11) and a "wretched planet" (*TI*, p. 12) that suffers from the colonial crimes committed by its commis-

---

[101] For more information on anti-imperialist movements in Britain, see Mira Matikkala, *Empire and Imperial Ambition: Liberty, Englishness and Anti-Imperialism in Late-Victorian Britain. Library of Victorian Studies. Vol. 4* (London *et al.*: I. B. Tauris, 2011).

sioner. The underlying notion of the meaninglessness of Earth opposes Judeo-Christian belief since it implies that the planet is a small and thus insignificant place in the universe. Furthermore, classifying Earth as a "backward little dump" emphasizes the superiority of the nuls once more, and it implies a certain arrogance since the conquest of such a "backward" planet must have been an easy operation.

Conquest is followed by the transformation of the planet, and involuntarily by degeneration. The main export product of Earth is timber and, during two thousand years of nul rule, most of the planet's surface has been turned into a forest (cf. *TI*, p. 17). In order to grow and harvest the wood most efficiently, the nuls have introduced mass-production. Human cities have been abandoned and human industry or agriculture are not mentioned in the novel. In contrast to the 'natives', the nuls run refineries, factories, mills and farms (cf. *TI*, p. 26). Their enterprises as well as the monoculture for wood-based industry indicate that Earth underwent tremendous changes, and these changes serve the purpose of making profit. The nuls even dried the English Channel, as we assume (cf. *TI*, p. 27) and introduced a new form of cattle, called "affrizians" (cf. *TI*, p. 21). Timber is "tended and harvested by Earth men" (*TI*, p. 17). Apart from the fact that the nuls exploit human resources as well, this illustrates that mankind has changed, too. Instead of trading, running businesses and expanding their own industries, the people work for the aliens, and we can hypothesize that research and development are at a standstill. This inevitably alters the attitude of men towards their work: as semi-slave labourers, they lose the will to accomplish their tasks or improve their efficiency. Consequently, mankind has degenerated under alien influence. Culture (in all its different forms) might suffer, too. Under alien domination, people lose their individuality and, kept in serfdom, they might not have the possibility to cultivate their traditions and customs. Basically, the Partussians 'silence' their colonial subjects. The theory of backward development is corroborated by the fact that the only notable economic activity on Earth is silvicultural, which is an activity of the primary economic sector. A country's economy that relies mainly on the primary sector bears traits of underdevelopment. To sum up, the nuls transform the planet in a way that they hinder progress. As Forlie states in his accusations against the commissioner, "[i]f his [Par-Chavorlem's] rule continues, all Earth culture will be obliterated in another generation" (*TI*, p. 12).

Par-Chavorlem is the emblem of imperial crimes. By narrating his scheming in detail, Aldiss hints on notions of postcolonial guilt since the nul's wrongdoings bear parallels to crimes committed by European colonizers. Par-Chavorlem transgresses the laws dictated by the Partussian charter in various ways and, due to his wit, he succeeds in deceiving the inspection envoy. Synvoret learns about the crimes in an indirect way: Wattol Forlie sends him copies of instructions and reports signed by the Earth Commissioner. These documents form "a sketch of systematic enslavement and robbery of the local population" (*TI*, p. 13). For instance, Par-Chavorlem imposes "racial restrictions" on men, he supports the employment of "forced terrestrial labour gangs", and he allows the military to "shoot on sight any terrestrial found within half a mile of any main road" (*ibid.*). His army exceeds the stipulated number by a factor of three (cf. *TI*, p. 18), and he embezzles two *byaksis* (the nul currency) for every exported tree (cf. *ibid.*). Par-Chavorlem also confiscates human works of art (cf. *TI*, p. 109), a parallel to nineteenth-century explorers who robbed cultural artefacts from Egypt or Greece for display in museums. What is more, the city with its palace for the commissioner is twice as large as the statutes allow. The narrator draws a parallel between the city and the wrongdoings, or maybe even the monomania, of the commissioner: "[t]he big city was illegal, a gigantic material witness to their misrule" (*TI*, p. 123). Therefore, in contrast to the cities of the Masters in the *Tripods* trilogy (cf. chapter 1.2), Commission City is not a symbol of dominance and grandeur, but a symbol of Par-Chavorlem's greed and vanity.

The commissioner makes elaborate plans to disguise his crimes from the inspection team. First of all, he understands that the huge city must be concealed. That is why he has a smaller city built and hides the big one "behind negavision screens" (*TI*, p. 31). His plan is successful; Synvoret does not realize that there is a gigantic Commission City on Earth. The commissioner keeps the human rebels, i.e. Rivars and his band, alive in order to shed a bad light on mankind and, as long as there is human resistance, the nuls can justify "restrictive measures." They do not seriously fear the rebels since the weapon systems of the humans are not powerful enough to defeat the aliens (cf. *TI*, p. 25). In addition, Par-Chavorlem's subordinates stage a civil war between bipeds on Earth in order to please the commissioner and reveal the hostile nature of humans. Thus, they transfer five thousand natives from Starjj to Earth – which is forbidden – and equip them with weapons to fight men (cf. *TI*, p. 33). Ironically, the nuls believe that a Starjjan can easily be mistaken for a human despite the "vestigial tail, webbed feet [...] and some slight modifications in the sexual organs" (*TI*, p. 32). This illustrates that, for the nuls, all bipeds are alike. During the civil war, certain attacks are fake, i.e. launched by the nuls. The aliens even accept the destruction of some of their forest land (cf. *TI*, pp. 72f.). Moreover, they construct an artificial war zone for the investigation envoy:

> Accordingly, a fake Ashkar was established in an area of perfect safety that had been cleared of Rivar's forces. The native labour which had been wounded at Ashkar had been transported here to lend realism to the scene. Fires were started. Other people were brought from the City to increase the confusion. Partussian soldiery in operational kit moved about in businesslike fashion, occasionally discharging annihilators at an imaginary enemy. (*TI*, p. 69)

This scene is reminiscent of a grotesque theatre play with casualties as props, and it stresses Par-Chavorlem's unscrupulousness. Yet, it must be admitted that the humans are not innocent. The two biped races do actually fight each other. This shows that bipeds have a hostile nature to a certain extent. The rebels destroy oil wells, wasting important resources (cf. *TI*, p. 67). Hence, *The Interpreter* does not only depict the wrongdoings of the nuls, but it also denounces negative aspects of human beings.

The chief interpreter, Gary Towler, plays a crucial role in Par-Chavorlem's deceits. At this point, Aldiss' novel emphasizes the importance of language as a means of power. The commissioner bribes his interpreter to give false translations when Synvoret interviews the natives, and Towler is lured by the prospect of living a free life with Elizabeth on Partussy (cf. *TI*, pp. 55f.). He decides to mistranslate what a human woman, who plays a refugee in the staged war, tells the inspection team, and to wait for the opportunity to present evidence against Par-Chavorlem to Synvoret. Yet, Synvoret realizes that the interpreter censors the interview (cf. *TI*, p. 71), and he provokes a discussion about the role of language in a colonial context:

> 'Commissioner, does it not seem to you that for some understanding of the native's habits, his laws, his customs, his religion, his ceremonies, his philosophy, his literature, his history; for some understanding of all or any of these vital things, does it not seem necessary to you to have a knowledge of his language?'
>
> 'You are assuming, Signatory, sir, that an understanding of these things helps a governor to govern. On this wretched planet it is not so.' (*TI*, p. 72)

Here, Synvoret holds that a nation is unable to rule its colonial subjects without understanding them, and understanding equals native language skills. However, only the inferior, i.e. the humans, learns the language of the Other. In *The Conquest of America*, Tzvetan Tordorov emphasizes the historical and political importance of interpreters. By giving the example of La Malinche, a female Indian slave who spoke Spanish, Nahuatl (the language of the Aztecs) and the Mayan language, Tordorov shows that the interpreter was an indispensable tool for the *conquistadors*. La Malinche made communication between the Spanish and the Indians possible and, due to her role, she was despised as a servant of European domination.[102] We can imagine that the aliens in *The Interpreter* would not be able to deal with the humans or exploit the planet on a large scale without the help of interpreters. Towler faces the same problems as La Malinche: the other terrestrials do not trust him since they think he collaborates with the nuls. Inter-

[102] Cf. Tzvetan Todorov, *The Conquest of America. The Question of the Other*, translated by Richard Howard (New York, NY: Harper & Row, 1984), pp. 100f.

estingly, the nuls hold that “there is no terrestrial language, only a series of dialects with which no serious nul could trouble himself” (*TI*, p. 115). They evidently consider the human languages ‘inadequate’ and, as a consequence, the human mind must be ‘inadequate’ as well. This is a further reason for them to control and govern the natives.

A famous play that centres around the work of interpreters and translators in a colonial context is Brian Friel’s “Translations” (first performed in the Guildhall Theatre in Derry, Ireland, in 1980). The three-act play is set in Baile Beag (“Smalltown”) in nineteenth-century rural Ireland and raises awareness of British cultural imperialism. The British military draw maps of Ireland and translate Gaelic place names into English, a task that one of the officers considers a severe intervention into Irish language and culture. Towler’s misinterpretations in *The Interpreter* are surprisingly similar to a scene in Friel’s play. Owen, a man from Baile Beag who has joined the British Army, interprets Lancey’s (i.e. his superior’s) words at the local hedge-school:

> LANCEY: [A new map is being made] so that the entire basis of land valuation can be reassessed for purposes of more equitable taxation.
>
> OWEN: This new map will take the place of the estate-agent’s map so that from now on you will know exactly what is yours in law.
>
> LANCEY: In conclusion I wish to quote two brief extracts from the white paper which is our governing charter: (Reads) ‘All former surveys of Ireland originated in forfeiture and violent transfer of property; the present survey has for its object the relief which can be afforded to the proprietors and occupiers of land from unequal taxation.’
>
> OWEN: The captain hopes that the public will cooperate with the sappers and that the new map will mean that taxes are reduced.
>
> […]

LANCEY: 'Ireland is privileged. No such survey is being undertaken in England. So this survey cannot but be received as proof of the disposition of this government to advance the interests of Ireland.' My sentiments, too.
OWEN: This survey demonstrates the government's interest in Ireland and the captain thanks you for listening so attentively to him.[103]

As we can see, Owen intends to manipulate his fellow Irishmen out of personal motives (he is on the pay-roll of the British Army), and he thereby acts as an agent for the imperial ruler.

Furthermore, Friel's play demonstrates that "[c]olonial discourse erased prior constructions of the land, allowing it to be seen as an empty space, ready to receive their own inscriptions."[104] In fact, new "inscriptions" are also made by the nuls. They classify the different planets according to the type of resources and the atmosphere. Earth is a 5c planet, "the '5' standing for natural products, the 'c' indicating an oxygen-nitrogen world" (*TI*, p. 17). By reducing a planet to a number and a letter, the aliens deprive it of its individuality, and so removing any sense of beauty of the colonized world. What matters to them is the profit they can make. Despite this, however, the traces of the previous character of Earth (before the appropriation of the planet by extraterrestrial invaders) remain intact within man's consciousness, an idea that is referred to as 'palimpsest' in postcolonial studies.[105]

To come back to Par-Chavorlem, the commissioner is depicted as being abnormally cruel. One of his interpreters, Cy Chettle, explains: "Cruelty, extortion, oppression, they're not a way of life to him, they're a hobby" (*TI*, p. 57). This implies that cruelty arouses pleasure in the nul. For the people on Earth, it means that they are left to the mercy of the tyrant. Par-Chavorlem also in-

[103] Brian Friel, *Translations* (London and Boston, MA: Faber & Faber, 1980), p. 31.

[104] Cf. Bill Ashcroft, Gareth Griffiths and Helen Tiffin, *Post-Colonial Studies. The Key Concepts* (London and New York, NY: Routledge, ²2007), s.v. 'palimpsest'.

[105] Cf. *ibid.*

dulges in sexual violence against human women. In a particularly revealing scene, he forces his servant, Clotilda, to recite poetry. Par-Chavorlem stares at her mouth, which is intimately intrusive to nuls and resembles looking at genitalia for humans:

> She babbled, he did not listen. In strained intensity he stared through the separating glass, drinking in the movements of her jaw, chin, eyes, lips, mouth, tongue. These things should be hidden away in all but the ultimate situation. Yet here was a life-form, this flimsy, hateful, biped lifeform [*sic*], flaunting the bright moving bits of itself. It was obscene, revolting. Yet Par-Chavorlem could not tear himself from the sight. (*TI*, p. 50)

Apparently, the sight of the mouth excites the nul in a sexually perverted way. The act of sexual harassment illustrates that he treats human beings, especially females, like objects or possessions. When the servant is released, the omniscient narrator relates that "[t]hese creatures [do] not always escape so lightly" (*ibid.*). Here, the narrator alludes to murder. Later in the novel, a conversation between the interpreters clarifies the allusion; Elizabeth claims that "Chav's getting worse every day. He nearly killed Clotilda early this afternoon. Yesterday one of the computer girls disappeared and it looks as if he took her" (*TI*, p. 57). Therefore, the commissioner is dangerous and morally corrupt; he does not feel pity for his subjects. As Aldiss' novel has a political overtone, these crimes might also raise questions about the crimes committed by the British commissioners in the colonies. Nevertheless, there is no hint in the text that the narrator blames commissioners *per se*.

To conclude, the nuls are portrayed as Other but not too alien. Analogous to human invaders, they are driven by recklessness and greed or, at best, rationality. The jurisdiction, the organization and the size of their empire is reminiscent of the British Empire in the nineteenth century. Par-Chavorlem is a flat character. He is the morally depraved criminal that treats his colonial subjects like vermin. We can imagine that this is the main reason why the people still revolt against the aliens, even though the nuls have been ruling the planet for about two thousand years. Synvoret explains why corruption and other colonial crimes flourish in an empire of enormous size: "the cost of sending impartials investigator to any outlying planet [is] colossal" (*TI*, p. 45). He understands that the greater the empire, the more difficult it is to control the governors of the different planets. Incidentally, the British were alleged of colonial crimes such as genocide in Uganda in the late 1800s,[106] the bloodshed during the Indian mutiny in 1857,[107] or the torture of the Kenyan Mau Mau people in the 1950s.[108] The novel thus raises awareness of the violence and corruption that might lurk beneath the 'grandeur' of an empire.

In *The Interpreter*, the reader also learns in what way the nuls perceive the humans. Interestingly, the depiction of mankind is largely based on orientalist paradigms. In *Orientalism*, Said claims that the concept of the 'Orient' – as opposed to the 'Occident' – has been constructed by European scholars. Yet, as this picture is influenced by imperialist thinking, it is rather stereotypical and barely objective.[109] Among other topics, Said elaborates on the advanced/backward dichotomy that is central to late-nineteenth-century Orientalism and explains the role of the 'Orientals' in an imperialist context:

> Along with all other peoples variously designated as backward, degenerate, uncivilized, and retarded, the Orientals were viewed in a framework constructed out

[106] Cf. "Ugandans sue Britain over colonial era 'crimes'," in: *The Telegraph*, Tuesday 2 February 2010, available on http://www.telegraph.co.uk/news/worldnews/africaandindianocean/uganda/7139493/Ugandans-sue-Britain-over-colonial-era-crimes.html (2011-06-07).

[107] Cf. Peter Marshall, "British India and the 'Great Rebellion'," last updated 2011-02-17, *BBC Online*, available on http://www.bbc.co.uk/history/british/victorians/indian_rebellion_01.shtml (2011-06-07).

[108] Cf. "Mau Mau torture files were 'guilty secret'," in: *The Independent*, Monday 9 May 2011, available on http://www.independent.co.uk/news/world/africa/mau-mau-torture-files-were-guilty-secret-2281456.html (2011-06-07).

[109] Even though Said's work was published after Aldiss' novel, the concept of Orientalism is a historical one. The idea that representing the Other by a construct of false assumptions has, according to Said, a long tradition. Thus, his theories can be applied to Aldiss' novel.

> of biological determinism and moral-political admonishment. The Oriental was linked thus to elements in Western society (delinquents, the insane, women, the poor) having in common an identity best described as lamentably alien. Orientals were rarely seen or looked at; they were seen through, analyzed not as citizens, or even people, but as problems to be solved or confined or – as the colonial powers openly coveted their territory – taken over. The point is that the very designation of something as Oriental involved an already pronounced evaluative judgment, and in the case of the people inhabiting the decayed Ottoman Empire, an implicit program of action. Since the Oriental was a member of a subject race, he had to be subjected: it was that simple.[110]

Representing natives as "problems" that require a "program of action" might be seen as a definition of "subject race" within the constellation of ideas of nineteenth-century imperialism. Accordingly, the nuls portray the terrestrial Other in a way that confirms its role as subject race: man is perceived as irrational, naïve, 'backwards' and entirely different. One of the orientalist paradigms the nuls mention frequently is the bellicose nature of terrestrials (cf. *TI*, pp. 92, 114). In this context, the aliens also refer to the Other as an "emotionally unstable species for whom violence is irresistible" (*TI*, p. 116). This idea has two implications. On the one hand, it characterizes man as brutal, barbaric and morally inferior to the nuls, which corresponds to the irrationality and depravity of the stereotypical 'Oriental'. On the other hand, we can imagine that the author, who served in India and Burma during World War II, criticizes violence. Even though the nuls manipulate the humans as they import Starjjans, the two biped races do fight each other, and it seems to have been a predictable event. Consequently, it becomes evident that Aldiss does not criticize imperialism in general (let alone as harshly as Said does), but what he does condemn is cruelty and criminal offences.

---

[110] Edward W. Said, *Orientalism*, p. 207.

To come back to the nuls' construct of the Other, the aliens refer to human beings as "primitive" (cf. *TI*, pp. 75, 115). Synvoret explains before the Colony Worlds Council: "These bipeds are very primitive, [...] they have had the benefit of only a thousand years of our supervision" (*TI*, p. 115). Synvoret does not specify primitiveness, but we assume that he refers to man's social and intellectual faculties, which classifies the people on Earth as child-like or "lamentably alien"; they have to be "subjugated". Moreover, the idea that nul supervision is beneficial is taken up by the investigator when he observes the civil war on Earth: "Seeing this sort of barbarism makes me more than ever aware that we Partussians have a mission in the galaxy" (*TI*, p. 106). This bears parallels to the civilizing mission of Europeans. Just like in Aldiss' *Non-Stop* (cf. chapter 3.2), it alludes to intervention into so-called 'primitive' cultures. In the latter work, the political evaluation remains ambiguous. In *The Interpreter*, though, the nuls evidently oppress and exploit the humans. Hence, their civilizing mission – if existent at all – only serves the purpose of making profit.

The aliens also represent humans through a big/small dichotomy. Physically, the nuls are much bigger and stronger. They can easily kill a man. The aliens compare the Other to "pygmies" (*TI*, p. 110), a standard orientalist attribute of an inferior culture. When they watch the civil war from a helicopter, the nuls – literally – look down on the bipeds, i.e. they take the "godlike view" (*TI*, p. 106). Synvoret even likens man to lice: "Picked out by telescopes, the tiny figures crawled like lice over a rumpled counterpane, their actions interesting for a while but without significance" (*ibid.*). Therefore, the people are not only inferior but maybe even parasites to the nuls, or mere "problems to be solved" in Said's terms. This is also the reason why the aliens regard them "as beyond rational compassion" (*TI*, p. 110).

Representation of the Other enables the nuls to exercise power over terrestrials. Apart from reckless exploitation, their rule also manifests itself in enslavement of human beings. Gary Towler is a slave in Commission City, punished for a minor (unmentioned) crime (cf. *TI*, p. 23), and his girlfriend, Elizabeth, faces the same fate. As to Elizabeth, we learn that her father was found guilty of tax evasion, and that the aliens force his only daughter to work in

Commission City as a punishment (cf. *TI*, p. 22). The unfair treatment of an innocent woman reveals the nuls' lack of compassion as well as their tyrannical ways of ruling their subjects. The slaves are kept in the City, without any contact to the world outside. Basically, they feel like they are living in a 'pocket universe':

> The City kept its own time, was its own world, marked its own crisis. For most of its oppressed terrestrial inhabitants, it might have been a spaceship adrift in intragalactic night, so slight was their contact with their native Earth. (*TI*, p. 59)

Despite living on Earth, the slaves still strongly perceive the alienness of their surroundings. They seem to be imprisoned in another world. Incidentally, the author takes up one of the main ideas of *Non-Stop* in this quote (cf. chapter 3.2). The description of the people's "native quarters" in the City expresses hopelessness and monotony:

> The streets of the native quarters were almost deserted. They held no beauty; nor were they interestingly ugly. They had been designed by a nul architect on Castacorze, Sector HQ planet, who had seen bipeds only on sense-screens. His vision had materialized into a series of dog kennels. (*TI*, p. 22)

It is worth noting that even architecture reveals the nuls' picture of human beings: the aliens associate humans with dogs, and they have created the accommodation they consider appropriate. Again, it is evident that they feel superior to mankind.

As *The Interpreter* is a novel about racial inequality, it also deals with racism. Aldiss' work is part of a tradition of science fiction novels of the 1950s and 1960s which pinpoint "mistakes that have been made, or crimes committed, in the past when 'superior' races came across 'inferior' ones."[111] Just like in numerous

---

[111] Edward James, "Yellow, black, metal and tentacled: the race question in American science fiction," in: *Science fiction, social conflict and war*, ed. by

other works of that time, mankind is portrayed as one united race and juxtaposed to the alien Other. In addition, even though the theme of racism seems to be more prominent in US-American science fiction,[112] it is also a British topic since the 'science' of race is a British one: on the basis of phrenology and other pseudosciences, the British purported to show that the white race – especially the Anglo-Saxon one – is superior to blacks, for example.[113] Naturally, this 'result' is a major justification of dominance over other cultures in a colonial context. In Aldiss' novel, the nuls are blatantly racist. For instance, they impose "racial restrictions" (*TI*, p. 13) on human beings that recall segregation in the USA or Apartheid in South Africa.[114] Furthermore, the nul Wattol Forlie

---

Philip John Davies (Manchester and New York, NY: Manchester University Press, 1990), 47.

[112] Edward James points out that early works of science fiction depict 'the Yellow Peril', i.e. the US-Americans' fear of conquest by Asian races. Moreover, he convincingly demonstrates the similarities between robots struggling for equality with human beings and blacks in the US after World War II. This topic is dealt with in Isaac Asimov's fiction, for example in the short stories collected in *I, Robot* (1950). Cf. *ibid.*, 40ff.

[113] Cf. *ibid.*, 26.

[114] One of the most popular science-fiction films about racism is perhaps Neill Blomkamp's *District 9* (2009). It shows how aliens (not humans as in *The Interpreter*) become victims of racism. The movie obviously deals with the Apartheid-era in South Africa: when an alien spaceship breaks down over Johannesburg, the refugees – called "prawns" by the people – are taken to the city and forced to live segregate from the population. They stay in District 9, a fenced, impoverished township much like Soweto. The "prawn" embodies stereotypes formerly associated with *kaffirs* (a derogative term for blacks in South Africa): uneducated, lazy and violent, they live in filth and roam garbage heaps. In District 9, Nigerian gangsters sell tinned cat food and slaughterhouse waste to the aliens, control interracial prostitution and traffic weapons. Signs saying "No non-humans" are put up in the city, at bus stops, parks and shops. The plot unfolds around a white Afrikaner, Wikus van de Merve, who works for a private multinational defence and security corporation, MNU. MNU secretly experiment with alien DNA and weaponry, and they are responsible for 'alien affairs'. During a relocation program for the "prawns", Wikus is exposed to an alien fluid and transforms into the Other; in terms of imperial romance, the white man 'goes native'. He finally changes from a human who treats the aliens according to some sort of Apartheid-like protocol into one of them and fights for their acceptance. In the end, two aliens manage to escape from Earth and return to their mothership. About 1.8 million other extraterrestrials – Wikus among them – are relocated to District 10, a mere concentration camp. Thus, the film offers no solution for the two species

makes clear that "[t]he fact that they [human beings] are biped has told against them historically – as it seems to have done against biped races everywhere" (*TI*, p. 12). Consequently, the people on Earth are discriminated against due to physical features. Here, racist paradigms shift: what used to be (and still is) the black skin colour or the Jewish religion, for example, is the number of legs in the science-fiction novel. It becomes clear that the author criticizes discrimination since the 'reason' for racial inferiority (bipedal) appears arbitrary.[115] What is more, a nul weapons expert, Ibowitter, "murdered some two thousand bipeds in an experiment with this new [stereosonic] weapon" (*TI*, p. 25). This form of slaughter would be classified as genocide or as a crime against humanity, and it certainly implies cruelty and hatred for bipeds. Since humans are like "lice" (*TI*, p. 106) for nuls, it might also recall vermin extermination and emphasize the aliens' superiority. Generally speaking, Aldiss raises awareness about the dangers of racial prejudices: they can develop into racism and inhuman crimes. Aldiss' strategy of pinpointing these aspects of colonialism appears like an expression of postcolonial guilt. What is more, showing mankind as a united race in various works of science fiction might emerge from the desire to overcome "an unhappy past of racial misunderstandings and conflicts."[116] In this respect, *The Interpreter* carries the same didactic message as many US-American works of the 1950s and 1960s.

---

living together on Earth; the Other is better off 'at home'. Cf. *District 9* (USA 2009, directed by Neill Blomkamp). For a detailed discussion of the film, see for example Michael Valdez Moses, Lucy Valerie Graham, John Marx *et al.*, "*District 9*: A Roundtable," in: *Safundi: The Journal of South African and American Studies* 11:1-2 (2010), 155-175.

[115] Reducing complex human beings to 'bipedal' appears emotionless as well, and the nuls might associate them with cattle since the number of legs is a marker for the categorization of animals. Incidentally, these notions of rationality, sterility and scientific provability are opposed to the imagination, emotionality and playfulness of children in Charles Dickens' *Hard Times* (1854). The teacher in Dickens' novel, Thomas Gradgrind, makes his pupils describe a horse as "Quadruped. Graminivorous. Forty teeth, namely, twenty-four grinders, four eye-teeth, and twelve incisive. […]." Charles Dickens, *Hard Times* (London *et al.*: Penguin Popular Classics, 1994), p. 4.

[116] Cf. Edward James, "Yellow, black, metal and tentacled: the race question in American science fiction," 47.

Due to the maltreatment of the terrestrial Other, the latter revolt against Partussian rule. Yet, human resistance in *The Interpreter* is carried out by only few brave individuals, i.e. it is not a mass movement, and Earth is eventually not liberated from extraterrestrial domination – a major difference to other works of alien-encounter science fiction. Basically, there are two resistance groups: the guerrillas led by Rivars and the interpreters. The rebels are generally depicted as famous and determined but unsuccessful. Rivars has romantic and naïve ideas about the rise of man, symbolized by the wreck of a ship:

> That's the mast of an old ship. It must be twelve hundred years old at least. All this area used to be sea bed just a few centuries ago. That ship sunk through a series of accidents; now it's been raised up again through another series. The same thing will happen to Earth. Our job is to engineer the right accidents. (*TI*, p. 40)

Obviously, Rivars speaks like a patriotic military leader trying to motivate his troops. His repertoire of hollow phrases also includes "The result will undoubtedly be justice and restitution for our people", "we shall win through at last" and "The way is clear!" (*TI*, pp. 40f.). Rivars' plan of action is to present evidence of Par-Chavorlem's crimes to the inspector, Synvoret (cf. *TI*, p. 108). Relying on the nul's incorruptibility and integrity, he imagines Synvoret as man's saviour. As Rivars is sure of his plan, he drinks "to forthcoming freedom" (*TI*, p. 41). The rebel leader even orders another interpreter, Peter Lardening, to kill Towler since he neither trusts the latter nor understands the difficulties of dealing with the aliens in Commission City (cf. *TI*, p. 109). Rivars thus embodies the committed but irrational guerrilla fighter. Lardening and Towler criticize the fact that Rivars is incapable of diplomacy (cf. *TI*, pp. 41, 119).

However, the interpreters finally learn that diplomacy does not help them to bring down the nuls. For this reason, they decide to attack the aliens directly. They hide in an ambush at a disposal plant, shoot some nuls, take over their vehicles and weapons and destroy the Atmosphere Plant of the City so that the nuls suffocate (cf. *TI*, pp. 122f.).[117] The people also manage to hold the City and defend themselves against the nuls with stereosonic weapons; superior technology leads to victory. In *The Interpreter* and numerous other works, the events take place in an environment where technology is an agent or a tool of imperial expansion and dominance. Thus, superior technology guarantees the victory over the Other and is used to maintain the hegemonic position.

Towler eventually becomes the new leader of the insurgents, ends the war with the Starjjans and spreads notions of hope for the people (cf. *TI*, pp. 122ff.). Earth is freed from nul rule, but as the Partussian Empire includes countless other planets, their empire does not fall after the loss of one colony. The nuls are well aware of the disadvantages of a vast empire; they take into account that the odd planet or two might regain independence:

> [T]he larger the Empire grows, the more thinly its forces are spread. As time goes by, we are less and less able to spare nuls and weapons from the perimeter areas to cope with trouble far behind their lines. Too much pressure on the frontier and the whole balloon collapses. That is why, recently, some rebel planets have been allowed to triumph and retain their independence. Only a comparatively weak blow is needed to knock them flat again. But that weak blow is often not worth the expense. In the future we must hold what we have. (*TI*, p. 75)

Hence, there are limits to the extension of an empire; the nuls admit that they are unable to govern a growing number of planets. The balloon analogy might appear simple and unreliable, but it proves accurate when we consider the fate of Earth. Nevertheless, Earth is not yet ruled by its people. After Par-Chavorlem has been removed from office, a new commissioner of an alien species,

---

[117] The idea that the aliens can be defeated through fire power and divergent biological requirements is taken up in John Christopher's *Tripods* trilogy: when the boys of the resistance group destroy the domes of the Cities, the aliens die from breathing oxygen, and mankind is free (cf. chapter 1.2).

called “Dlotpodite”, is sent to the planet. The men hope that the new ruler sympathizes with them and that they might regain complete independence in the future (cf. *TI*, p. 126). The end of the novel, especially the posting of a new commissioner to Earth, mitigates the notions of success and victory for man. The reader receives the impression that mankind, after two thousand years of Partussian rule, is unable to govern itself. Here, Aldiss highlights that it takes some time to transform from a subject race into an independent people.

To conclude, *The Interpreter* illustrates the effects of protracted colonial governance. The people have changed into a subject race that is exploited under the jurisdiction of the imperial ruler, with the interpreters serving as their mediators and tools for dominance. Due to their Protegé Charter, the nuls are ‘legally unfair’. The novel also deals with racial inequality. Representations of the Other presuppose structures of power. The aliens are depicted as superior to man, for instance they have more advanced technology, an elaborate system of governance and efficient ways of exploiting natural resources. However, they are greedy and racist, and the Commissioner of Earth is the emblem of colonial crimes. *The Interpreter* harshly criticizes mismanagement and reckless exploitation, and it illustrates that crimes committed by the imperial ruler – no matter how ‘fair’ this ruler is according to its own regulations – are not always detected and prosecuted due to a lack of financial resources. Consequently, Aldiss’ work reveals postcolonial guilt. We can imagine that depicting aliens instead of Europeans as imperial tyrants is a means of avoiding negative criticism to a certain extent. Additionally, human beings, or bipeds, are characterized in a way that inevitably marks them as colonial subjects. Equipped with orientalist paradigms, the ‘primitive’ Other necessitates nul tutelage. Men also become victims of racism, much like blacks in times of slavery and of racial segregation in the USA or during the Apartheid-era in South Africa. Human rebellion is considered a brave and noble endeavour, but only if it is carried out in the right way, i.e. not by guerrilla activity or placing trust in an alien investigator (Synvoret fails to reveal the crimes). Finally, Earth is freed from the nuls, but it is not liberated from the rule of a new commissioner and remains a ‘subject planet’.

1.2 Mind Control: John Christopher, The *Tripods* Trilogy

John Christopher (Christopher Samuel Youd, 1922-2012) was one of the most important British authors of juvenile science fiction and widely published in the USA. His literary *œuvre* contains about fifty novels and short-story collections. Among his best known juvenile novels are the *Tripods* trilogy (1967-1968), the *Fireball* trilogy (1981-1986) and *The Guardians* (1970). The latter won the Guardian Award in the UK, the Christopher Award in the United States and the Jugendbuchpreis in Germany.[118] John Christopher also published adult novels such as *The Winter Swan* (1949) and *The Death of Grass* (1956). Recurring themes in his works are post-catastrophic worlds, neo-medievalism and teenage rebellion against adult authority and against the social order in general.

While taking up classic themes of alien-encounter science fiction, the focus of interest of the *Tripods* trilogy lies in the treatment of authority and ideological education. The novels reflect both the Great Terror and the Red Scare (as manifestations of oppression and fear thereof), as well as the political youth movement of 1968, which exemplifies acts of liberation from ideological straightjackets. The *Tripods* trilogy comprises *The White Mountains* (1967), *The City of Gold and Lead* (1967) and *The Pool of Fire* (1968). The British Broadcasting Corporation (BBC) created a television adaptation in 1985. Initially, each of its three seasons was planned to cover one novel of the trilogy. However, after the success had faltered, a third episode was never filmed.[119] In 1988, Christopher published a prequel to the trilogy, *When the Tripods Came*. The predominant themes of *The White Mountains* are freedom, self-determination, the friendship between the teenage protagonists Will Parker, his cousin Henry and their French friend Jean-Paul (called Beanpole), as well as the threat to them by the aliens. Will is a first-person narrator, which implies that his report shapes our

---

[118] Cf. John Newsinger, "Rebellion and Power in the Juvenile Science Fiction of John Christopher," in: *The Science Fiction Foundation* 47 (1989), 46.

[119] Cf. John Christopher, Preface to *When the Tripods Came* (New York *et al.*: Simon Pulse, 2003), p. iii. All subsequent references to this edition are in brackets in the text.

understanding of the world under the rule of the Tripods. In the novel, Earth is controlled by extraterrestrial Masters. The Masters use huge metallic tripods for transport and live in domed "Cities" that meet their biological needs. They maintain their rule by "Capping" the humans, i.e. at puberty, they fix a metallic "Cap" on every person's head and thereby indoctrinate and control mankind. However, Will, Henry and Beanpole are not yet "Capped" and dread the ceremony. They decide to join a resistance group, the "Free Men", and travel to a stronghold that is located in an ancient railway tunnel within what we presume is Mont Blanc.

The City of Gold and Lead centres around the aim of the resistance group to establish freedom for mankind. In their three Cities, the Masters hold numerous human slaves. The homodiegetic narrator Will and his companion Fritz are sent on a mission to discover any weaknesses the aliens might have. The novel depicts the miserable conditions of the slaves in the City: at best, they are treated like pets; at worst, they are beaten and abused by their Masters. Due to the hard labour, the humid and hot climate and increased gravity, the slaves usually die within a year. Nevertheless, Will manages to escape and informs the insurgents about the Masters' plan to change the atmosphere of Earth and destroy all life on the planet.

In *The Pool of Fire*, the perseverance and the willpower of the resistance group are eventually crowned with success: they bring down a Tripod, capture a Master and study it. As they find out that alcohol has a paralyzing effect on the alien, they decide to use it against the Masters. Insurgent agents travel around the world to set up resistance cells of "Uncapped" teenagers. They intend to infiltrate the Cities again and simultaneously poison the water system with alcohol. That gives them time to switch off the Pool of Fire, i.e. the City's energy source. Two missions succeed, but the attack in the third City fails. Finally, they destroy the City with explosives launched from air balloons. The end of the trilogy remains ambiguous: after the liberation of mankind, national resentments reemerge. The prequel, *When the Tripods Came*, is set in the late twentieth century. The homodiegetic narrator Laurie, a teenage boy like Will, elaborates on the way the Masters conquer Earth: they brainwash humans through a TV programme, the *Trippy Show*, and make them gladly accept the Caps. The Capped men then force the Uncapped ones to wear the device. Laurie and his family flee to Switzerland where they establish the resistance stronghold in the Alps. The ending of the prequel builds up a notion of anticipation and hope.

When interpreting Christopher's *Tripods* novels, most critics focus on the aspect of initiation and development of the teenage protagonists. In this analysis, however, I would like to elaborate on the Masters conquering Earth as it is crucial to the works. This is due to the fact that, without the invasion of the Tripods, the world of the novels would not provide a basis for the teenage heroes to rebel against authorities and undergo tremendous developments. Not only do the protagonists revolt against the beliefs of adults but their predominant aim is the victory over the extraterrestrial conquerors. Generally speaking, the reader learns that the Master have "been rulers of the earth for more than a hundred years"[120] when the trilogy starts, i.e. their regime begins in the late twentieth century. Their arrival on the planet is depicted in the prequel *When the Tripods Came*. What is interesting is that people are surprised rather than scared when they see the first Tripod. They quickly consider it awkward and ridiculous. The Tripod's appearance is called a "cosmic farce" (*WTC*, p. 15), and the humans wonder why the Tripods "don't even have infrared" (*ibid.*). Moreover, "a single sortie from a single air force squadron [is] sufficient to reduce [the Tripod] to mechanical garbage" (*ibid.*). This shows that, despite the impressive size of the Tripods, people do not take them seriously, let alone dread the metal monsters. In addition, the machines from space are described as little menacing: "The Tripod was coming on in its awkward skittering motion, a metal spider that had lost all but three of its legs.[…][I]t looked small, unthreatening" (*WTC*, p. 147). The comparison of the Tripod to a small animal like a spider that could easily be squashed underestimates its power and size, though this portrayal will change in the course of the trilogy.

In order to gain control over mankind, the Masters eventually find an efficient way to condition human beings: by broadcasting the *Trippy Show* on TV, they brainwash the people and turn them

---

120 John Christopher, *The City of Gold and Lead* (New York *et al.*: Puffin Books, 1984), p. 10. All subsequent references to this edition are in bracket in the text.

into faithful followers, the "Trippies" (cf. *WTC*, p. 37). Initially, the print media understands the danger. For example, the homodiegetic narrator of the prequel, Laurie, tells us that the *Daily Mail* publishes an article about the strange behaviour of the Trippies: a boy set fire to his parents' house, a girl tried to stab her father with a knife, and numerous children leave their families in order to live together in so-called "Trippy communes" (cf. *ibid.*). On the one hand, this article comprises adults' fears of losing control over their children. The idea of a commune recalls the rebellion against society and the traditional concept of the family that emerged in the 1960s. Young people decided to live together in a way that undermined the set of values of the previous generation. In a way, this is what the Trippies do as well. Yet, on the other hand, we learn that the Trippies gradually become a serious threat to the public order. For instance, they form mobs and riot in the streets. Even though police and politicians are alarmed, they do not interfere at this point (cf. *WTC*, p. 45).

What follows is the second arrival of the Tripods on Earth. Fanatically welcomed by the Trippies, they tower near the big cities and Cap the first humans (cf. *WTC*, pp. 46ff.). We receive the impression that a new religion has developed; a priest even calls it "the Second Coming" (*WTC*, p. 92). The Trippy community grows and mankind is soon split into two parties, the Capped and the Uncapped. The situation approaches a civil war:

> The order came in a radio announcement; television had vanished in a welter of jammed transmissions. All free citizens were to take immediate action to help counter the activities of the Capped. This must involve total collaboration with the armed forces and police, who had authority to restore order by any means at their disposal. The situation was difficult, but could be overcome by free men and women fighting in defence of liberty. Meanwhile, the use of all sea and air routes was confined to government-authorized personnel. As far as possible, people should remain in their homes, avoid using motor transport except for emergencies, and listen for official announcements. (*WTC*, p. 75)

This is the moment when people understand that the invasion of the Tripods and its consequences for man must be taken seriously as there is the danger of losing control. As to the Masters' strategy, the example of Julius Caesar in France is brought up (cf. *WTC*, p. 89). During the Gallic Wars (58-51 BC), Julius Caesar claimed to support one tribe when fighting against another, and he subsequently succeeded in defeating all of the tribes. Generally speaking, the Romans stand for imperial power *par excellence*. Comparing the Tripods to them emphasizes the aliens' status of conquerors of the planet.

Eventually, the Capped form the majority on Earth and only few free men remain. The Capping of adolescents is a central element that pervades the trilogy which is set about one hundred years after the arrival of the metal monsters. The autodiegetic narrator of the trilogy, Will Parker, explains that the Masters rule men with the help of the Caps:

> They governed simply and effectively, by dominating the minds of men. This was achieved through the Caps, meshes of silvery metal which fitted closely round the skull and were woven into the very flesh of their wearers. Capping occurred in one's fourteenth year, marking the point at which one ceased to be a child and became an adult. It was taken for granted, an expected, looked-for thing, attended by feasting and celebration. (*CGL*, p. 10)

Thus, the Caps deprive the people of their free will and dehumanize them, turning them into "slaves" (*WTC*, p. 143). In the opening credits of the BBC series, we see a golden web that might symbolize the nervous system. The web then dissolves and transforms into the triangular shape of the Cap. This implies that the Capped are mind-controlled and lose their individuality. In the novels, the Capped are twice referred to as "cattle".[121] Therefore, mankind is not only a colonized race but also comparable to animals that exist to be exploited. This corresponds to the fact that the Masters hold

[121] John Christopher, *The Pool of Fire* (New York: Aladdin Paperbacks, ²1988), pp. 8, 186. All subsequent references to this edition are in brackets in the text.

slaves in their Cities. In addition, it is reminiscent of the discussions about slavery in the eighteenth and nineteenth centuries. Western nations exploited the colonies' resources as well as the indigenous population and, just like the Masters in Christopher's novels, treated the slaves like cattle. Hence, history is reflected in the science-fiction works. In addition, slavery is a recurrent theme in several famous novels about British imperialism. However, in contrast to the slaves, the Capped gladly accept the symbol of serfdom. They believe that the Cap is a rite of passage for a boy or a girl on the way to adulthood. Yet, due to the Cap, adulthood is attended by the loss of independent thought. This implies that Capping is a parody of traditional initiation rites. Additionally, only few teenagers question the ceremony. For most of them, Capping Day is an event to look forward to since they consider the Cap an honour. Therefore, within a mere hundred years, the Masters have established new traditions and crucially altered society. This illustrates their superiority over mankind. However, the new social order will be discussed later in this chapter.

The trilogy also features individuals whose Caps do not completely deprive them of their self-determination. These people are called "Vagrants", and they are usually ostracized by society. Will explains:

> Vagrants were people for whom the Capping had proved a failure. They had Caps, as normal people did, but they were not working properly. If this were going to happen, it usually showed itself in the first day or two following a Capping: the person who had been Capped showed distress, which increased as the days went by, turning at last into a fever of the brain. In this state, they were clearly in much pain. […] [The Vagrants'] minds, certainly, had been affected. None of them could settle to a train of thought for long, and many had visions, and did strange things.[122]

---

[122] John Christopher, *The White Mountains* (New York *et al.*: Simon Pulse, 2003), pp. 11f. All subsequent references to this edition are in brackets in the text.

It seems that the Vagrants become insane. In the BBC series, there is an additional scene that depicts Vagrants. In episode 11 of the first season, Will, Henry and Beanpole escape from a French village after having stolen food. In an adjacent forest, they encounter a group of Vagrants who are dressed like stereotypical savages: their faces are painted black and white, and they wear feathers in their hair. Their dwelling place is surrounded by skulls stacked on poles. These strongly resemble the skulls near Kurtz's hut in Joseph Conrad's *Heart of Darkness* (1899).[123] Obviously, the skulls symbolize savagery and superstition. What is more, they are an orientalist stereotype of 'primitive' decoration and frequently associated with cannibalism. It is striking to encounter this *idée reçue* in a science-fiction novel. However, it demonstrates how close the parallels between this genre and nineteenth-century colonial literature can be. The fact that there are savages in the forest also implies that the Vagrants' minds have deteriorated due to the unsuccessful Capping; they are wild and primitive. Hence, even though these people are not properly Capped, they have lost their independent thought to a certain extent and turned into madmen.

One of the Vagrants who wanders through the village where Will and Henry live is Ozymandias. Ozymandias is about thirty years of age, "a powerfully built man, with red hair and a beard" (*WM*, p. 22). The mysterious and apparently insane Vagrant speaks in poetic language and announces: "I am the king of this land. My wife was the Queen of a rainy country, but I left her weeping. My name is Ozymandias. Look on my works, ye mighty, and despair" (*ibid.*). The man's strange name reminds Will of a poem, and it is obvious that the boy thinks of Percy Bysshe Shelley's eponymous sonnet. Ozymandias is another name of the Egyptian pharaoh Ramses the Great, and the sonnet features a traveller who sees the shattered statue of the pharaoh lying in the sand. The major theme of Shelley's poem is the fall of a mighty leader.[124] Thus, the Va-

[123] Joseph Conrad, *Heart of Darkness & Other Stories*, p. 85.

[124] The third stanza of Shelley's poem reads:
"And on the pedestal these words appear:
My name is Ozymandias, king of kings:
Look on my works, ye Mighty, and despair!"

grant in Christopher's novel makes it clear that even leaders as powerful as the Masters could eventually fall, and he indirectly expresses that there is hope for mankind. This can be interpreted as *prolepsis*. Will subsequently finds out that Ozymandias only pretends to be a Vagrant. He actually wears a false Cap and recruits boys to join the resistance group in the White Mountains (cf. *WM*, pp. 34f.).

Ozymandias eventually convinces Will to refuse the Cap and leave the village in order to work for the Free Men. Even before he meets the false Vagrant, Will questions the Capping procedure since he understands that it is accompanied by the loss of independent thought. Apparently, the name Will is not randomly chosen by the author: it emphasizes the boy's claim for free will and thereby sets him apart from the Capped "automatons".[125] Will comes to the conclusion that he "would rather die than wear a Cap" (*WM*, p. 39), i.e. he is an intelligent, free-thinking teenager. Even though he has grown up in a society that generally takes Capping for granted, he is critical of the procedure and, after having spoken to Ozymandias, against it. He appears mature for his age (Will is thirteen). As to the Masters, they underestimate adolescents: even though the teenagers are rather young, they are capable of understanding the system of mind-control and of making their own decisions. What is more, by refusing the Cap, Will rebels against two authorities: the Masters as well as the parents. The former depend on mind-control in order to maintain the social order they have imposed on man; the latter have been indoctrinated and cannot imagine that a teenager does not want to be Capped, neither do they allow this idea. Thus, apart from showing disobedience to the Tripods, Will's reluctance also demonstrates that he opposes adult values and beliefs. This usually appeals to the adolescent readers of Christopher's works as they are given the possibility of identifica-

---

It is evident that the Vagrant directly quotes from the poem. Cf. Percy Bysshe Shelley, *Percy Bysshe Shelley, Poetical Works*, ed. by Thomas Hutchinson (Oxford *et al.*: Oxford University Press, ²1970), p. 550.

[125] Cf. Claire Walsh, "From 'Capping' to Intercision: Metaphors/Metonyms of Mind Control in the Young Adult Fiction of John Christopher and Philip Pullman," in: *Language and Literature* 12 (2003), 237.

tion with the teenage heroes.[126] The adolescents in the novels develop individual personalities. As a consequence, the trilogy bears certain traits of a *Bildungsroman* or *Entwicklungsroman*.

As the trilogy was written in the late 1960s, it reflects the counterculture of that time. The hippie culture, which developed mainly in the USA and in Great Britain, widely changed the Western way of living. Many young people rebelled against those middle-class values their parents had taught them since they held that conservative beliefs impeded their freedom of personal expression and development. They also felt that they had to get involved in the debates about nuclear weapons and about social and racial difficulties. In 1958, approximately eighty thousand pacifist protesters stood up against a-bombs in Trafalgar Square, London. This demonstration developed into the 'ban the Bomb' movement. Incidentally, the famous peace symbol was created in this context. In addition, protests against the war in Vietnam (1964-1975) played a crucial role. In the USA, the demonstrations started in Berkeley, California, in 1965. There were student strikes, anti-Vietnam war marches and other forms of protests. These demonstrations soon spread throughout the USA, and the university turned into a political arena. The protests ended when the last American troops were withdrawn from Vietnam, and the country was eventually liberated from foreign colonizers. Part of the anti-war movements was a growing disillusionment with the traditional interpretation of the American Dream. Young people pursued different lifestyles characterized by sexual freedom, the liberation from hierarchical social structures and a turning-away from material values. With regard to Christopher's novel, Ozymandias bears traits of a free-thinking young man during the 1960s, and it is obvious that Will is impressed with the way Ozymandias revolts against the authority of the extraterrestrial Masters.

In the second novel of the trilogy, *The City of Gold and Lead*, the Masters' outward appearance is described in detail. In general, they are characterized by grotesque and repulsive features: they are

126 Welsh and Newsinger come to the same conclusion. Cf. Claire Walsh, "From 'Capping' to Intercision: Metaphors/Metonyms of Mind Control in the Young Adult Fiction of John Christopher and Philip Pullman," 238, and John Newsinger, "Rebellion and Power in the Juvenile Science Fiction of John Christopher," 47.

of a greenish-brown colour, have three thick, short legs, three tentacles, three eyes and two mouths, and they look identical at first sight (cf. *CGL*, pp. 83ff.). Will describes them as "disgusting" but simultaneously "ridiculous" monsters (cf. *ibid.*). Thus, the Masters must appear completely alien to human beings. The Masters also emblematize the Other. In colonial literature, alterity is a means of characterizing indigenous peoples on the one hand, and of self-definition on the other. Therefore, even though the Capped are mind-controlled, they are less Other and clearly more human than the Masters. Yet, Christopher mitigates the antitheses between men and aliens, i.e. a human being is not depicted as the binary opposite of a Master. For example, the Capped are rather automatons than self-determined beings, and Masters can have human qualities such as a sense of humour (cf. *PF*, pp. 79f.) or curiosity (cf. *CGL*, p. 108). Thus, 'man' and 'Master' are not mirror images. As to the Masters' physical features, they are approximately twice as tall as men and very strong (cf. *CGL*, p. 83). This might indicate superiority or even a more advanced state of evolution. Additionally, just like in *Childhood's End* (cf. chapter 2.1), men are repeatedly referred to as "pygmies" (*PF*, pp. 88, 132, 157), which is an orientalist paradigm. This might imply that they are deemed to be inferior to the colonizing race and that their resistance is considered feeble.

Under the rule of the Masters, human society has regressed, and it seems that man has taken the role of the 'native' in colonial encounters. For instance, everyday items such as watches have become rare. For Will, wearing his father's watch is something special – and forbidden (cf. *WM*, p. 4). We also learn that people live without electricity. When the boys visit the ruins of a substation, they cannot understand that the letters "LECT CITY" on the rusty metal plate refer to electricity. Instead, they wonder if it is the city where the metal plate was made (cf. *WM*, pp. 8f.). Apart from creating humour, the idea that watches and electricity are mysterious to man makes clear that the world of the novels is crucially different to the reader's reality. The reader can find points of reference, i.e. the world has not entirely changed (as is the case in other science-fiction works). Nonetheless, the reader understands that, due to the dominance of the Masters, society has undergone tremendous changes; he or she gradually increases his or her understanding of the new world order in the novels by comparing the setting of the texts to his or her own environment and culture.

It is striking that the Masters' dominance is not entirely based on their futuristic technology. Actually, the aliens do not posses any technology that might be considered far advanced. They do have spaceships, but this cannot be called astonishing from the perspective of the late 1960s. The humans are even surprised that the aliens switch on white searchlight beams at night instead of using infrared (cf. *WTC*, p.15). Furthermore, their transport machines, the Tripods, are repeatedly described as rather clumsy and awkward (cf. *WTC*, p. 147; *PF*, p. 57). Finally, the Masters can be deceived: Ozymandias and other human beings wear false Caps. Thereby, they are not controlled by the aliens, and we must assume that the latter are ignorant of the fraud. Instead of basing their rule on advanced technology, the Masters deprive people of their forefathers' achievements. This renders them different from alien races in other science-fiction novels such as Wells' *The War of the Worlds* and Clarke's *Childhood's End*.

The Capped believe that technology and science have become redundant. Laurie, the homodiegetic narrator of the prequel, understands that "[s]cience [is] a part of independent thinking, and that [it is] over for the human race" (*WTC*, p. 123). When he talks to his friend Andy about ice statues, we realize that Laurie is nostalgic since he knows that there will not be any new inventions as long as the Masters rule:

> He [Andy] was fascinated by a life-size ice motorcar, and pointed out it must have been carved more than seventy years ago because it was a model of an early Ford. I [Laurie] thought of how much things like motorcars and airplanes had changed in those seventy years. It was as though mankind had been a surfboarder, riding a high wave of invention. Who could tell what wonders would still have lain ahead? But now, thanks to the Tripods, it had all ended. (*WTC*, p. 136)

Eventually, society finds itself in a pre-industrial era; the achievements of the former generations have gradually been forgotten. The most crucial evidence for this thesis is that the Capped are conditioned in a way as to avoid the "great-cities" of the ancients (cf. *WM*, p. 78). Approximately one hundred years after Laurie muses about the end of innovation, Will tells us that the cities where man dwelt before the invasion of the Tripods are deteriorated and uninhabited: "[The cities] were little talked of, and then with disapproval and a shade of dread. No one would dream of going near them. [...] Those were the cities where all the murdering and sickness were" (*WM*, p. 13). In order to avoid the Capping and to join the resistance group in the Alps, Will and his friends travel through France. On their way, they come to a city which we assume to be Paris. After some hesitation, the boys decide to walk through it, and they encounter numerous things that are unfamiliar to them, for example cars. Additionally, what they find interesting are the great shops and the items that are still on the shelves; Will even finds himself a watch (cf. *WM*, pp. 79ff.). The atmosphere Christopher creates is claustrophobic and threatening. The depiction of the deserted and ruined city reminds the reader of post-apocalyptical films such as *I am Legend*[127], *Resident Evil*[128] or *Mad Max*[129]. Incidentally, in the *Tripods* series, the city is still inhabited: the boys are followed by a group of Vagrants and dogs, whom they manage to chase away by throwing hand grenades.[130] In the novel, they also find grenades, but they just take them and wait for a later point in time to attack a Tripod (cf. *WM*, pp. 88ff.). It becomes clear that the scene in Paris has a certain function in the novel: it shows that the knowledge of the former generations has been completely lost. The Caps have transformed intelligent and curious human beings into ignorant and naïve slaves.

The Masters have imposed a new social order on man: they have replaced a technologically advanced civilization by a feudal one. What might be termed 'neo-medievalism' manifests itself in

---

[127] *I am Legend* (USA 2007, directed by Francis Lawrence).

[128] *Resident Evil* (USA 2002, directed by Paul W.S. Anderson).

[129] *Mad Max* (Australia 1979, directed by George Miller).

[130] Cf. *The Tripods* (UK 1984, directed by Graham Theakston), season 1, episode 4.

various forms. For instance, when watching the BBC series, we see the pastoral landscapes of England and France, the costumes of the characters bear medieval traits, and the upper class dwells in castles. The teenage protagonists stay with a Comte and his family. Thus, several *topoi* of the Middle Ages are brought up. On the one hand, neo-medievalism implies that man is back in the 'dark ages', i.e. there is little or no scientific progress and the majority of the population is uneducated. On the other hand, though, the fact that man lives without electricity, running water, *et cetera* turns them into stereotypical savages. They live in a 'savage' state as they appear primitive compared to the human civilization that existed a hundred years before them. The reason for putting humans into this state is evident: the Masters have chosen a form of social order that takes serfdom for granted. Under the feudal system, the people had to serve a superior. The king was at the top with the nobles, barons, lords and knights below him. In return for service, individuals received protection by their superiors. In the trilogy, however, the people are not protected. Instead, the Masters brainwash them, thereby making them submissive. As a consequence, we might say that they obviously exploit mankind. This is reminiscent of Kurtz in Conrad's *Heart of Darkness*: the greedy and insane ivory trader makes the Congolese population believe that he is something like a god and ruthlessly exploits the resources as well as the people. Clearly, he has also managed to brainwash the 'primitives'.[131] Hence, similar mechanisms of mind control and enforcement are applied. To come back to the Middle Ages, man did not know scientifically advanced weapon systems. From the prequel, we know that a Tripod can easily be defeated with a missile (cf. *WTC*, p. 11). Thus, the Masters protect themselves by making people ignorant and obedient.

In the trilogy, the emblem of feudalism is the Château de la Tour Rouge. During the protagonists' journey through France, Will suffers from a fever and collapses. Seeking shelter in a hut, the boys are caught and taken to the castle. There, the Comtesse and her daughter Eloise kindly take care of Will and allow Beanpole and Henry to stay in the esquires' quarters (cf. *WM*, pp. 105ff.).

[131] Cf. Joseph Conrad, *Heart of Darkness & Other Stories*, pp. 91ff.

The nobles are exceedingly kind, gentle and honest. Will even falls in love with the beautiful Eloise (cf. *WM*, p. 111). Incidentally, the topic of love is extended in the BBC series: the audience sees the two flirting and kissing, and Eloise's father eventually announces their marriage.[132] Above all, the nobles offer to adopt Will; the King of France might even grant him nobility (cf. *WM*, p. 120). Nonetheless, the adoption would imply Capping. At this point of the novel, the teenage protagonist seriously thinks about what is best for him, i.e. he oscillates between freedom of thought and pleasant captivity. On the one hand, staying at the Château is like stepping out of time for the boy. He feels relief after the hardships of the journey and enjoys spending time with Eloise. The break with traditional time is symbolized by his watch falling into the river (cf. *WM*, pp. 125f.). In addition, Will understands that the Cap does away with his insecurities and misgivings:

> Before Capping there might be doubts and uncertainties and revulsion; perhaps these people had known them, too. When the Cap was put on, the doubts vanished. How great a loss was that? Was it a loss at all? The Tripods, apart from the act of Capping itself, did not seem to interfere much with men. […] Ozymandias had spoken of men working in mines underground to get metals for the Tripods, of the Tripods hunting men, of human beings serving them in their cities. But even if those things were true, they must happen far away. None of it touched this secure and pleasant life. (*WM*, p. 123)

These thoughts, as well as his love for Eloise, make the teenager want to stay with the noble family.

---

[132] Cf. *The Tripods* (UK 1984, directed by Graham Theakston), season 1, episode 6. John Christopher comments on the differences between the novels and the BBC series in the preface to *When the Tripods Came*. He states: "For the first half of the first series the producer had followed my story line reasonably closely, but in the second half he made a lot of changes, and in the second series even more. It eventually reached a point where I found it difficult to trace any connection with the original." (*WTC*, p. iii) We receive the impression that the author does not agree with the vast discrepancies between his novels and the series.

Yet, on the other hand, Will also muses about continuing the journey to the White Mountains. He feels that he must be loyal to his friends who have already left to join the resistance group (cf. *WM*, p. 127). Eloise is Capped and thus "belong[s], irretrievable, body and soul, to the Enemy" (*WM*, p. 116). This implies that the Masters take away the possibility of love and govern people's feelings to a certain extent. Will also understands that, at the castle, every year is similar to the preceding one: in summer, there are the tournaments, the hunting and the Harvest Feast in autumn, the Christmas Feast in winter, hawking in spring, and then come the tournaments again (cf. *WM*, p. 122). In fact, this sounds very much like *ennui*. We receive the impression that the nobles are happy but lethargic. We can also assume that they have lost any interest in innovations and adopted automatic behaviour patterns. The Comtesse and her *entourage* have lost their independent thinking due to the Caps and, if Will were Capped and stayed with them, he would be a "sheep among sheep" (*WM*, p. 121).

The idea of beautiful but lethargic beings that are compared to cattle recalls H.G. Wells' *The Time Machine* (1895). In the novel, an anonymous Time Traveller finds out that mankind has evolved into two species in the far future: the carnivorous, ape-like Morlocks and the beautiful but childish Eloi (in fact, the name 'Eloise' sounds like 'Eloi'). When the Time Traveller meets the Eloi, he soon realizes that the little people are easily fatigued and lack interest and intelligence, because there is no struggle in the world of AD 802,701.[133] They spend their time playing, laughing, sleeping and eating, and they are "cattle" for the Morlocks.[134] The Eloi are therefore comparable to the nobles at the Château. Due to her beauty, Eloise is elected Queen of the Tournament (cf. *WM*, p. 131). However, this honour has a terrible consequence: she must leave her family and serve the Masters in their City. What is striking is that the girl is very happy about this as she has been conditioned (cf. *WM*, pp. 135ff.). Will experiences a strong feeling of "[h]orror" (*WM*, p. 137), and he eventually leaves the castle to catch up with his friends. His looking back to the Château de la Tour Rouge is a symbolic scene: from a distance, he does not only

---

[133] Cf. Herbert G. Wells, *The Time Machine* (London: Phoenix, 2004), p. 28.
[134] Cf. *ibid.*, p. 38.

make out the castle but also a Tripod "standing sentinel among the rushing waters of the river's other branch" (*WM*, p. 139). This means that life at the castle is not free since the people's minds are dominated by the Masters. The nobles' empire has become the empire of the Tripods.

For the Capped, life on Earth appears to be comparable to a utopia. Generally speaking, the reader learns that the Masters' rule covers the whole world, i.e. all civilizations – including the technologically advanced ones that were once the colonial powers – have been transformed into feudal ones. Ironically, this implies that all men are slaves and therefore finally equal. Moreover, the Masters have abolished war: "The Tripods stalked the earth, guiding and helping their followers against bands of men whose weapons were puny, or non-existent. In the end, there was peace" (*CGL*, p. 115). What is more, the Capped do not doubt the legitimacy of the Tripods' rule and they are happy in general (cf. *WTC*, p. 57). A similar society is depicted in Arthur Clarke's *Childhood's End* (cf. chapter 2.1). Nevertheless, in Christopher's novels, we cannot speak of utopia as peace and happiness are enforced by the Masters. Instead, the Masters control and exploit human beings; these are characteristics of Empire. Istvan Csicsery-Ronay points out:

> The model of Empire is grounded in the history of real empires. Utopia is crafted from an abstract conjunction of community and natural harmony; Empire is energized by a more concrete relationship: the conjunction of might and right. Even in its most idealized form, Empire is a complex machine that distributes – and thereby produces – force. In utopias, force is occasionally rationalized as a way of protecting the balance between people and state, and insuring the inviolability of the enclave. In Empire, it is the vitalizing condition of possibility. All the social and creative endeavors of imperial peoples are shot through with the institutional violence that makes them materially possible. Imperial

> violence is so powerful that it must expand; contained, its society would implode like a black hole.[135]

Brainwashing the Capped might be termed imperial violence. In addition, the ability to establish peace and order through imperial violence is a recurrent issue in imperialism. Among other qualities, the imperial powers justified their rule with it. As to the abolition of war, the British ended tribal conflicts in Africa and India, for instance, and protected India from the Russians. British missionaries were proud of imposing Christian values on the 'heathens'. For example, they forbade superstition and cannibalism. Yet, these 'noble' ideas served as a moral basis for imperialism and exploitation.

There are numerous examples of Europeans that bring peace to the 'savages' in the classical romances of Empire. One of the most famous works is probably Sir Henry Rider Haggard's *King Solomon's Mines* (1885). *King Solomon's Mines* is Haggard's first African romance adventure. It narrates the quest for the fabled treasures of King Solomon in the unexplored regions of southern Africa. Together with the autodiegetic narrator Allan Quatermain, a hunter and adventurer, the British aristocrat Sir Henry Curtis and his friend Captain Good search for Sir Henry's brother who has disappeared during an expedition for Solomon's mines. One of their servants is a native Zulu, Umbopa. Following Quatermain's mysterious map, the party travels over a desert and crosses mountains until they reach the fertile valley of Kukuanaland. The Kukuanas are ruled by the ferocious king Twala and the evil witch Gagool. Umbopa then reveals that he is the rightful king of Kukuanaland and a rebellion breaks out. However, Umbopa's army and the three British men overpower Twala and capture Gagool. Their purpose is noble as they fight for the installation of the rightful king. They finally beat Twala's army and Sir Henry kills the tyrant. We receive the impression that the Kukuanas are actually noble savages that cannot lead a happy life due to the scheming of their ruthless and cruel king. Furthermore, this lays a basis for the intrusion of the whites into Kukuanaland; they free the natives from

[135] Istvan Csicsery-Ronay, "Science Fiction and Empire," 236f.

their oppressor and therefore 'deserve' the Solomonian treasure. Umbopa becomes King Ignosi and thereby restores order and peace in Kukuanaland. Yet, it is evident that the installation of the legitimate and 'good' king was only possible with the help of Quatermain, Sir Henry and Captain Good.[136] The ability to establish peace and happiness is a quality shared by the Europeans and the alien Masters. It might eventually be used as a justification for exploitation.

Generally speaking, the Masters' dominance is expressed by two symbols: the Tripods and the Cities. The Tripods are the aliens' means of transport. As they cannot survive in the atmosphere of Earth, the Masters depend on the huge machines whenever they leave their Cities. One hundred years after the arrival of the aliens, the Uncapped are afraid of the Tripods; initially, they also equate them to the Masters. The dread is due to the size of the machines as well as to the mystery that surrounds them. Will narrates the coming of a Tripod in his little village as follows:

> At last we heard, above the clang of bells, the deep staccato booming in the distance, and there was a kind of sigh from everyone. The booming came nearer and then, suddenly, we could see it over the roofs of the houses to the south: the great hemisphere of gleaming metal rocking through the air above the three articulated legs, several times as high as the church. (*WM*, p. 15)

Men are as small as "insects" (*PF*, p. 198) compared to the Tripod. Additionally, the BBC series features red Tripods with laser guns. These look even more aggressive and threatening than the silver ones.[137] Incidentally, the special effects in the *Tripods* series were sophisticated and unprecedented. This rendered the series one of the most expensive adaptations of the BBC. Even though the Tripods are only shown for approximately sixty seconds per episode, they seem to be omnipresent, creating an eerie atmosphere. In the

---

[136] Cf. Henry Rider Haggard, *King Solomon's Mines* (Oxford *et al.*: Oxford University Press, 2008).
[137] *The Tripods* (UK 1984, directed by Christopher Barry), season 1, episode 13.

depiction of the Tripods, Christopher owes a lot to H.G. Wells: the tripods in *The War of the Worlds* are very similar to the ones in Christopher's works. For instance, one of them is described as "a walking engine of glittering metal, striding now across the heather; articulate ropes of steel dangling from it, [...] a great body of machinery on a tripod stand."[138] At the bottom side of the hemisphere, the tripod has a gate that might be comparable to a mouth, and its picking up humans can be seen as 'swallowing' them.

Before the resistance group brings down a Tripod and captures a Master, they do not even know if the Tripods are mere machines or partly sentient beings (cf. *PF*, pp. 65ff.). In fact, human or animal features sometimes seem to blend with robotic ones when a Tripod is described in detail. For instance, a Tripod that attacks a ship is characterized as a "vicious boy" (*CGL*, p. 48), which is a rather awkward portrayal of a machine.[139] The tentacle that grips human beings is perceived as "hard metal but weirdly resilient, pulsing with what seemed like life" (*CGL*, p. 72). This illustrates the unknowability of the machines and the resulting fear by the Uncapped. When the Tripods search for the teenage heroes, Christopher creates an uncanny and claustrophobic atmosphere. The boys are surrounded by about a dozen machines that try to find them with their light beams at night. Will, Henry and Beanpole hide in a stone crevice until the Tripods are gone. They are close to the stronghold of the resistance group and, after all the hardships and dangers of the long journey, they finally encounter the Free Men (cf. *WM*, pp. 183ff.). Naturally, scenes like these create suspense and appeal to the adolescent readers.

The second symbol of the Masters' rule is their City. We learn that the Masters, just like the Martians in Wells' *The War of the Worlds* and the nuls in Brian Aldiss' *The Interpreter* (cf. chapter 1.1), cannot survive in the atmosphere of Earth (cf. *CGL*, p. 129). When Will is taken to the City in Germany, he describes it as "an

---

[138] Herbert G. Wells, *The War of the Worlds*, pp. 55f.

[139] Incidentally, the Tripods in the water might make the reader think of the Maunsell Sea Forts, gun emplacements constructed in the Thames Estuary area during World War II. The bulky towers, which provided anti-aircraft fire during the war, stand in the water on stilts. For photos of the Maunsell Sea Forts, see http://www.undergroundkent.co.uk/maunsell_towers.htm (2012-05-09).

enormous bubble of green-tinged crystal" with a roof "of gleaming gold, on which flashed a titanic emerald" (*CGL*, p. 75). This description might make the reader think of an impressive religious building such as the Dome of the Rocks in Jerusalem. Given the idea that society in the trilogy bears neo-medievalist traits, the heroes entering the Masters' City might have crusading elements. Furthermore, the massive shiny building reveals the power as well as the technological and architectural faculties of the aliens. What is striking is that the City is so disconnected from the landscape that it appears to be an illusion. Will narrates: "The eye […] could almost imagine that the City was not there at all – that if one looked hard enough, the illusion would vanish, and there would be just the river running through ordinary fields" (*ibid.*). Thus, the City has certain qualities of a fairy-tale castle; it is beautiful, mysterious, unreal and threatening at the same time.

The inside of the City appears repulsive and hostile for human beings. For instance, the air is damp and hot, and everything is shed in a green light (cf. *CGL*, pp. 76ff.). Incidentally, green might be associated with illness, which stresses the idea that the Masters are perceived as 'parasites' on Earth. Moreover, Will feels as if he were "far down in a thick forest" (*CGL*, p. 76). In numerous garden-pools grow "ugly, somber-colored plants [that look] like menacing sentient beings themselves" (*PF*, p. 110). A forest or jungle is a recurrent setting in colonial literature. Again, the most prominent example is probably the jungle at the banks of the Congo River in Joseph Conrad's *Heart of Darkness*. Conrad's novella is narrated by an anonymous frame narrator who tells the story of the master mariner Marlow. Marlow is employed as a riverboat captain with the Company, a Belgian enterprise that organizes trade in the Congo. While undertaking the difficult and dangerous journey up the Congo River, Marlow receives the impression that

> [g]oing up that river was like travelling back to the earliest beginnings of the world, when vegetation rioted on the earth and the big trees were kings. An empty stream, a great silence, an impenetrable forest.

> The air was warm, thick, heavy, sluggish. There was no joy in the brilliance of sunshine.[140]

For Marlow, it feels like stepping out of reality: "We were wanderers on a prehistoric earth, on an earth that wore the aspect of an unknown planet."[141] Although Conrad's and Christopher's works are crucially different, it is interesting to note how similar Will's and Marlow's impressions are; both find themselves in an environment that should actually be avoided since it is characterized by darkness, obscurity and desolation.

In Christopher's science-fiction novels, the City of the Masters is not a jungle. Instead, the boys perceive it as an enormous maze (cf. *CGL*, pp. 80f.). What is striking is that all the buildings have the shape of pyramids (cf. *ibid.*). This might be an allusion to the ancient pyramids of the Egyptians or the Mexicans. These pyramids were built for eternity and they symbolize power and sacredness. As the pyramids are triangular, the number three seems to play an important role for the Masters (they use Tripods and have three legs and three eyes, much like the nuls in Aldiss' *The Interpreter* [cf. chapter 1.1]). The pyramid is also the ideal shape for displaying hierarchy and surveillance. This thesis was elaborated on by the French philosopher Michel Foucault (1926-1984) in *Discipline and Punish: The Birth of the Prison* (1975):

> [T]he disciplinary gaze did, in fact, need relays. The pyramid was able to fulfil, more efficiently than the circle, two requirements: to be complete enough to form an uninterrupted network – consequently the possibility of multiplying its levels, and of distributing them over the entire surface to be supervised; and yet to be discrete enough not to weight down with an inert mass on the activity to be disciplined [...].[142]

---

[140] Joseph Conrad, *Heart of Darkness & Other Stories*, p. 61.
[141] *Ibid.*, p. 63.
[142] Michel Foucault, *Discipline and Punish: The Birth of the Prison* (New York, NY: Vintage Books, ²1995), p. 174.

Thinking about architecture and surveillance, the Capping of humans might bear parallels to the Panopticon (a prison building that allows the overseers to observe the prisoners without letting them know that they are being watched): the Masters are able to monitor the Capped and maybe even read their thoughts. Likewise, the utilitarian philosopher Jeremy Bentham (1748-1832) described the Panopticon as "a new mode of obtaining power of mind over mind [...]."[143] Even though this idea was developed in the late eighteenth century, we can clearly see the parallels to the concept of Capping; both Capping and the Panopticon serve as means of surveillance and, indirectly, control. What is more, the fact that the Masters build Cities, i.e. implanted settlements, on Earth gives them the quality of not only an imperial but also a colonial power.

Inside the City, slaves work for the Masters: "Slaves, or sacrifices. After all, though hundreds of men and women each year entered the City, none had yet been known to come out" (*CGL*, p. 63). All over the world, humans take part in sports tournaments, the winners of which then go to the City to serve the Masters. In order to gain knowledge on the aliens, the resistance group has worked out the following plan: Will, Beanpole and a German boy, Fritz, are to travel to the games in Germany and enter the City as spies. Eventually, Will and Fritz win the competitions and are taken to the City in a Tripod (cf. *CGL*, pp. 63f.). On entering the City, the three discover that human slaves perform various tasks for the Masters. For instance, they tidy homes, cook food, change the damp moss in which the aliens sleep, and prepare their Masters' baths as the latter are fond of lying in hot water (cf. *CGL*, pp. 99f.). Will and Fritz are dismayed by the bad state of health of the slaves. Due to the moist heat and the high gravity in the City, the slaves are ill, exhausted and age much more quickly. In the BBC series, there are slaves that look as if they were in their sixties, but the boys find out that these men are actually not much older than the teenage protagonists.[144] This tells us that the slaves live under horrifying conditions. However, due to the Caps, they are happy and

[143] Cf. Derrick Jensen and George Draffan, *Welcome to the Machine: Science, Surveillance, and the Culture of Control* (White River Junction, VT: Chelsea Green Publishing, 2004), p. 8.

[144] *The Tripods* (UK 1985, directed by Bob Blagden), season 2, episode 5.

consider serving the Masters an honour; they obey as if they served gods. The slaves' lives in the City are very short and when they realize that they are no longer strong enough to serve the Masters, they choose to die at the "Place of Happy Release":

> Some crumpled up and died almost at once; others lasted a year, two years. Fritz had met a slave who had been more than five years in the City, but he was exceptional. When the slave knew that death was on him, he went, of his own volition, to the Place of Happy Release, and died in the glad assurance that he had served the Masters to the utmost of his ability and the last atom of energy. (*CGL*, p. 98)

This implies that the Capped slaves dedicate their lives entirely to the Masters. It also illustrates that the life of a Capped person is not worth anything; the slaves only exist to serve. However, reducing a person's life to serfdom deprives him or her of essential human qualities. We might say that the slaves do not live but they only fulfil a function.

Not only this, the aliens abuse their slaves. For example, Fritz' Master frequently beats the boy, although the maltreatment is not the consequence of any wrong-doings. Instead, Fritz' Master is sadistically cruel. Fritz tells Will: "I howl and shriek a lot, which pleases him" (*CGL*, p. 97). The fact that some Masters inflict pain on 'inferior' beings like slaves shows that they are morally depraved. Will is not physically abused, but mentally. In fact, his Master treats him like a pet. In chapter seven of *The City of Gold and Lead*, "My Master's Cat", Will describes the relationship between him and his Master in detail. We learn that the Master initially treats the teenager with respect and kindness. Due to this, Will even considers himself "fortunate" (*CGL*, p. 88). It is only later that Will understands what lies behind his Master's behaviour: the alien expects his slave to keep him company and talk to him. The teenager feels like his Master's "cat" (*CGL*, p. 101) or "kitten" (*CGL*, p. 107). The repulsive alien even cuddles Will (cf. *ibid.*), which might add a bizarre erotic subtext to the novel. After having questioned the boy about friendship, the Master announces:

"You will be my friend" (*CGL*, p. 109). Will takes advantage of his Master's ignorance and of the strange relationship to tell the alien lies and investigate the Masters' intentions. He discovers that they have a terrible plan:

> [O]ur atmosphere was as poisonous to them as theirs to us. This meant that outside the enclaves of the Cities they could only be masked; and not just head-masked as we slaves were here, but with their whole bodies covered by a clinging greenish envelope, because the brightness of the sun's light hurt their skins also. [...]
>
> All this, though, could be changed and would be. The success of the expedition, the conquest of this world, had been reported back to the home planet. Samples had been taken – of air, water, other natural constituents. Their wise men had studies them, and in due course the message had been sent: the earth's atmosphere could be altered to enable the Masters to live naturally in it. [Mighty engines] would take in our air and breathe out an air suited to the Masters. (*CGL*, pp. 129f.)

Will immediately realizes that the changes in atmosphere and climate would be followed by the death of flora and fauna. This would also be the end of the human species. The Master then reveals that the spaceship bringing the machines will arrive on Earth in four years (cf. *CGL*, p. 131). This means that the resistance group is running out of time to set up a plan to defeat the aliens, preventing the planet being completely taken over by the Masters. This goes even beyond occupation and exploitation. In imperial terms, the annihilation of the human race might be compared to a settler colony – but on a global scale.

To come back to the slaves in the City, it is striking that there is also a movement against slavery.[145] The movement is briefly men-

[145] Even though the time reference of the novels obviously lies in the counterculture of the 1960s, the anti-slavery movements in the Cities of the Tripods might also recall the discussions about the abolition of slavery in Victorian times. One of

tioned in *The City of Gold and Lead*. We learn that some of the Masters protest against human slavery in the Cities (*CGL*, p. 92). Yet, in contrast to the anti-slavery movements in Victorian times that emphasized Judeo-Christian values and advocated the equality of the races of man, the Masters generally consider the humans inferior (cf. *CGL*, p. 128). In fact, their movement against slavery is "based on fear, not that the slaves might revolt, because no one doubted their docility, but that the Masters, in accepting the personal service of other creatures, were somehow weakened and degraded" (*CGL*, p. 92). We receive the impression that the aliens are reluctant to admit any weaknesses as this would undermine their 'right' to conquer and colonize Earth.

However, the structures of domination in the BBC series are different from the ones in the novels. In the novels, the aliens' aim is to colonize new territories whereas, in the series, their motives are governed by so-called "Cognoscs". The Cognoscs are countless immaterial entities that consist of pulses of energy and form the "Space Brain".[146] The latter is comparable to the Overmind in

---

the most famous opponents of slavery was Charles Darwin. Generally speaking, *The Descent of Man* might also be read as a pamphlet against slavery. Even though Darwin's *The Voyage of the Beagle* features the idea of a 'racial ladder', his more mature work, *The Descent of Man*, does not include this theory. In his later work, Darwin explains that "[s]lavery, although in some ways beneficial during ancient times, is a great crime; yet it was not so regarded until quite recently, even by the most civilised nations" (Charles Darwin, *The Descent of Man, and Selection in Relation to Sex*, pp. 141f.). This is a very clear statement that criticizes the ideology of the Empire before 1833, i.e. before the abolition of slavery. The Darwins had for a long time been committed in the abolitionist movement and, when the Beagle reached Brazil in April 1832, Darwin was appalled to find slavery in the country. In his journal, he writes: "It may be said there exists no limit to the blindness of interest and selfish habit" (Charles Darwin, *The Voyage of the Beagle. Journal of Researches into the Natural History and Geology of the Countries Visited during the Voyage of HMS Beagle round the World, under the Command of Captain Fitz Roy, RN.*, ed. by Tom Griffith, with an introduction by David Amigoni [Ware: Wordsworth Classics, 1997], p. 26). The overarching subject of *The Descent of Man* are the races of mankind, their origin as well as the reasons for diversification. Darwin's work can be interpreted as a proof of the unity of the human races; all races must be classified under the same species. It also becomes evident that racial diversity (a possible basis for slavery) is natural and has developed due to sexual selection. This means that one race is not superior to another.

[146] *The Tripods* (UK 1985, directed by Bob Blagden), season 2, episode 8.

Childhood's End (cf. chapter 2.1). The Masters' task is to provide the physical environment the Cognoscs require. For example, Will learns that the Cognoscs 'dwell' in the peaks of the pyramids in the City and are all connected to the Pool of Fire, i.e. the City's source of energy. The Cognoscs know about every individual's psychological functions.[147] This implies that the Space Brain is aware of the fact that Will and Fritz wear false Caps and belong to a human resistance group. Therefore, Will is taken to a Cognosc. Coggy, as the entity calls itself, does not have a physical existence, and so it is not depicted as a character in the series. Instead, Will is lifted up to a bright empty space where he hears Coggy's voice. What is interesting is that the 'cell' of the Space Brain seems to mock the teenager. For example, it laughs at the idea of resistance and the "depths of human desperation".[148] In addition, the Cognosc plays with Will's mind: Will suddenly finds himself dancing with his beloved Eloise on a clock face. When a bell tolls, Eloise runs away and leaves Will with a glass shoe in his hands. He then sees Eloise in a glass coffin and breaks the shoe. Will is painfully reminded of the fact that he is not a fairy-tale prince as in "Cinderella" but a slave in the City of the Masters.[149]

One of the central topics of the trilogy, human resistance, manifests itself in two different (albeit interrelated) ways. The teenage protagonists' objectives are liberation from the extraterrestrial conquerors *and* self-determination, i.e. freedom from the ideological norms the Masters have imposed on man. Strikingly, the Cognosc encourages Will to fight for these aims.[150] Even though the entity refuses to collaborate with the resistance group, we receive the impression that it does not agree with the Masters' plan to destroy Earth. Furthermore, apart from telling the insurgents not to under-

---

[147] The name "Cognosc" derives from the Latin verb 'cognoscere', which means 'to become acquainted with' and 'to know'.

[148] *The Tripods* (UK 1985, directed by Bob Blagden), season 2, episode 8.

[149] "Cinderella" is not the only fairy tale that might be thought of. K. V. Bailey points out that the protagonists' acquisition of knowledge to destroy the Masters recalls "Hansel and Gretel" and "Jack the Giant-Killer". Cf. K. V. Bailey, "Masters, Slaves, and Rebels: Dystopia as Defined and Defied by John Christopher," in: *Science Fiction for Young Readers*, ed. by C.W. Sullivan (Westport *et al.*: Greenwood Press, 1993), 111n6.

[150] *The Tripods* (UK 1985, directed by Bob Blagden), season 2, episode 9.

estimate themselves, Coggy helps Will to escape from the City. As Coggy has decided to leave the planet, the entity collects huge amounts of energy and thereby causes an emergency at the City's power station. Due to the high demand for cooling water, the current of the river increases and the filters in the water are opened. The Cognosc ascends into the sky in a blue ball of light and Will leaves the City through a canal. We can only speculate why the screenwriters included the Cognoscs in the plot. On the one hand, the idea of a Space Brain, i.e. an immaterial futuristic entity, might appeal to the audience. On the other hand, the inclusion of the Space Brain in the storyline crucially alters the hierarchical structures as the Masters are turned into mere 'servants' of the Cognoscs. The Cognoscs govern the Masters and are clearly superior to the aliens. Will's Master even admires Coggy.

In the novel, Will also escapes through the river. Accompanied by his friend Beanpole, he travels back to the White Mountains (cf. *WM*, pp. 152ff.). The most important piece of information Will has gathered is that the Masters intend to annihilate all life on Earth. Generally speaking, the ending of the trilogy remains ambiguous. *The Pool of Fire* initially narrates major successes of the human resistance group: they establish cells of insurgents in various countries, infiltrate the Cities again and break the golden domes so that the aliens are poisoned. This is a difference to *The War of the Worlds* since the aliens in Wells' novel are not defeated by man but by bacteria.[151] In both works, though, mankind is free in the end. What is striking is the fact that Christopher's rather inexperienced teenage heroes develop into brave and committed men in the course of the story. The group of insurgents they join clearly has military structures, and the liberation of mankind from the rule of the Masters equals a war. These military elements recall the conquests of the colonies in the eighteenth and nineteenth centuries as well as the struggles for independence. In the case of the *Tripods* trilogy, the colonized race defeats the imperial power and regains its freedom. We also learn that the Caps lose their function as soon as the Masters are dead. Thus, the minds of the people are no longer controlled (cf. *PF*, p. 137). After the victory over the Masters,

[151] Cf. Herbert G. Wells, *The War of the Worlds*, p. 195.

science and technology gradually return. For example, the human beings reinvent diesel-electric trains and ships (cf. *PF*, pp. 203f.). The leader of the resistance group, Julius, announces a "glorious future" as the people are eager to reacquire and maybe also improve the achievements of the previous generations (cf. *PF* p. 210). Thus, mankind seems to undergo a second Industrial Revolution, and the reader might expect that society can go back to its normal state within a relatively short period of time.

Nevertheless, Christopher subsequently portrays the negative consequences of freedom as the question remains who will rule Earth after the liberation from the aliens and the resulting power vacuum. Thus, delegates from all countries meet in the White Mountains. The Conference of Man is held by Julius, the leader of the Council. The latter has specific ideas on how to govern the planet:

> [F]reedom had been achieved, and local governments had arisen, all over the world, each administering its own territory. International affairs, the control of science, and so on, fell into the jurisdiction of the Council.
>
> It was clearly the interest of everyone that some such system should continue. But it was also essential that it should come under the democratic control of the peoples of the world. For this reason, the Council was prepared to dissolve itself and hand over its authority and functions to a similar, though possibly larger, body which would be properly representative. (*PF*, p. 211)

First of all, the delegates discuss the appointment of a leader for the new Council. Yet, despite all his achievements, Julius is not reelected. This result starts resentments and discord between the different nations. For instance, the delegate of the United States calls the Conference a "farce" and withdraws (cf. *PF*, p. 216). Subsequently, the Chinese, the English and other delegates leave as well. The Germans even insult the French and threaten them with military power (cf. *PF*, pp. 216f.). Eventually, the Conference ends in chaos and no aim is reached. Indeed, this is a surprisingly negative ending for a trilogy that narrates the perseverance and the heroic actions of the human resistance group. Furthermore, the feelings of antipathy, suspicion and the preconceptions that are displayed during the Conference would not have been possible under the rule of the Masters. This is due to the fact that the Caps generated conformity and peace. Hence, the question arises what is more beneficial for mankind: freedom but discord or pleasant captivity – the same question Will had to answer at the Château de la Tour Rouge. The novels contain criticism of contemporary politics and the division of power, but they do not offer a solution, let alone indicate any utopian alternatives. In the end, the teenage protagonists set themselves a new target: they intend to "get men to live together, in peace as well as in harmony" (*PF*, p. 218), free from the restraints of being Capped. However, they seem to be painfully aware of the fact that this new fight will be "a longer, less exciting one, with no great triumphs at the end" (*ibid.*).

To conclude, I hope to have shown that the Masters in John Christopher's *Tripods* trilogy are colonizers of Earth. The mechanisms of enforcement and control generally parallel a colonial situation: the extraterrestrials generate tremendous psychological changes as they brainwash and dehumanize their colonial subjects, they impose a new social order on them, and they subsequently enslave and exploit mankind. These features are also depicted in nineteenth-century colonial literature. The Tripods as well as the Cities serve as symbols of dominance. In addition, instead of introducing highly advanced alien technology on Earth, the aliens deprive human beings of the knowledge and the scientific achievements of their forefathers, so that mankind find itself in a 'savage' state and takes the role of 'natives' in colonial encounters. The idea that former colonial nations – just like all other humans on Earth – undergo experiences of exploitation, slavery and death might absolve them from past sins.

Despite the establishment of peace and equality on a global scale, society is not a utopia. Instead, the situation bears traits of Empire as it generates force and violence. The Masters' most crucial weakness is that they underestimate the adolescents; just like the generation of 1968, the Uncapped rebel against adult authority and, simultaneously, against the rule of the Masters. Within the context of the counterculture of the 1960s, the Uncapped bear traits of young people undermining conservative middle-class values. In fact, the protagonists are intelligent and free-thinking young men, and it is due to their perseverance and courage that the human resistance group is able to defeat the aliens. Both the conquest of Earth and the struggle for independence resemble wars in the colonies. The trilogy also includes elements of social criticism since the end remains ambiguous: after the liberation of mankind, bias and national conflicts re-emerge; the question who will rule the planet eventually remains unsolved.

1.3 Conquest of Space and Time: Stephen Baxter, *Timelike Infinity*

Stephen Baxter was born in Liverpool, England, in 1957. He holds degrees in mathematics from Cambridge University, in engineering from Southampton University and in business administration from Henley Management College. Baxter had worked as a teacher of mathematics, physics and information technology before he became a full-time author in 1995. His first science-fiction story, "The Xeelee Flower", was published in *Interzone* in 1987. Baxter is one of the most famous English authors of hard science fiction.[152] He has published more than thirty novels, several works of non-fiction and numerous short stories collected in *Resplendent* (2006), *The Hunters of Pangaea* (2004) and *Phase Space* (2002), among others. Baxter also wrote alternate history. One example is *Time's Tapestry* (2008), a novel in which Hitler successfully invades Britain.[153] Moreover, the author contributed to TV productions for the BBC and Sky One, and his novel *Voyage* (1996) was dramatized and broadcasted for BBC Radio. Finally, Stephen Baxter is a Chartered Engineer and Fellow of the British Interplanetary Society.[154]

Many of Baxter's novels have won awards such as the British Science Fiction Association Award for Best Non-Fiction (*Omegatropic*, 2001), the Philip K. Dick Award for Best Novel (*Vacuum Diagrams*, 1999, and *The Time Ships*, 1997) and the award of the Oxford University Science Fiction Group for best novel published in paperback in the preceding academic year (*Coalescent*, 2005). Among Baxter's most popular works are those of the *Xeelee* se-

---

[152] As mentioned in the introductory chapter, hard science fiction purports to create 'realistic' scenarios based on scientific theory. Naturally, it is debatable if all the events depicted in Baxter's novel, and all the theses they are supposed to be based on, can be taken seriously. For example, Baxter takes pains to describe black holes, singularities, *et cetera*. This is to give his storyline a touch of realism, but I doubt that physicists, astronomers and other experts would agree to what he writes. Needless to say, when we read science fiction, we should leave our doubts as to the credibility of the events behind and embrace the idea of escaping into a world of future possibilities.

[153] Cf. http://www.stephen-baxter.com/articles.html#nazis (2011-10-05).

[154] http://www.stephen-baxter.com/author.html (2011-10-05).

quence, a series of seven novels and various short stories in which different alien species invade Earth.[155] *Timelike Infinity* (1992) is the second novel in the *Xeelee* sequence. Discussing this work in my study might surprise as it does not explicitly treat imperial history. In contrast to other narratives, the novel's focus does not lie in depicting the new world order extraterrestrial rulers impose on man. Instead, the novel as a work of hard science fiction is characterized by its technology-dominated way of narration and detailed references to the natural sciences. The language generally suggests scientificity and, even if tropes such as time travel, hyperdrive, singularity cannons and an alien creature as spaceship are, of course, far from realistic, the readers allow themselves to get engaged with the universe of the novel. However, *Timelike Infinity* goes beyond the traditional features of hard science fiction; it illustrates that a socio-political topic like imperialism can also provide good material for the subgenre. Just like in 'soft' examples of alien-encounter science fiction, the subject race is portrayed as inferior to the invader. The merit of Baxter's novel is that it highlights the reasons for this difference between the two species, a difference that is one of the bases of imperial rule: science and technology serve as the 'measure' of civilization and facilitate power over others. Thus, the novel places the reasons *why* the Qax invade Earth and what they *do* there (form of rule, occupation laws, *et cetera*) into the background. Rather, it demonstrates *how* the dominant position of the Qax is gained – and how they eventually lose it.

The plot of *Timelike Infinity* allows for a portrayal of various tropes of hard science fiction. In the far future, i.e. around AD 5400, the turbulent-liquid aliens, called "Qax", have ruled Earth for about two hundred years and mankind has degenerated: space-

[155] The novels are *Raft* (1991), *Timelike Infinity* (1992), *Flux* (1993), *Ring* (1994), which are collected in an omnibus (cf. Stephen Baxter, *Xeelee: An Omnibus*. With an Introduction by Paul McAuley [London: Gollancz, 2010]), *Coalescent* (cf. Stephen Baxter, *Coalescent: A Novel. Destiny's Children Book One* [New York, NY: Del Rey, 2004]), *Exultant* (cf. Stephen Baxter, *Exultant. Destiny's Children Book Two* [New York, NY: Gollancz, 2004]) and *Transcendent* (cf. Stephen Baxter, *Transcendent. Destiny's Children Book Three* [New York, NY: Gollancz, 2005]). A timeline of the *Xeelee* sequence can be found on Stephen Baxter's homepage. Cf. http://www.stephen-baxter.com/articles.html#xeelee (2011-11-21).

travel is banned, immortality treatments are forbidden, and the belief in human technology is shattered. Thus, a group of fanatics from the future, the "Friends of Wigner", travel back through time in order to change history and influence the ultimate destiny of man with the help of an Interface portal, or wormhole, designed by the human engineer Michael Poole. The plan of the Friends of Wigner threatens Qax domination, and the alien governor of Earth has his own portal built in order to receive help from the future. Yet, shortly before the future Qax governor arrives, humans manage to destroy the alien spaceship and close the Interface. The destruction of the wormhole eventually 'disarranges' space-time: Michael Poole travels five million years into the future, where he is transformed into an immaterial entity and observes a new beginning of the era of man. The novel is narrated through the eyes of human beings – more specifically of the ambassador Jasoft Parz, the engineer Michael Poole and his colleague Miriam Berg – which is different from the more complex narrative situation in Brian Aldiss' and Gwyneth Jones' works (cf. chapters 1.1 and 3.3). Naturally, the characters evaluate the aliens and their actions from a human point of view. This has implications for the depiction of the aliens as Other and as colonial power: the reader sympathizes with the people from Earth and condemns alien domination.

With regard to the depiction of the Other, information about the aliens as species is scarce. The Qax only reveal themselves to two men and, apart from giving some background information on the aliens, the narrators lay emphasis on the first-contact experience. First, the reader learns what the Qax governor of Earth tells Jasoft Parz. Generally speaking, the Qax appear entirely Other to the ambassador. They are quasi-immaterial "turbulence" inhabiting the ocean of their home planet: "A sea, much like the primaeval [*sic*] ocean of Earth, covered the world from pole to pole. Submerged volcano mouths glowed like coals. The sea boiled: everywhere was turbulence […]."[156] The governor also explains that there are only a limited number of Qax individuals due to their massive size: "The greatest of [them] span miles" (*ibid.*). In addition, Qax convection cells "can readily be renewed and replaced" (*TII*, p. 45),

[156] Stephen Baxter, *Timelike Infinity* (London: Voyager, 1997), p. 44. All subsequent references to this edition are in brackets in the text.

which renders the aliens immortal. Naturally, humans would not associate these characteristics with organic beings; the Qax are clearly Other. Nevertheless, Parz's reaction is rather moderate, and he asks the governor more questions. The second character that sees a Qax is Jim Bolder, protagonist of Baxter's short story "Blue Shift" (1989) which is also set during the Qax occupation of Earth. In contrast to Jasoft Parz, Bolder is actually taken to the planet of the Qax. This direct confrontation with the Other evidently overwhelms him. His reactions are restricted to silence and sudden movements. He narrates: "I jumped, whirled around", "I bristled" and twice "I stared". Neither is Boulder able to focus on the voice of the Qax in the "translator box". The scene ends abruptly with a leap in time.[157] It becomes obvious that the first contact with the Other in its alien environment traumatizes him. As to colonialism, the Otherness of the aliens characterizes them as unknowable and thereby threatening.

Concerning the Qax as colonial power, the reasons why they occupy Earth are unambiguous. What is striking is that the human narrators mention how easy it was for the aliens to gain control over Earth. After a short "honeymoon period" of trading and cultural exchange, the Qax realized that they could effortlessly take over the planet: "As soon as the Qax had found out how weak and naïve humanity really was, [their] warships had moved in" (*TII*, p. 10). Thus, the aliens simply take the opportunity to gain power. Furthermore, the Qax are portrayed as "natural traders" (*TII*, p. 17) whose intentions centre around short-term profit – like so many extraterrestrial species in alien-encounter science fiction. Their trading empire spans "hundreds of star systems" (*TII*, p. 62), and the Qax function as "independent corporations, in pure competition" (*TII*, p. 17). Parz imagines the laws that govern their society in the following way:

> [The Qax] would swim in a sea of perfect information about each other's activities and intentions, kept in some semblance of order only by the operation of the laws of economics. [...] And trading relationships

[157] Cf. Stephen Baxter, *Vacuum Diagrams. Stories of the Xeelee Sequence* (New York, NY: Eos, 2001), pp. 181f.

> would be their natural mode of approaching other species, once they started spreading beyond their own planet. (*ibid.*)

Hence, the Qax are 'naturally' driven by greed. The idea that a Qax works like a corporation deprives it[158] of any characteristics associated with a biological creature, a theory that is corroborated by the fact that the aliens are immaterial and practically immortal (cf. *TII*, pp. 44f.). A Qax resembles a company that exploits its employees (the subject races) for the sake of profit. This reflects the concept of company rule in the colonies. For instance, the British East India Company governed India from 1757 to 1858, the British East Africa Company controlled Kenya between 1888 and 1893, and the British South Africa Company under Cecil John Rhodes colonized what is today Malawi, Zambia and Zimbabwe from 1887 to 1923. Just like the Qax on Earth, the main target of these companies was the material gain through exploitation of the natives' land and natural resources. This led to forced labour policies, dispossession of the indigenous population and deteriorated living-conditions.

In the universe of Baxter's novel, competition is presented as something natural, i.e. the different species can neither be blamed for their striving for domination nor for the means they employ to reach a superior position over their competitors – a theory that will be further elaborated on in the course of this chapter. The concept clearly recalls capitalism. In the context of imperialism, capitalism aggravated the discrepancy between 'civilization' and 'savagery', as John Rieder makes clear:

> As local economies ravaged by the new extractive industries (oil, rubber, tin, copper, precious metals) and regional specialization of agriculture (cotton, sugar, pineapple) became "underdeveloped" and dependent, so too the cultures that the traditional economies had supported often were thrown into shock and disarray.

[158] A Qax will be referred to as 'it' since it has no material form, let alone biological sex or social gender. The voices in the translator boxes sound masculine in some instances, and feminine in others (cf. *TII*, pp. 12f., 74).

> What the dominant ideology recognized as the relation between civilization and savagery, and between modernity and its past, can be read at least in part as a misrecognition of the corrosive effects of capitalist social relations on the traditional cultures of colonized populations and territories.[159]

Accordingly, the 'underdeveloped' humans, whose scientific achievements have been banned by the Qax, are regarded as backward and dependent. Due to the capitalist universe, even the former imperialist nations on Earth have been transformed into subject races.

Since the Qax as traders operate "in pure competition" (*TII*, p. 17), the so-called 'Scramble for Africa' comes to the reader's mind. Before 1884, only the coastal regions of Africa were ruled by Europeans. The competitive rush for the rest of the continent was initiated by the Berlin Conference (or *Kongokonferenz* in German) in 1884 and 1885. The European powers divided Africa into fifty colonies and thereby superimposed new geographical borders on the indigenous population. The British and French held the largest territories: France governed much of northern Africa, and Britain dominated the east and the south. Germany ruled what is now Namibia and Tanzania, and the other African countries were taken by Italy, Portugal, Spain and Belgium. Thus, between 1885 and 1910, the commercial and political rivalries of the European nations resulted in the fact that almost the entire African continent (except Liberia and Ethiopia) was colonized in only twenty-five years.[160] With regard to the aliens in Baxter's novel, we can imagine that they divide their empire like Europeans did, which implies that the planets are conquered and plundered without the

---

[159] John Rieder, *Colonialism and the Emergence of Science Fiction*, p. 26.

[160] For more information on the 'Scramble for Africa', see for example Stig Förster, Wolfgang J. Mommsen and Ronald E. Robinson, *Bismarck, Europe, and Africa: The Berlin Africa Conference 1884–1885 and the Onset of Partition* (Oxford *et al.*: Oxford University Press, 1989); Thomas Pakenham, *The Scramble for Africa: White Man's Conquest of the Dark Continent from 1876 to 1912* (London: Abacus, 1991); Mia Carter and Barbara Harlow (eds.), *Archives of Empire. Vol. 2: The Scramble for Africa* (Durham, NC, and London: Duke University Press, 2003).

consent of the natives. This stresses the greed and ruthlessness of the Qax.

As a work of hard science fiction, Baxter's novel highlights the crucial role of scientific and technological achievements of a society or species in the struggle for dominance. The idea that discoveries in natural sciences and machines serve as a 'measure' of a nation directly originates in nineteenth-century European thinking. Europeans considered their historical experience unique and felt that they differed from others due to, amongst others, their technological skills. Distinctness was based on simple polarities:

> The polarities were numerous and obvious: metal versus wood; machine versus human or animal power; science versus superstition and myth; synthetic versus organic; progressive versus stagnant. All aspects of culture could be linked to these polarities, to the fundamental dichotomy between industrial and preindustrial societies.[161]

This way of thinking shaped the concept of the Other since there was the widespread belief that non-Western peoples could be evaluated and 'ranked' according to their level of industrialization, which eventually generated stereotyping and prejudices. For example, African cultures were considered incapable of scientific thinking, and people thought Black Africans used only the most primitive technology. Thus, nineteenth-century observers speculated that the massive stone edifices in the colony of Southern Rhodesia (which is now Zimbabwe) could not have been built by the indigenous population. India's level of science and technology was deemed to be roughly comparable to that of Europe in the Middle Ages – and even inferior in arts and agriculture. These prejudices were largely shaped by one specific work, James Mill's *History of British India* (1817), which pays particular attention to the backwardness of Indian science and technology – a major 'proof' of a low level of civilization. Other Orientalists held that India used to be highly civilized but subsequently stagnated due to various rea-

[161] Michael Adas, *Machines as the Measure of Man. Science, Technology, and Ideologies of Western Dominance*, p. 144.

sons, for instance climate, government and 'racial inertia'. Even Gustave Le Bon, who had a high regard for Indian art, architecture, religion, *et cetera*, argues in *Les civilisations de l'Inde* (1887) that Indians were truly inferior to the Western world with regard to scientific discoveries, and that this feature led to British domination. Just like India, China was seen as a once sophisticated society that had fallen into long-term deterioration. European scholars named the despotic Chinese regime and the refusal to accept foreign innovation and skills as reasons for the decline. They also believed that the plans for impressive scientific and artistic achievements (like the Great Wall) were not originally from China but imported by Caucasians from Persia, 'Aryan' invaders or peoples from the Middle East. Furthermore, numerous writers commented on China's feeble military power as evidence of its low level of development, which was revealed in particular during the Opium War of 1839-1842.[162]

The major attribute that set Europeans off from other cultures was science and technology as a manifestation of the triumph over Nature. Non-industrialized peoples were considered victims of every 'natural caprice' (such as floods, hostile climate or impassable terrains) and unable to make use of Nature's resources. This indicated a low level of civilization, as illustrated in the works of Charles Darwin (1809-1882), for example. Therefore, Europeans argued that those people required paternalistic tutelage, and the agents in their 'mission to civilize the savages' were technological accomplishments such as railroads, steamships, telegraphs and factory machines. Technology was supposed to ensure commercial growth, to decrease poverty and hunger, and even to do away with social evils like cannibalism, human sacrifice and polygamy. Hence, people thought that the living-conditions in the colonies could only be improved by Western science and technology, which simultaneously justified Europe's global hegemony. Naturally, prejudices towards the 'savages' might come across as Western arrogance from nowadays' perspective, and assumptions of European superiority have been criticized by European intellectuals themselves.[163] However, it is undeniable that Europeans had (and

---

[162] Cf. *ibid.*, pp. 133ff.

[163] Cf. *ibid*, pp. 204ff.

still have) advantages over other peoples due to scientific and technological achievements, and that these achievements have generated living-conditions in the Western world which are far better than the ones in most other regions.

In *Timelike Infinity*, science and technology have various facets. First, they are the basis of the Qax trading empire. The Qax governor explains:

> [M]y cells can operate as independent factories, assembling high technology of a miniaturized, biochemical nature. [...] Our biochemical products had enormous market value, and we were able to build a trading empire – by proxy – spanning light-years. (*TII*, p. 45)

This is a parallel to the Aleutians' production of biotechnological goods in Jones' works (cf. chapter 3.3). The aliens' technology appears highly advanced and establishes a superior status over man. Incidentally, miniaturized technology, or nanotechnology, is of a high market value today as well, for instance as a coating of metal or textile products, in colour screens and mobile phones or in disease diagnostics. Nowadays, less developed countries such as India, Thailand and the Philippines have already started to harness nanotechnology in order to solve development problems. However, these countries still require assistance of the international community to make sustainable progress. In the context of neo-imperialism, the countries might depend on the financial means and innovative potential of their former colonizers.[164]

Second, *Timelike Infinity* broaches the issue of mobility in space and time. Mobility in space has always been a decisive factor in imperial history. Europe's 'mastering' of space largely influenced thinking as the Europeans believed they excelled all other peoples due to their achievements in measuring distances and dimensions, their understanding of geography and cartography, and

---

[164] Cf. Fabio Salamanca-Buentello, Deepa L. Persad, Erin B. Court, *et al.*, "Nanotechnology and the Developing World" (2005), available on http://www.plosmedicine.org/article/info:doi/10.1371/journal.pmed.0020097 (2011-10-09).

the invention of telegraphs (and later telephones), railways and steamships.[165] With regard to the latter, is undeniable that the British Empire with its overseas colonies could only exist due to seafaring. Apart from the fact that seafaring made the journey to and the conquest of the colonies possible, it is also a prerequisite for flourishing trade networks – and profit for Europe. The establishment of global networks revolutionized commerce and consequently generated an imbalance in power:

> Europe and its North American offshoots, which had once been peripheral areas exporting mainly raw materials, had become the global centers for manufactured and finished goods, investment capital, and entrepreneurial and technical skills. India and China, which for millennia had been major sources of handicraft manufactures avidly sought in long-distance trade, were reduced to supplying cotton, tea, and raw silk to Euroamerican industries and consumers. Having set these changes in motion, the Europeans turned to transforming the very cultures of Africans and Asians to bring them into accord with modes of thought and behavior the colonizers deemed rational, efficient, and thus civilized.[166]

The world was split into the metropolises as centres of industrial production and capital and mere 'cropland' for raw materials. Until today, this development has contributed to a widening of the gap between rich and poor countries.

Accordingly, in Baxter's novel, the Qax would not be a colonial power if it had not been for their Spline carriers since they enable the Qax to invade other planets. Due to their biological requirements, the Qax can only travel in their mother ocean, which is a major constraint on their mobility. Hence, the Qax hire another alien species, the so-called "Spline", for transport. A Spline is an interesting amalgam of organism and machine:

---

[165] Cf. Michael Adas, *Machines as the Measure of Man. Science, Technology, and Ideologies of Western Dominance*, pp. 259ff.

[166] *Ibid.*, p. 205.

> [The] Spline vessels employed by the Qax were derived from immense, sea-going creatures with articulated limbs, which had once scoured the depths of some world-girdling ocean. […]
>
> They had plated over their flesh, hardened their internal organs – and had risen from the surface of their planet like mile-wide, studded balloons. They had become living ships, feeding on the thin substance between the stars.
>
> The Spline had become carriers, earning their place in the universe by hiring themselves out to any one of a hundred species. (*TII*, p.11)

Consequently, the Spline serve other species, thereby avoiding being colonized themselves. The narrators experience a journey in a Spline vessel as oppressive, unnatural and repulsive.[167] Yet, the Qax depend on the Spline whenever they leave their home planet. The Spline's stomach hosts a globe surrounded by the turbulent brown liquid that the Qax is made of (cf. *TII*, p. 43). In addition, the vessels are symbols of Qax domination: "There was a Spline looming over every human city now, a constant reminder of the power of the Qax – the ship's owners and [man's] overlords."[168] The Qax rule Earth like gods in the sky, literally looking down upon humanity.

In several works of science fiction, the empires of the techno-science era add a further (or a fourth) dimension to mobility: the travel in time. Generally speaking, *Timelike Infinity* treats time travel in an ambiguous way. On the one hand, it demonstrates the opportunities of time travel: people might escape from oppression and exploitation, and they may find answers to those questions and riddles that cannot be solved within their base-reality. On the other

---

[167] The Spline is an example of the popular trope of techno-monstrosity in science fiction. Prototypes of works depicting techno-monstrosity might be Mary Shelley's *Frankenstein, or The Modern Prometheus* (1818) and Herbert G. Wells' *The Island of Doctor Moreau* (1896). Yet, example in contemporary literature, video games and film are too abundant to be listed here, and the conceptual frameworks are likewise numerous: techno-monstrosity is portrayed in works about mad scientists, dystopian worlds, cyborgs, genetic engineering, *et cetera.*

[168] Stephen Baxter, *Vacuum Diagrams. Stories of the Xeelee Sequence*, p. 178.

hand, opening portals in time bears perils; enemies from the past or future might arrive on Earth, and the consequences of meddling with space-time are usually uncontrollable. Moreover, Baxter's work highlights the paradoxes of time travel. Future beings (such as the Friends of Wigner) appear backwards, whereas 'past' humans – like the scientist-protagonists of the novel – seem to be more advanced, rational and intelligent. These anachronisms dislocate the time travellers, and their experiences and feelings bear parallels to encounters between the 'savage' and the 'civilized' in colonial history and narrative. Incidentally, Herbert G. Wells' *The Time Machine* (1895) is concerned with exactly the same aspects. The Time Traveller of Wells' novel narrates that, in AD 802,701, man has developed into two distinct species: the gentle, but feeble Eloi, who spend their time playing and laughing in the garden-like Thames valley (cf. chapter 1.2), and the apelike, carnivorous Morlocks who prey upon the Eloi in the dark. Since both species can be characterized as degenerate, the Time Traveller encounters 'savages', i.e. he experiences mankind's own past. Subsequently, the Time Traveller makes two more stops on his journey through time: in the distant future, the world is shed in eternal twilight and inhabited by giant butterflies and monster crabs and, in AD 30 Million, the Time Traveller finds a dark and chilly Earth. The only living beings on the dying planet are shapeless things, and he returns into present time. The next day, he departs again and it is left open whether he ever returns.[169]

Wells' novel shows that degeneration is a threat to national stability. If the Victorians, who consider themselves a superior race, do not improve social conditions, they might end up like Eloi and Morlocks. Due to the process of degeneration, roles might change, and men, despite all their achievements, might regress into brute and simpleminded beings. Interestingly, one hundred years after the publication of *The Time Machine*, Stephen Baxter wrote a sequel to Wells' novel, *The Time Ships* (1995), in which he solves the mystery around the Time Traveller's disappearance. Determined to save Weena, the Time Traveller undertakes another journey into the future. The novel then provides visions of alternate

[169] Cf. Herbert G. Wells, *The Time Machine*.

past and future scenarios, and of a universe that is eventually ruled by human consciousness.[170] In contrast to Wells' novel, *The Time Ships* avoids the paradoxes of time travel by creating a universe in which parallel timelines branch off whenever time travellers arrive.[171]

Timelike Infinity does not only feature alien technology, it deals with human innovation as well. Yet, in order to maintain their dominant position over the 'natives', the Qax ban human science and technology on Earth. Before the arrival of the aliens, the planet was on its way to become a utopia. Man began to explore the universe and "banished many of the ills, social as well as physiological – hunger, disease, untimely death [...]" (*TII*, p. 216). Thus, humanity was progressing and thriving towards perfection, much in the accordance with Darwinian evolution. However, the Qax change this development. Most importantly, they forbid space travel to prevent human beings from escaping and developing defence mechanisms. The Qax recall all human-built spaceships from the Solar System and thoroughly destroy them, the last of which is destroyed around AD 5400 (cf. *TII*, p. 114). This implies that approximately 3450 years of research and the enormous amounts of resources that humans invested into space travel have been in vain – a massive setback with regard to self-esteem and prestige. Additionally, the Qax eradicate man's victory over illness and death. Before Qax occupation, the people on Earth used "AntiSenescence" technology that stopped them from aging (cf. *TII*, p. 8). The Qax banish this treatment to control the number of humans and to be one of the only immortal species in the Solar System, as we assume.

Human innovation in the form of a wormhole designed by Poole poses a serious threat to Qax rule. The wormhole, or "Interface project", consists of two portals: "One tetrahedral framework was left in orbit around Jupiter, while the other was transported at

---

170 Cf. Stephen Baxter, *The Time Ships. An Astonishing Quantum Voyage to the Far Future* (New York, NY: Eos, 2000).

171 For a detailed discussion of time-travel paradoxes in *The Time Ships*, see Joan-Pau Rubiés, "Foundation Forum: The Logic of Time Travel," in: *Foundation* 69 (1997), 80-85. The article also contains Stephen Baxter's comment on Rubiés' theses.

sublight speeds away from Earth, in the direction of the Centre of the Galaxy" (*TII*, p. 14). These portals function as a time machine, "a tunnel through time which connects [man] to the humanity of fifteen centuries ago" (*TII*, p. 15). As we expect from a work of hard science fiction, Baxter elaborates on the theoretical background of wormholes in much detail (cf. *TII*, p. 27). Yet, for my line of argument it is more important to know that the novel is set at exactly that point of time when the second portal returns and the 'time machine' can actually be used. Generally speaking, there is the risk that people escape to the past, when Earth was a free planet. This shows that human technology, which has been forbidden as much as possible, can still harm the alien invaders. It also means that human beings have an advantage over the Qax due to technology, which would deprive the alien occupiers of their superior position.

In *Timelike Infinity*, Earth has changed under the rule of the alien invaders. The fact that people are not allowed to leave the colony puts them into the position of prisoners or even slaves. Since the Qax exploit the planet for economic purposes, we can imagine that human beings are forced to work for the aliens. The Qax run plankton farms on Earth. These farms alter the image of the planet from space, a disturbing idea for the female protagonist, Miriam Berg:

> Cities flattened. The continents bordered by thick, chlorophyll green: offshore farms. The produce from what's left of the planet's arable dry land is exported off-planet. The complex molecules are highly prized, apparently, and raise a good price. For the Qax. […] [T]hey've turned the planet into a damn factory. (*TII*, p. 97)

It becomes evident that Miriam longs for the pre-occupation time and that the Qax' use of the Earth's resources seems to be unjustified to her; the invaders ruthlessly steal from the subject race. Unfortunately, the novel does not treat labour conditions under the aliens, a topic that is explored in Brian Aldiss' *The Interpreter* (cf.

chapter 1.1) and in John Christopher's *Tripods* trilogy (cf. chapter 1.2).

Just like the nuls in Aldiss' novel, the Qax institutionalize their rule. The crucial figures are the governors since domination and exploitation of the colonies depend on their competence. In the course of *Timelike Infinity*, mankind is confronted with two different governors. The first one has had a diplomatic relationship with the human ambassador, Parz, for a long time, as we learn in the beginning of the novel. The reader receives the impression that the governor treats the man with respect since it requires information. For instance, the governor interviews the ambassador about the Interface portal, and it becomes obvious that the Qax does not understand the technology but is aware of its dangerous potential (cf. *TII*, pp. 13ff.). In addition, this scene reveals that the Qax governor is not "some huge god" (*TII*, p. 14). As it depends on Parz' information, it displays weakness and ignorance, notions that run counter to imperial domination. Here, suspense builds up: the reader sees a chance for humanity to overthrow the invader, which opens up a variety of possible future events and arouses the reader's interest.

The second governor of Earth, i.e. the one that travels through the wormhole from the future, clearly keeps the sympathy of the reader on the side of the humans. Generally speaking, this governor is a tyrant. It kills its predecessor for being a "failure" and "hesitant" when confronted with insurgents and subsequently justifies the murder as "a strengthening of [its] species through the elimination of the weak" (*TII*, p. 76). The intentions of the Qax might be fatal for mankind: the governor from the future wants to travel further back in time and wipe out the entire human species (cf. *TII*, p. 109). Just like in numerous other works of alien-encounter science fiction, the colonizer from space eventually poses a threat to the survival of the human race, and the people on Earth transform from a passive subject race into an active enemy. This also implies that the Qax' attitude towards man changes: the species that was once effortlessly invaded is now considered a dangerous opponent – an idea that will be further discussed within the context of human resistance.

To come back to the Qax' institutionalization of power, they have introduced "Occupation laws" on Earth (cf. *TII*, p. 9). The reader knows that the aliens control the activities of man from their massive battleships in orbit around Earth (cf. *TII*, p. 10). The image of spaceships in the sky with aliens inside that few humans have ever seen must be oppressive and fearful to the people. In this respect, the Qax appear godlike, at least to those who have not detected their weaknesses yet. Nevertheless, *Timelike Infinity* neither gives details about the occupation laws nor does it narrate by what means the Qax enforce the laws. As mentioned before, it rather focuses on how the invaders gain their dominant position.

Interestingly, the novel evaluates Qax occupation by comparing it to man's colonial history. This has two implications: first, the Qax hold a mirror up to mankind, especially to the former imperialist nations; second, bringing man's colonial past (projected on alien oppressors) back into the present is an expression of postcolonial guilt. As to the first aspect, Parz muses that "it was as if the Qax were an externalized embodiment of man's treatment of man, a judgement of history" (*TII*, p. 35). Thus, the Qax are an anachronism: humanity 'travels' into its own past and witnesses a colonial encounter that occurred in a comparable way in Africa, Canada or India, for example. Moreover, the alien invasion generates a reversal of perspective on two different levels. The protagonists of *Timelike Infinity* are a politician and two scientists who come from the Western world, as we deduce from their names. In fact, Western scientists and politicians used to be the ones who felt intellectually and technologically superior to the Other, i.e. over the colonial subjects. However, in Baxter's novel, these people find themselves in a position inferior to the alien invaders – a phenomenon that John Rieder detects in Herbert G. Wells' *The War of the Worlds* (1898) and other early works of the genre.[172] The English protagonist in Wells' novel mutates from the one who looks into the one who is looked at, which eventually reverses the structures of power and hierarchy. Analogously, the Qax are the ones that look at humanity and administer the planet from their Spline ships in the sky. Just like the Overlords in *Childhood's End* (cf.

[172] John Rieder, *Colonialism and the Emergence of Science Fiction*, p. 7.

chapter 2.1), they try to grasp human behaviour and technology, as if they were human ethnologists studying an indigenous tribe. In order to gain more information on humans, the governor interviews Parz (cf. *TII*, pp. 13ff). Apart from the reversal of perspective on the individual level of the protagonists, the "colonial gaze" establishes itself on a national level (if we presume that Earth has not become a post-national state under the Qax). The former imperialist nations have been transformed into colonial subjects of the aliens. What follows is that they are deprived of their human rights to a certain extent (the Qax definitely limit freedom). In addition, the reader assumes that all human beings are treated equally by the invaders – no matter if they live in industrialized or underdeveloped countries. Basically, all achievements with regard to innovation and living-standards do not count any more, and humans are exploited on the plankton farms.

Through the eyes of Jasoft Parz, the narrator expresses a rather extreme theory with regard to postcolonial guilt. Parz claims that mankind itself is to blame for occupying the position of a subject race:

> Paradoxically he had always found it hard to blame the Qax for this sort of action. To establish control of Earth and its sister worlds the Qax had merely had to study history and adapt methods used by humans to oppress their fellows. There was no evidence that the Qax had ever evolved such tactics as means of dealing with each other. The Qax were acting as had oppressors throughout human history, Parz thought, but still humanity had only itself to blame [...]. (*TII*, p. 35)

Thus, humans served as 'teachers' for the alien invaders, an idea that is taken up in Baxter's short story "The Switch" (1990): "[*The Qax*] *had to learn the techniques of oppression from humans themselves. Fortunately for the Qax, human history wasn't short of object lessons....*"[173] This implies that human beings are, in a way, accomplices of the aliens. As to the "techniques of oppression", the

[173] Stephen Baxter, *Vacuum Diagrams. Stories of the Xeelee Sequence*, p. 173, italics by S. Baxter.

narrator might refer to the introduction of new laws, surveillance and punishment of disobedience. Another technique of oppression might be brainwashing, but there is no hint in the text that the aliens use this method. Moreover, the narrator of *Timelike Infinity* plays down the cruelty and humiliation of alien domination by making clear that human beings used to be worse: "Two centuries of Qax occupation had left few visible scars on Earth's surface – far fewer, in fact, than those wrought by humans during their slow, haphazard rise to technological civilization" (*TII*, p. 7). Here, Parz alludes to slavery, industrialization and the exploitation of the colonies, and the reader might detect an underlying notion of *nemesis*, i.e. Western nations somewhat 'deserve' to be treated as colonial subjects since they subjugated other peoples in the past. Thus, human beings do not take the role of pure and innocent natives; instead, they are painfully aware of their own 'complicity' with the invader. Nevertheless, these feelings of guilt appear rather disproportionate since *Timelike Infinity* is set four thousand years after the halcyon days of the British Empire.

Additionally, Baxter's novel portrays imperialism as a 'natural' process that accompanies a species' "rise to technological civilization" (cf. *TII*, p. 7). What also seems to be 'natural' in the universe of the novel is the interplay of dominance and subjugation, which recalls a struggle for survival. Consequently, those races which dominate others now might occupy the position of colonial subjects in the future. This is why Parz feels respect and maybe even sympathy for the dead Qax governor. He understands that, one day, the Qax will be overthrown by a human being, Jim Bolder, and explains: "Poole, one day humans are going to bring about the destruction of the Qax home world. We'll almost wipe them out" (*ibid.*). Parz even mourns the dead governor of Earth, a reaction that causes outrage in Michael Poole (cf. *TII*, p. 186). To summarize, Baxter's novel evaluates Qax occupation in an ambiguous way. On the one hand, the Qax as oppressors of man are enemies and, on the other hand, by juxtaposing their rule and man's colonial past, the negative implications of alien dominance are moderated; the aliens are not truly the ones to blame for the exploitation of Earth and its inhabitants – a crass expression of postcolonial guilt. Alien occupation is part of the 'natural order' of the universe in the far future.

In *Timelike Infinity*, human resistance does not culminate in a glorious victory over the alien oppressors. Humans do defeat the Qax but, in a universe that takes wars and exploitation for granted, victory over one invader does not guarantee the freedom of mankind. Since the novel combines alien occupation and time travel, it allows a diachronic view on mankind under the Qax. With regard to the human species, it becomes apparent that they have degenerated / will degenerate under Qax occupation. Interestingly, in order to demonstrate the development, Baxter does not portray the general public on Earth (as do Gwyneth Jones and John Christopher, for example) but merely a resistance group about one thousand five hundred years from the future. Baxter's novel unfolds a paradigmatic shift as he changes the function of the insurgents from threatening the rule of the occupants into proving that the aliens are highly detrimental to the development of mankind; the latter being victims of the extraterrestrial rulers. The theory that the rebels, i.e. the "Friends of Wigner" (*TII*, p. 95), are only a minor threat to Qax power is corroborated by their depiction. Basically, the Friends are anti-heroes whose plans are bound to fail. The Friends have secretly assembled a spaceship – a piece of English ground with Stonehenge on top (cf. *TII*, p. 63) – with which they travel back in time, when the Qax had no influence on man (cf. *TII*, p. 36). They intend to transform Jupiter into a time capsule that stores the human genome and influences the Ultimate Observer[174] to change timelines in favour of mankind (cf. *TII*, p. 210). However, the reader eventually learns that there is no Ultimate Observer in the universe. Thus, a noble idea that could have brought benefits for the human race turns out to be completely unfounded.

---

[174] Obviously, the existence of an Ultimate Observer is not a question of physics. However, in some recent works of quantum physics, scholars make clear that there might be something like an Ultimate Observer, and that it might even be God. For more information, see Daniel Lazich, "How Science Discovered God," available on http://www.cienciayreligion.org/articulos/pdfs/how_science_discovered_god.pdf (2011-10-31).

In contrast to the insurgents in John Christopher's (cf. chapter 1.2) or Brian Aldiss' works (cf. chapters 1.1 and 3.2), the Friends of Wigner are flat characters portrayed as backwards and irrational. The individual depicted in most detail is a twenty-five-year-old female called Shira. Despite the fact that the Friends come from the future, the characterization of Shira truly negates any notions of progress. For instance, her complexion is "quite poor, the skin around her eyes bruised-looking and tired" (*TII*, p. 92). We can imagine that the shaven skull – a custom among the Friends (cf. *TII*, p. 52) – adds to her haggard appearance. Moreover, Michael Poole describes Shira as a "shabby girl with her flavourless food" (*TII*, p. 97), dressed in a "single-piece coverall [...] of some coarse, cheap-looking artificial fabric" (*TII*, p. 92). As he notices her "inner deadness" and "flat interest", he realizes that "life [holds] no meaning for this girl" (*TII*, p. 102). In addition, the Friends suffer from illnesses such as dental caries (cf. *TII*, p. 53) and rickets (cf. *TII*, p. 122) since the Qax have banned AntiSenescence technology. The insurgents seem to function as evidence that evolution moves backwards under Qax domination: instead of far advanced 'superhumans', the people from the future have evolved into the opposite direction.[175] Naturally, this shocks the scientists Miriam

[175] This idea clearly recalls the degeneration debate of the *fin-de-siècle* era. In the aftermath of Darwin's theory that the species were not individually created but evolved from lower forms, degenerationists such as Bénédicte Augustin Morel reversed the idea of evolutionary progress and founded the theory of the biological and social decline of man. Among others, Cesare Lombroso (1835-1909) and Max Nordau (born Simon Maximilian Südfeld, 1849-1923) took up the concept and transferred it to their fields of studies. Hence, even though the theory of degeneration is based on biology, it soon spread through medicine, arts, criminology and politics. In his *Traité des dégénérescences physiques, intellectuelles et morales* (1857), Morel makes clear that "degeneration [is] a morbid deviation from a perfect primitive type" that leads to physical deformity and insanity. The symptoms of degeneration are passed on to the offspring, and – due to accumulation – a family line could become extinct in four generations: "When under any kind of noxious influences an organism becomes debilitated, its successor will not resemble the healthy, normal type of species, [...] but will form a new sub-species, which, like all others, possesses the capacity of transmitting to its offspring, in a continuously increasing degree, its peculiarities [...] – gaps in development, malformation and infirmities." (Cf. Bénédicte Augustin Morel, *Traité des dégénérescences physiques, intellectuelles et morales de l'éspèce humaine et des causes qui produisent ces variétés maladives*, cited in Kelly Hurley, *The Gothic*

Berg and Michael Poole; where they expected "*progress* [and] dignity" (*TII*, p. 97, italics by S. Baxter), they are actually confronted with creatures from the past, creatures that cannot be man's saviours. To sum up, just like the Qax, the Friends of Wigner are anachronisms – and once more it becomes apparent that the novel deals with time travel in a very elaborate way: the characters can neither trust their theories about striving for a better future, nor can they rely on physical theses from the twentieth century. As a consequence, the individuals affected by time travel seem dislocated and helpless.

The philosophy of the Friends of Wigner – or at least the philosophy of the thirty Friends that inhabit the Stonehenge spaceship – is presented as contradictive: the Friends assembled their spaceship beneath a historical site as the Qax do not interfere with religious practices on Earth; Stonehenge thus served as a 'smokescreen' (cf. *TII*, p. 57). However, the reader receives the impression that its camouflage function is not the only reason why the Friends appreciate Stonehenge. In fact, their culture seems to bear notions of primitivism.[176] It appears as if they yearn for a long-lost

---

Body. Sexuality, Materialism, and Degeneration at the Fin de Siècle [Cambridge *et al.*: Cambridge University Press, 1996], p. 66). Accordingly, Qax rule might be interpreted as a "noxious influence" in Morel's words, and the Friends of Wigner physically and mentally resemble those individuals that would have been classified as 'degenerates' around 1900. We might even theorize that the criminal anthropologist Cesare Lombroso would have identified the Friends of Wigner as "mattoids" since a "mattoid" is "an offender who champions an idealistic and often altruistic political or religious cause but is in fact mentally unstable and dangerous" (cf. Cesare Lombroso, *Criminal Man* [London and Durham, NC: Duke University Press, 2006], p. 405).

[176] Primitivism is a problematic concept in postcolonial studies as it is not clearly defined and was frequently used as a derogative category. In art history, primitivist works are usually characterized by simplicity of form and theme, as in the works of Paul Gauguin (1848-1903), Constantin Brâncuşi (1876-1957) and Joan Miró (1893-1983). Pablo Picasso (1881-1973) deliberately reproduced primitivist art for its liberating potential. Primitivist works in literature display an uncomplicated style and employ simple themes such as peasant life. In contrast, my characterization of the lifestyle of the Friends of Wigner as primitivist rather refers to a much broader definition that takes colonial history into account. Hence, primitivism is understood as bearing parallels to early human culture as well as to alternative cultural and artistic endeavours. In history, primitivist art and culture evoked prejudices centring around savage crudity, naivety and immaturity, which fre-

past, when people lived without the restraints of a civilization in the techno-science era, for instance invasions from outer space, intergalactic empires and competition for the resources of planets. They might long for less abusive relationships – between man and Nature as well as between the Self and the Other. It is clear that the Friends associate notions of innocence, peace and community with the past. In contrast, the present is characterized by the interplay of dominance and subjugation, which requires fighting spirit rather than nostalgic desires. The Friends have transformed a historical religious site into a battleship, and their philosophy suggests scientificity and futurity – a harsh contrast to their appearance as 'savages in tepees' (cf. *TII*, p. 95). This philosophy is based on elaborate theories of quantum physics and highly advanced alien technology, and it becomes clear that it is both a fantasy of apotheosis and an escapist strategy from the suppression of human technology that accompanies Qax domination. The name "Friends of Wigner" is taken from a quantum physicist of the twentieth century, Eugene Paul Wigner (1902-1995), who enquired into the philosophy of mathematics, physics and reality:

> Wigner and his co-workers had tried to evolve a philosophy in response to the fact that quantum physics, while universally accepted, was saturated with dazzling paradoxes which suggested that the external world had no well-defined structure until minds observe it. (*TII*, p. 39)

As a result, the Friends believe that reality is only created by observation. They also theorize that, at the end of time – or at "timelike infinity" respectively – the "Ultimate Observer" will make the

---

quently led to the process of Othering. For instance, the artworks of Black Africans, Pacific Islanders and Australian Aborigines were described as 'primitive' or 'savage' respectively. Cf. Bill Ashcroft, Gareth Griffiths and Helen Tiffin, *Post-Colonial Studies. The Key Concepts*, s.v. 'primitivism'. In the universe of intergalactic imperialism depicted in Baxter's novel, the insurgents as 'primitive' people seem to be less 'civilized' than the scientist-protagonists and might therefore be considered the inferior Other by those characters. For more information on primitivism, see for example Susan Hiller (ed.), *The Myth of Primitivism. Perspectives on Art* (London and New York, NY: Routledge, 1991).

"last Observation" and retrospectively create the history of the universe (cf. *TII*, p. 205). As mentioned before, the Friends intend to influence man's higher purpose by directly 'addressing' the Ultimate Observer. According to their philosophy, humanity will finally find itself in a state of "shining" or "optimal state" (cf. *TII*, p. 206), which recalls apotheosis and which implies that all the traumata in human history, for example Qax occupation and the exploitation of Earth, do not matter any more. Yet, in contrast to the scenario of apotheosis in Arthur C. Clarke's *Childhood's End* (cf. chapter 2.1), the theories of the Friends of Wigner appear at best unreliable, if not megalomaniac and fanatic. The reader learns that, in the far future, history repeats itself without being influenced by humans (cf. *TII*, pp. 252f.). In short, the mission of the insurgents turns out to be a failure.

Apart from the debatable theories of the quantum physics of the universe, the mission of the Friends of Wigner is based on advanced alien technology. Basically, they use "a stolen Squeem hyperdrive device" (*TII*, p. 58) to power their spaceship. This implies that humans depend on alien discoveries in order to fight the Qax. Shira expresses the pride of the insurgents in their achievements:

> Our craft has successfully traversed the portal, without significant damage or injury. Our supplies – and our recycling gear – should suffice to sustain us in the orbit around Jupiter for many years. Long enough for our purposes. […] Yes, we have done well. (*TII*, p. 60)

In addition, the Friends have the means to release "singularities from their electromagnetic nets and propel them […] towards Jupiter" (*TII*, p. 130) in order to store data for the Ultimate Observer within the destroyed planet. Again, we realize how important technology is for the self-esteem of the insurgents and the completion of their mission – even though they have not developed the technology themselves. Naturally, the fanatic rebels' plan involves perils for the human race (and maybe even for the entire universe) as it might shatter space-time (cf. *TII*, p. 48). This renders them more dangerous than the invaders from outer space, and the reader does not consider them rational and heroic at all. In comparison to the brave and intelligent insurgents in other works, the Friends of Wigner lack cunning, a reliable strategy and efficient organization. Since their endeavours cannot be characterized as noble, the Friends bear no resemblance to the famous leaders of resistance in colonial history such as Simón Bolívar (1783-1830) or Mahatma Gandhi (1869-1948). The rebels in *Timelike Infinity* are rather victims of the alien invaders, i.e. they provide evidence for the idea that Qax occupation is detrimental to the human race in the long run.

Ironically, victory over the aliens is eventually brought about by "a simple military assault" (*TII*, p. 62), i.e. by exactly that strategy which the Friends of Wigner refuse to apply. Finally, it takes two attempts to overthrow the invaders. The first one forms the climax of the action of *Timelike Infinity*. Strikingly, the Qax governor of Earth does not perceive the natives as a serious threat: "'They cannot harm us,' the Qax said, sounding uninterested" (*TII*, p. 142). Nonetheless, Jasoft Parz believes in the potential of his species and likens the situation to a battle between 'civilized' Europeans and 'savage' islanders:

> Qax, listening to you I can hear the voice of the commander of a twentieth-century atomic carrier disdaining the painted, dugout canoes of islanders, drifting out to meet him on the curve of some sea. Still, though, the most primitive weapon can kill…" (*ibid.*)

It becomes evident that Parz understands how superior the aliens actually are. Yet, he warns the governor, cautioning him on being overconfident. The comparison of high-tech ships and canoes of indigenous islanders recalls encounters between the Europeans and non-Westerners in overseas territories. For example, the reader might think of Captain Cook's last voyage to Hawaii in 1779. Despite the apparent superiority of his massive ship (the Resolution), the firearms and the courage of the crew, Captain Cook and four of his mariners were killed by the indigenous population on the beach. To come back to *Timelike Infinity*, the Qax governor is simultaneously attacked by three parties: Parz starts a fire on the carrier (cf. *TII*, pp. 173f.), Poole tears it open with his own spaceship (cf. *TII*, p. 175), and the Friends of Wigner along with Miriam Berg fire at the Spline with "singularity cannons" (cf. *TII*, p. 174). As the spaceship is destroyed, the governor, who is "embedded in the consciousness of the Spline" (*TII*, p. 177), dies. However, the destruction of one Qax individual is not sufficient to overthrow the invaders.

The ultimate collapse of Qax occupation is eventually accomplished by Jim Bolder, as we learn in *Timelike Infinity* and in the short story "Blue Shift". Bolder steals a spaceship from the Qax and approaches the sun of the aliens' home planet. The Qax ruthlessly attack him:

> 'Starbreakers were used. In the confusion and panic, they brushed the Qax sun. It was enough to cause the sun to become unstable – ultimately, to nova.
>
> The Qax were forced to flee. Dozens of individuals died in the exodus. [Their] power was lost, and the occupation of Earth crumbled…' (*TII*, p. 119)

More than half of the Qax population expires, and humans regain control over their planet. Hence, Bolder is the saviour of the human race; he achieves what the Friends of Wigner failed at. It seems that Baxter criticizes religious fanaticism and meddling with space and time as nobody can foresee the consequences. He also illustrates that the courage and cunning of a single individual count more than elaborate theories and technology. To sum up, Bolder is a truly human hero for the reader. Unfortunately, Bolder remains a shadow throughout the course of the novel.

Both *The Time Machine* and *Timelike Infinity* feature the last man who observes the end of the world or universe respectively.[177]

---

[177] The last man is a trope that goes back to Romanticism. Early examples are Jean-Baptiste Cousin de Grainville's *The Last Man, or Omegarus and Syderia* (1806, cf. Jean-Baptiste Cousin de Grainville, *The Last Man, or Omegarus and Syderia*, translated by I. F. Clarke and M. Clarke, introduction and critical materials by I. F. Clarke [Middleton, CT: Wesleyan University Press, Reprint 2003]), Mary Shelley's *The Last Man* (1826, cf. Mary Shelley, *The Last Man*, introduction and notes by Pamela Bickley [Ware: Wordsworth Classics, 2004]) and Thomas Campbell's eponymous poem (1823, available on

However, the endings of the novels differ tremendously. The Time Traveller escapes from the Morlocks into the year AD 30 Million, where he catches a glimpse of the dying world. Wells refers to the concept of entropy[178] by making his protagonist experience eternal winter, cold, death and silence,[179] i.e. the end of life on Earth appears to be a state after which nothing is left. In contrast to *The Time Machine*, Baxter's novel treats history as an eternal loop or a cyclical repetition of events. Michael Poole destroys the time portals and is subsequently hurled into space in the far future (around AD 5 Million), where he receives a tragic gift: out of "curiosity", the "antiXeelee" (an immaterial being that travels back in time and alters the evolution of the Xeelee alien race) transforms the human scientist into "quantum functions" and allows him to observe space at timelike infinity (cf. *TII*, pp. 249ff.). In fact, Poole does not witness the end but a new beginning:

> There was a box, drifting in space, tetrahedral, clear-walled.
>
> From around an impossible corner a human walked into the box. A rope of woven bark trailed behind him. The human was dressed in treated animal skins. He

http://www.poemhunter.com/poem/last-man-the/ [2012-05-11]). In the Victorian era, the last-man trope was treated for example by Edgar Allan Poe in "The Conversation of Eiros and Charmion" (1839, available on http://classiclit.about.com/library/bl-etexts/eapoe/bl-eapoe-conversation.htm [2012-05-11]) and by Herbert G. Wells. Apart from *The Time Machine*, Wells' short story "The Star" (1897) describes the end of the world witnessed by a single individual (cf. H.G. Wells, "The Star", available on http://www.online-literature.com/wellshg/17/ [2012-05-11]). The topic has been popular ever since. A theme anthology is *Last Man on Earth* (1982), edited by Isaac Asimov, Martin Harry Greenberg and Charles G. Waugh (cf. Isaac Asimov, Martin Harry Greenberg and Charles G. Waugh, *The Last Man on Earth* [New York, NY: Fawcett, [2]1985]). The best-known films that feature a solitary human survivor are probably *The Last Man on Earth* (USA and Italy 1964, directed by Ubaldo Ragona) and its remake, *I am Legend* (2007), both adaptations of Richard Matheson's novel *I am Legend* (1954, cf. Richard Matheson, *I am Legend* [London: Millennium, 1999]). Cf. John Clute and Peter Nicholls (eds.), *The Encyclopedia of Science Fiction*, s.v. 'end of the world'.

[178] According to the second law of thermodynamics, entropy is the degree of disorder or uncertainty in a closed system, and it serves as a measure of available energy. An increase in entropy thus means an increase in disorder.

[179] Cf. Herbert G. Wells, *The Time Machine*, pp. 74f.

> was gaunt, encrusted in filth, his skin ravaged by frost.
> [...]
> History resumed. (*TII*, pp. 252f.)

The savage in the box is a synecdoche for humanity, and it is assumed that man will undergo the 'process of civilization' again, i.e. repeat all accomplishments and mistakes. In fact, this idea is similar to Garry W. Trompf's "cyclical view", the paradigm of historical recurrence which is based on the belief that events pass through various stages, eventually return to the first and start the cycle anew.[180] The cyclical view implies an identical repetition of history, which is a concept that can also be found in Buddhist and Hindu writing.

In *Timelike Infinity*, historical recurrence has a negative overtone. It seems that there is no way out of the cycle; neither Poole nor other creatures are able to influence or alter human history. As a consequence, man will develop from a rather innocent 'savage' into a 'civilized' being whose universe is governed by greed, competition and the urge to dominate the Other. That is the reason why Michael finds nothing but "relics of war" in the far future (cf. *TII*, p. 251). An influential philosophical text that enquires into the process of civilization is the *Discourse on the Origin and Foundations of Inequality among Men*, or *Second Discourse*, by Jean-Jacques Rousseau (1712-1778). Rousseau wrote both the *First* and the *Second Discourse* on the occasion of contests held by the Académie de Dijon.[181] In the *Second Discourse*, the philosopher elaborates on the following question: "What is the origin of inequality among men and is it warranted by natural law?"[182] By depicting a hypothetical history of man, he comes to the conclusion that man has evolved in several stages: human beings develop from the "state of Nature" into societal savages; what follows are com-

---

[180] Cf. Garry W. Trompf, *The Idea of Historical Recurrence in Western Thought: From Antiquity to the Reformation* (Los Angeles, CA, *et al.*: University of California Press, 1979).

[181] Cf. Jerry Combee, "Rousseau's Noble Savage and European Self-Consciousness," in: *Modern Age* 17:2 (1973), 177. Incidentally, Rousseau did not win a prize for the *Second Discourse*.

[182] Jean-Jacques Rousseau, *Discourse on the Origin of Inequality*, translated by Franklin Philip (Oxford *et al.*: Oxford University Press, 1994), p. 21.

plex human societies and, finally, domination and slavery. Rousseau claims that the notions of property and society are the first step towards inequality among men since these ideas generate ambition and competition.[183] Thus, the history of mankind, including civilized Europe, is characterized by decline. This idea must have been disturbing for contemporary readers as it undermines the Europeans' notion of superiority over the 'savage': the 'wild' man is naturally good, free and strong, whereas the 'civilized' of the Enlightenment needs rules and punishment in order to behave morally correct.[184] Likewise, due to the "relics of war" Michael Poole sees in space, we must assume that *Timelike Infinity* demonstrates the negative effects of the process of civilization. In the end, man neither awaits a higher purpose nor can humanity be saved from cyclical historical recurrence.

To conclude, *Timelike Infinity* is a novel in a sequence of works about alien invasions which directly refers to and retrospectively evaluates colonial history. By means of comparison, Baxter's work holds a mirror up to former imperialist nations; humanity 'travels' into its own past. The treatment of the topic contains a reversal of perspective: once dominant nations are now subject races of the alien overlords. This appears to be some sort of *nemesis* as man used to be guilty of worse things, according to the overtone of the novel. Colonial history on Earth provided 'object lessons' for the invaders from outer space, a thesis that mitigates the humiliation that accompanies Qax rule and that finally puts the blame on humanity itself. In this respect, Parz expresses strong feelings of postcolonial guilt despite the long period of time that has elapsed since Europe actually had colonies. What is more, Baxter's novel lays emphasis on how the hegemonic position of the aliens is achieved by demonstrating the crucial role of scientific and technological achievements in colonial encounters. Science and technology form the basis of the Qax trading empire, and the aliens maintain their superior position by banning human innovation. Mobility in space is undeniably a prerequisite of colonialism without which the Qax' strategy of 'planetfall and plunder' would not be possible.

---

[183] Cf. Jean-Jacques Rousseau, *Discourse on the Origin of Inequality*, p. 60.
[184] Cf. Jerry Combee, "Rousseau's Noble Savage and European Self-Consciousness," 177.

Mobility in time is depicted as being dichotomous; *Timelike Infinity* shows the opportunities as well as the dangers.

The alien Others, i.e. the Qax, are portrayed as naturally driven by competition. Their ruling of Earth is comparable to company rule in India or in British South Africa, for example, and they have turned the planet into mere cropland. Their ways of conquering, subdividing and exploiting the interstellar colonies even recall the 'Scramble for Africa'. Nevertheless, the Qax also display weaknesses such as arrogance and ignorance with regard to human technology, an aspect that generates suspense. The insurgents in *Timelike Infinity*, the Friends of Wigner, provide evidence for the backward development of humanity rather than putting the superior position of the aliens under threat. In contrast to these degenerate antiheroes, Jim Bolder is the celebrated personality in the battle against the invaders, and he illustrates that courage and cunning are more effective than various guises of fanaticism. The novel ends with a notion of historical recurrence and demonstrates that the 'rise of civilization' is inevitably accompanied by greed, competition, war and exploitation.

2. Close Encounters of the Second Kind: Benevolent Alien Invasions

2.1 Man's Higher Purpose: Arthur C. Clarke, *Childhood's End*

Arthur C. Clarke (1917-2008) is one of the most famous British science-fiction writers. He published more than thirty novels and short stories. His key works of fiction include the *Odyssey Saga* (1968-1996), *The Deep Range* (1957), *A Fall of Moondust* (1961), *Dolphin Island* (1963) and *Rendez-vous with Rama* (1973). Incidentally, the latter novel won the Nebula and Hugo awards. Clarke also wrote non-fiction, such as *The Exploration of Space* (1951), *Voice Across the Sea* (1958) and *Voices from the Sky: Previews of the Coming Space Age* (1965). The author might be called an enthusiast of science. During World War II, he served as a radar instructor with the Royal Air Force. In 1948, he completed a Bachelor of Science degree at the University of London. In addition, he became chairman of the British Interplanetary Society and did research in oceanography around the island of Sri Lanka, his later place of residence. Apart from being a lecturer in the UK and the United States, Clarke was the presenter of the television series *Arthur C. Clarke's Mysterious World* (1980) and *World of Strange Powers* (1985).[185]

Clarke's most successful novel, *Childhood's End*, was published in 1953. It narrates the story of mankind facing its new role in the universe. The novel begins with the appearance of an alien life form, called "Overlords" by humans. The Overlords seem to benevolently conquer the planet and bring back the Golden Age.

---

[185] For a detailed biography of Arthur C. Clarke, see Robin Anne Reid, *Arthur C. Clarke: A Critical Compendium* (Westport, CT: Greenwood Press, 1997); Neil McAleer, *Arthur C. Clarke, The Authorized Biography* (Chicago, IL: Contemporary Books, 1992); David N. Samuelson, *Arthur C. Clarke: A Primary and Secondary Bibliography* (Boston, MA: G.K. Hall, 1984).

However, in the course of the novel it becomes clear that in freeing the world from poverty, war and disease the Overlords serve a higher purpose: at the command of a higher power they 'nurse' the human race in order to prepare it for its destiny. The children of man eventually become part of the ubiquitous and incomprehensible "Overmind". *Childhood's End* was influenced by Olaf Stapledon's concepts of metamorphoses in the future in *Last and First Men* (1930) and of an immaterial being similar to the Overmind in *Star Maker* (1937).[186] Interestingly, various musicians have adapted the novel into songs. For instance, the first song of the Genesis album *Foxtrot* (1972), "Watcher of the Skies", draws back on *Childhood's End*. The novel also provided material for bands such as Iron Maiden, Pink Floyd and Van der Graaf Generator.[187]

Childhood's End is subdivided into three parts of approximately the same length: "Earth and the Overlords", "The Golden Age" and "The Last Generation". Part I, developed from the short story "Guardian Angel" (1946),[188] is set in the 1950s and begins with the appearance of alien spaceships in the sky. The Overlords arrive during the second space race or, more precisely, directly before humans launch Mars expeditions and thereby herald "the century of the Solar System."[189] Clarke published two versions of the first chapter since he believed that either the Germans or the Russians would lead in space travel. What the different versions have in common is that two people, who are personally involved in the space race but on opposite sides, simultaneously witness the arrival of the extraterrestrials. The original text features two German scientists who parted after World War II: Reinhold Hoffman stayed in West Germany, whereas Konrad Schneider "chose the road to Moscow."[190] The completion of their projects is accompanied by

---

[186] Cf. David Norman Samuelson, *Studies in the Contemporary American and British Science Fiction Novel* (Los Angeles, CA: University Microfilms International, 1979), p. 96.
[187] Cf. Adam Roberts, "On Science Fiction Music," in: *Vector* 269 (2012), 22.
[188] Cf. Bruce A. Beatie, "Arthur C. Clarke and the Alien Encounter: The Background of *Childhood's End*," in: *Extrapolation* 30:1 (1989): 53-69.
[189] Arthur C. Clarke, *Childhood's End* (New York, NY *et al.*: Random House, 1990), p. 4. All subsequent references to this edition are in brackets in the text.
[190] Arthur C. Clarke, *Childhood's End* (New York, NY: Del Rey Impact, 2001), p. 5.

Cold-War paranoia: both scientists worry about the secret services, espionage, financial advantages of the competitor and national prestige. In the 1989 version, the notion of competitiveness is less apparent. The Russian cosmonaut Helena Lyakhow and the US Mission Commander Mohan Kaleer muse about the glorious beginnings of space travel in the mid-twentieth century. In both versions of the first chapter, the narrators stress the primitiveness of man's spaceships ("log canoes") compared to the Overlords' "great ships […] in their overwhelming majesty" (*CE*, p. 4). In fact, this is an anticipation of one of the novel's main themes.

The main events of *Childhood's End* centre around the relationship between the alien Supervisor of the Overlords, Karellen, and the human Secretary-General of the United Nations, Rikki Stormgren. Generally speaking, the reader receives the impression that the Overlords colonize Earth since they impose their rules upon mankind and profoundly change the world. For instance, they unify the nations by creating a "world state", eliminating poverty and war, and they ban cruelty in every form, be it towards human being or animal (cf. *CE*, pp. 9ff.). They also have a passion for order (cf. *CE*, p. 36). Consequently, the Overlords seem to make Earth a better place. It is for this reason that, apart from a small resistance group called the "Freedom League", nobody opposes the aliens' rule. Human beings accept the Overlords as masters of Earth since they understand that the aliens improve the quality of life (cf. *CE*, p. 21). As to a world without poverty, war and inequality, the concept of utopia comes to the reader's mind. This is further elaborated on in the interpretation of the second part of the novel.

The narrative perspective in *Childhood's End* is not always clear. Most of the events are narrated through the eyes of human beings, for example by Rikki Stormgren, George Greggson and Jan Rodricks. Just like in the works of exploitative alien invasions (cf. chapter 1), humans take the role of the natives in colonial encounters and tell the story from their 'inferior position'. This reversal of the "colonial gaze"[191] is a crucial difference to eighteenth- and nineteenth-century travel and adventure narratives, and it illustrates that science fiction plays with traditions in literature. What is more,

[191] Cf. John Rieder, *Colonialism and the Emergence of Science Fiction*, pp. 7ff.

the human narrative perspective creates suspense: the Overlords appear far advanced, awe-inspiring and beyond comprehension at the same time. This is due to the fact that, especially in the beginning of the text, their outward appearance and their motives remain a mystery. Nevertheless, the author is rather careless with regard to the narrator, i.e. occasionally, the reader does not know who tells the story. For instance, it seems that an omniscient narrator describes Karellen's revelation (cf. *CE*, pp. 59-61), comments on the changes on Earth (cf. *CE*, p. 62) and gives proleptic hints (cf. *CE*, pp. 130, 160, 170). In addition, some short scenes are narrated through the eyes of the alien: the reader learns that Karellen envies the fate of man (cf. *CE*, pp. 130, 211f.), a theory that will be discussed in the course of this chapter. On the whole, the narration is not always consistent, which weakens the concept of telling the story from the point of view of colonial subjects.

From the moment of their arrival, the Overlords rule Earth, and their language is clearly imperial. Several features define their superiority over mankind. Early in the novel, we learn that the Overlords possess intellectual super-powers. For instance, they have a perfect memory (cf. *CE*, p. 17) and their technology is much further advanced. They can even block out the sun in certain places that disobey their rule (cf. *CE*, p. 12). The Overlords generally represent "reason and science" (*CE*, p. 15), the key terms of the Age of Enlightenment. This implies that, compared to the Overlords, human beings of the twentieth century might be considered as 'ignorant' as man in the 'dark' Middle Ages. What is more, comparisons between the Overlords as European colonizers and human beings as a primitive race reoccur, for example considering mankind superstitious. Karellen tells Stormgren: "[Y]ou must remember that most of the world is still uneducated by any reasonable standards, and is riddled with prejudices and superstitions that may take decades to eradicate" (*CE*, p. 46). Superstition is indeed a feature that European colonizers frequently associated with the so-called savages. In *The Descent of Man, and Selection in Relation to Sex* (1871), Charles Darwin explains that "with the less civilised nations, reason often errs, and many bad customs and base superstitions come within the same scope [...],"[192] which implies that superstition is generated by ignorance. In *Childhood's End*, Karellen seems to reflect Darwin's point. In contrast to the Overlords, human beings are characterized as irrational due to their superstitious ideas. What follows is that they are considered inferior to the alien life form. This might serve as a justification for conquest. Eventually, humans accept the aliens as their "Overlords", a name that unambiguously defines the power relations in the colonial encounter.

What is more, the reader receives the impression that the aliens protect mankind from man-made dangers. Generally speaking, the themes protection and education are connected to a potential nuclear holocaust on Earth. Karellen explains to a group of human reporters:

> Your race had shown a notable incapacity for dealing with the problems of its own rather small planet. When we arrived, you were on the point of destroying yourselves with the powers that science had rashly given you. Without our intervention, the Earth today would be a radioactive wilderness.
>
> Now you have a world at peace, and a united race. Soon you will be sufficiently civilized to run your planet without our assistance. (*CE*, p. 129)

Thus, the imperial overtone is pre-eminent: the paternalistic conqueror prevents mankind from annihilating itself. Since the novel was written only a few years after atomic bombs had been dropped on Hiroshima and Nagasaki, the author hints at the disastrous effects nuclear weapons can have on the world. In fact, the generational fear of a nuclear holocaust which pervades Clarke's novel is symptomatic of science fiction of the early and mid-twentieth century. Before Hiroshima and Nagasaki, the dangers of nuclear disasters were pictured, for example, in Robert A. Heinlein's "Solution Unsatisfactory" (1941), Lester Del Rey's *Nerves* (1942) and Cleve Cartmill's "Deadline" (1944), which depicted an a-bomb in such

[192] Charles Darwin, *The Descent of Man, and Selection in Relation to Sex*, p. 681.

realistic detail that the US security forces suspected the editor of *Astounding Science-Fiction*, John W. Campbell Jr, of having access to government secrets.[193] After the war, nuclear power had become real rather than speculative and provided material for those works that treat its biological, mental and social consequences in a more realistic way. Several short stories discuss the responsibility of nuclear scientists for mankind, for instance Frederic Brown's "The Weapon" (1951), Poul Anderson's "The Disintegrating Sky" (1953) and "Progress" (1962) and L. Sprague Le Camp's "Judgement Day" (1955). Furthermore, "Atomic!" (1947) by Henry Kuttner, *Children of the Atom* (1958-1950) by Wilmar H. Shiras and *Aubade for Ganelon* (1984) by John Willet pinpoint the mutagenic effects of radioactivity.[194] An influential work in which a post-holocaust society repeats the errors of its forefathers is Walter M. Miller's *A Canticle for Leibowitz* (1960). The plot of Millers' single novel develops around the Catholic Order of Leibowitz that tries to preserve human knowledge after a nuclear holocaust. Just like in the *Tripods* trilogy (cf. chapter 1.2), mankind is back in the Middle Ages. Human beings slowly rediscover science and technology only to enter into a new global war, and the order builds a spaceship to escape the imminent second holocaust on Earth.[195] Hence, Miller portrays a negative view on cyclical historical recurrence, much like Stephen Baxter in *Timelike Infinity* (cf. chapter 1.3).

Obviously, Clarke's portrayal of man as "a kind of lemming bent on racial suicide"[196] influences the evaluation of postcolonial guilt in *Childhood's End*. The Overlords' intervention into man's "suicide" is their primordial reason for the conquest of the planet. The people on Earth, who seem to be immature and incapable of leading their lives independently rather than being self-reliant, require tutelage by a more advanced species. This implies that tutelage as the Overlords' 'duty' is necessary and positive, and that

[193] Cf. John Clute and Peter Nicholls (eds.), *The Encyclopedia of Science Fiction*, s.v. 'nuclear power'.
[194] Cf. *ibid.*
[195] Cf. Walter M. Miller, *A Canticle for Leibowitz* (London: Gollancz, 2001).
[196] John Clute and Peter Nicholls (eds.), *The Encyclopedia of Science Fiction*, s.v. 'holocaust and after'.

the extraterrestrial invaders pursue a noble course. Naturally, this image of benevolent aliens excludes notions of postcolonial guilt. What is more, the Overlords' 'duty' recalls the work of missionaries who 'educate' and 'civilize' the 'primitives'. In colonial literature of the early and mid-nineteenth century, for instance in Robert Michael Ballantyne's *The Coral Island* (1857), Christian missions are depicted as institutions that compassionately free the natives from savagery. It was only later that the missionaries received criticism since imposing the European system of values on the 'heathens' was often allied with the expansion of international trade networks and imperialistic practises.

In *Childhood's End*, Karellen makes clear that, once man is 'educated', the Overlords can begin their "real work" (*CE*, p. 52). Stormgren replies: "I have often wondered what that might be. Tidying up our world and civilizing the human race is only a means – you must have an end as well" (*ibid.*). He then wants to know if human beings will travel to the stars with the Overlords, and Karellen indirectly answers in the affirmative (cf. *ibid.*). This leads to the fact that Stormgren tries to evaluate the probability of failure: "But suppose, after all, your experiments fail with man? We have known such things in our own dealings with primitive human races." (*CE*, p. 53). It is striking that not only the Overlords but also Stormgren draws parallels between the human race and 'savages'. We can imagine that he thinks about 'primitives' that were brought to Europe in order to adopt a European way of life. In his *Journal of Researches* (1839), Charles Darwin tells us that that the captain of the Beagle, Captain Fitz Roy, had taken three Fuegian adolescents, called Jemmy Button, York Minster and Fuegia Basket, to England in order to provide a religious education for them. Aboard the Beagle, they return to their native country, where they are to help a missionary establish a mission.[197] After three years in England, the savages have undergone tremendous changes as the example of Jemmy Button shows: "Jemmy was short, thick and fat, but vain of his personal appearance; he used to wear gloves, his hair was neatly cut, and he was distressed if his well-

[197] Cf. Charles Darwin, *The Voyage of the Beagle. Journal of Researches into the Natural History and Geology of the Countries Visited during the Voyage of HMS Beagle round the World, under the Command of Captain Fitz Roy, RN.*, pp. 197f.

polished shoes were dirtied. He was fond of admiring himself in a looking-glass."[198] Thus, Jemmy has adapted the way of living of a gentleman, and Darwin finds Jemmy's development "wonderful".[199] Nevertheless, when the Beagle returns to Jemmy's dwelling place one month later, Jemmy has transformed into a 'barbarian' again, "a thin haggard savage, with long disordered hair, and naked, except a bit of blanked round his waist."[200] Therefore, Darwin doubts that the religious education in England was advantageous for the Fuegian.[201] We might say that Darwin gives an example of what Stormgren calls 'failure'.

The Overlords take the role of a superior life form that clearly acts as the colonizer of Earth. They change the political structures and impose their laws on man. In fact, the laws of the Overlords appear morally correct as they correspond to Judeo-Christian virtues in ensuring peace and the abolition of violence. As mentioned above, even the name "Overlords" emphasizes the aliens' superiority. What is more, Matthew Candelaria convincingly makes clear that the Overlords' rule is comparable to "not just European, but distinctly English" imperialist practices.[202] First of all, the aliens speak fluent English in a radio broadcast (cf. *CE*, p. 10). Second, their administrative technique is similar to the British system of indirect rule, i.e. power is mediated through local and traditional forms of government.[203] The Overlords meet with the human Secretary-General Stormgren instead of imposing a completely different structure of government on man. Third, "[t]he Overlords also manifest a paternalistic affection for their charges, similar to that claimed by administrators in the British colonial system."[204] Paternalism is exhibited in a notion of sympathy or affection between Stormgren and Karellen. For instance, shortly before his retirement, Stormgren thinks:

---

[198] *Ibid.*, p. 198.
[199] *Ibid.*
[200] *Ibid.*, p. 217.
[201] Cf. *ibid.*, p. 218.
[202] Matthew Candelaria, "The Overlord's Burden: The Source of Sorrow in *Childhood's End*," in: *Ariel* 33:1 (2002), 40.
[203] Cf. *ibid.*, 41.
[204] *Ibid.*

> Karellen had always treated him with unmistakable affection, despite his occasional devastating frankness, and now that their time together was drawing to its close he did not wish to do anything that might spoil that relationship. (*CE*, p. 50)

Naturally, paternalism in a colonial context is an illusion, i.e. the description of an ideal way of colonial administration. We can conclude that Clarke reflects British colonialism in his novel.

Resistance to the rule of the Overlords is feeble. In fact, people consider the aliens complaisant and become increasingly enthusiastic about their technologies. If there is resistance, it is expressed in colonial terms. For example:

> As pygmies may threaten a giant, so those angry fists were directed against the sky fifty kilometres above his [Stormgren's] head – against the gleaming silver cloud that was the flagship of the Overlord fleet. (*CE*, p. 7)

The image of the pygmy, i.e. a small 'primitive', is a colonial prejudice. Moreover, it expresses the inferiority of man. Clarke also compares resistance to the aliens to nineteenth-century India:

> They [human beings] felt, with good reason, much as a cultured Indian of the nineteenth century must have done as he contemplated the British Raj. The invaders had brought peace and prosperity to Earth – but who knew what the cost might be? History was not reassuring; even the most peaceable of contacts between races at very different cultural levels had often resulted in the obliteration of the more backward society. (*CE*, p. 21)

Thus, those who resist do not completely trust the notion of utopia. As we will later find out, there are indeed negative consequences of the "Golden Age". Incidentally, the example of India is significant since *Childhood's End* was published only four years after

India's independence from the British Empire. An organization that opposes the Overlords' invasion is the Freedom League (cf. *CE*, pp. 23ff.). However, when they kidnap the Secretary-General Stormgren and discuss the consequences of the invasion with him, they are unable "to mention one act that, in the ultimate analysis, hasn't been beneficial" (*CE*, p. 35). Therefore, the insurgents appear naïve rather than brave and self-determined.

Understanding the future of man is another manifestation of the Overlords' superiority. The aliens with their enormous mental faculties perfectly understand human nature and can thereby predict that mankind will eventually eradicate itself with nuclear weapons if it had not been for their invasion. This also expresses an orientalist paradigm: the colonized race is seen as children who have to be taken care of, as the title of the novel indicates. The adult Overlords perform the function of "midwives attending a difficult birth" (*CE*, p. 169), which makes them appear mature and necessary for mankind's well-being. Eventually, resistance does not play a significant role in Clarke's novel. In a colonial context, Clarke thus describes the situation of an empire that has never existed in reality. When we compare the aliens to British colonizers, we might say that "[t]he Overlords are everything the British would have liked to believe themselves to be in India and elsewhere, if only they had received the same kind of cooperation from their subjects."[205] In *Childhood's End*, man willingly succumbs to the alien life form.

Apart from characteristics of imperial rulers, the Overlords represent certain divine qualities. For instance, they live in a spaceship above Earth (cf. *CE*, p. 13). The dwelling place clearly recalls Heaven in Christian religion or Olympus in Greek mythology. Furthermore, they never reveal themselves; their outward appearance is a complete enigma to man and generates wild speculations (cf. *CE*, p. 21). Yet, many humans do not believe what they cannot see and become curious about the aliens and their powers (cf. *CE*, p. 40). This makes the reader think of the discussions about a proof of God's existence. The divine features of the Overlords add to their superiority; they make use of man's propensity to spiritualism

---

[205] *Ibid.*, 47.

and, in the course of the novel, we learn that they use this propensity as a means of manipulation. This idea will be further elaborated on in the context of the Overlords' revelation. In fact, mankind becomes exceedingly resentful about the mystery that surrounds the Overlords. In order to keep outrage and rebellion at bay, Karellen eventually announces that the Overlords will reveal themselves in fifty years (cf. *CE*, p. 46). Meanwhile, Stormgren repeatedly tries to see or even photograph Karellen, but all attempts fail. We receive the impression that the narration of these events only serves as a means to create suspense, as does the scene of Stormgren's abduction by a resistance group. These elements do not advance the plot. Part I ends with the 'prophecy' that man and Overlords will "go together into the future" (*CE*, p. 55).

Part II of *Childhood's End*, "The Golden Age", is set fifty years later than the first part. It begins with Karellen revealing himself to man. What is striking is the outward appearance of the alien; instead of a BEM (bug-eyed monster) that was the common depiction of an alien in science-fiction works of the 1940s and 1950s,[206] Karellen looks like the late-medieval portrayal of Satan:

> There was no mistake. The leathery wings, the little horns, the barbed tail – all were there. The most terrible of all legends had come to life, out of the unknown past. Yet now it stood smiling, in ebon majesty, with the sunlight gleaming upon its tremendous body, and with a human child resting trustfully on either arm. (*CE*, p. 61)

Generally speaking, the devil's personality is not described in a detailed way in the Bible. He frequently appears in the form of animals, for example as a serpent,[207] a dragon[208] or a lion.[209] In

---

[206] Bruce A. Beatie makes clear that the shift from the BEM to a benevolent alien is significant in Clarke's works. What is more, Clarke established a major trend. Cf. Bruce A. Beatie, "Arthur C. Clarke and the Alien Encounter: The Background of *Childhood's End*," 53.

[207] Cf. *The King James Bible*, Genesis 3.13 available on http://bartleby.com (2010-05-10).

[208] Cf. *Ibid.*, The Revelation of St. John the Divine, 20.2.

[209] Cf. *Ibid.*, The First Epistle General of Peter, 5.8.

contrast to this, the late-medieval depiction seems to be an anthropomorphized dragon, which might stand for the idea that the devil is deprived of beauty and harmony. The portrayal of Satan in Clarke's novel arouses fear in the spectators, and the scientist Jan Rodricks makes clear that this is due to a "racial memory", i.e. common ideas inherited from our ancestors[210]:

> There must be such thing as a racial memory, and that memory was somehow independent of time. To it, the future and the past were one. That was why, thousands of years ago, men had already glimpsed a distorted image of the Overlords, through a mist of fear and terror. (*CE*, p. 201)

It becomes obvious that the depiction of an alien life form as a medieval devil is a cultural construct that serves as a means to emphasize the Overlords' superiority. Even though we learn that the Overlords do not understand mysticism (cf. *CE*, pp. 176f.), they successfully use it in order to establish power over human beings. The oxymoron "memory of the future" can only be explained by an utterly different concept of time. In the novel, time is not understood as a rigid and linear system but it might become subject to 'play' in the postmodern sense of the word. Frederic Jameson explains that in science-fiction literature, there can be a "shift [...] from diachronic to synchronic – that is, to a view willing to consider the possibility of overlap, co-existence, sedimentation, unequal or 'non-synchronous' development within a single structure."[211] This implies that events which occur in the future might already be implemented in man's subconscious, which can be comforting on the one hand, and evoke fear and terror on the other (as is the case in Clarke's novel). Incidentally, the portrayal of Karellen as Satan contrasts with the idea that the alien represents "science and reason" (*CE*, p. 15). Moreover, the depiction is not one-

---

[210] Cf. Carl G. Jung, *Archetypes and the Collective Unconscious. The Collected Works of C. G. Jung Vol 1, Pt 1* (Princeton *et al.:* Princeton University Press, 1969).

[211] Frederic Jameson, "Towards a New Awareness of Genre," in: *Science Fiction Studies* 9:3 (1982), 323.

sided. As Karellen carries two children, he reminds the reader of Jesus blessing the little children.[212] This might mitigate the spectators' fear. To conclude, the outward appearance of the aliens functions as a basis for their superiority that is subconsciously 'understood' by the humans.

From the title of Part II, the reader learns that the rule of the Overlords brings back the Golden Age, i.e. the age of innocence and happiness. According to Hesiod (around 700 BC), mankind has undergone five stages of existence: the Golden Age, the Silver Age, the Bronze Age, the Heroic Age and the Iron Age. The concept of the Golden Age is taken up by Ovid in *Metamorphoses* (AD 8). Ovid describes a world that is free from fear, oppression and war. Furthermore, it is a happy and safe place since man is guided by conscience and uncorrupted reason, and Nature provides for everything humans need. In Clarke's novel, the Golden Age manifests itself in the form of a utopia:

> Ignorance, disease, poverty, and fear had virtually ceased to exist. The memory of war was fading into the past as a nightmare vanishes with the dawn; soon it would lie outside the experience of all living men. (*CE*, p. 64)

The Overlords have created "One World", i.e. a united Earth that does not know crime, stress and other problems of a highly-developed society (cf. *CE*, pp. 64f.). Instead, people occupy themselves with education (cf. *CE*, p. 65) and leisure activities (cf. p. *CE*, 104). In addition, they relish technical gadgets such as image-projectors and fully automated kitchens (cf. *CE*, p. 70). Due to a "completely reliable oral contraceptive" and "an equally infallible method [...] of identifying the father of any child," (*CE*, p. 60) interpersonal relationships are characterized by sexual freedom. Here, Clarke seems to foreshadow the sexual revolution after the invention of the birth control pill in the 1960s and the advent of the DNA tests in the 1980s. Last but not least, the Overlords' technol-

---

[212] Cf. *The King James Bible*, The Gospel according to St. Matthew, 19.13-15, The Gospel according to Mark 10.13-16, The Gospel according to Luke, 18.15-17.

ogy in the form of a TV that shows the past leads to the fact that "[w]ithin a few days, all mankind's multitudinous messiahs [...] lost their divinity" (*CE*, p. 67). This means that religion is effectively non-existent in the techno-science world. On the whole, the changes on Earth appear to be positive.

However perfect the situation on Earth may appear, some characters in the novel experience boredom and a lack of adventure. This manifests itself, for example, in the fact that few human beings are still passionate about scientific research (the Overlords have already made most of the discoveries) and about creative arts (the artist needs conflict for inspiration) (cf. *CE*, p. 68). As to works of art, man still "liv[es] on the glories of a past that could never return" (*ibid.*). The idea that high-quality art will occupy a rather insignificant place in the future world is not original. In fact, it came up in the discussions about degeneration and degenerate art at the turn of the century. In his famous work *Entartung* (*Degeneration*, 1892), the Jewish philosopher, author and physician Max Nordau writes about the future of art:

> [T]he march followed hitherto by civilization gives us an idea of the fate which may be reserved for art and poetry in a very distant future. That which originally was the most important occupation of men of full mental development, of the maturest, best and wisest members of society, becomes little by little a subordinate pastime [...].[213]

During the Golden Age depicted in *Childhood's End*, works of art are still produced, but they lack quality. Moreover, we might conclude that the amateur artists only occupy their minds with art because they are bored; mankind falls into decadence.

One of the characters that experience a feeling of nostalgia is the adventurous young scientist Jan Rodricks. The reader learns that Jan is "romantic not only in his heart but also in mind", and that he would like to explore space (cf. *CE*, p. 85). However, Jan cannot 'legally' fulfil his dreams since the Overlords have banned

---

[213] Max Nordau, *Degeneration* (Lincoln and London: University of Nebraska Press, 1993), p. 543.

space travel for human beings (cf. *ibid.*). In a *séance* with an Ouija board that is initially presented as a comical farce, Jan actually finds out the location of the Overlords' home planet in the constellation Carina[214] (cf. *CE*, pp. 89ff.). After having carried out some research in the Catalogue of Stars (cf. *CE*, p. 101), Jan makes an adventurous plan: in order to travel to the planet of the Overlords as a stowaway in the aliens' ship, he is going to hide in an artificial whale the Overlords have ordered for their museum (cf. *CE*, pp. 115ff.). Naturally, this is compared to the Biblical story of Jonah as well as to the Trojan horse (cf. *CE*, p. 117). Jan carefully prepares his journey and finally departs in the Overlords' spaceship (cf. *CE*, p. 125).

Part II of Clarke's novel closes with Karellen's prophetic statement "*The stars are not for man*" (*CE*, p. 130, italics by A. C. Clarke). The Overlord then announces the end of the Golden Age on Earth:

> They [human beings] would never know how lucky they had been. For a lifetime, mankind had achieved as much happiness as any race can ever know. It had been the Golden Age. But gold was also the colour of sunset, of autumn: and only Karellen's ears could catch the first wailings of the winter storms.
>
> And only Karellen knew with what inexorable swiftness the Golden Age was rushing to its close. (*CE*, p. 130)

Despite the fact that the poetic – nearly Shelleyan – language appears rather inappropriate for a 'rational' alien, Karellen's contemplation creates suspense; the reader expects radical changes. Ironically, we will find out that the stars are not for the Overlords, either.

The third part of the novel, "The Last Generation", is set in the artists' settlement "New Athens". After having been invited by the

---

214 Today, we know that Carina covers an area of 494 square degrees and has eight stars with planets. Its brightest star is Canopus, or Apha Carinae repectively. Cf. http://www.constellation-guide.com/constellation-list/carina-constellation/ (2012-05-23).

New Athens artists, the Greggson family, i.e. the stage director George, his wife Jean and the children Jeffrey and Jennifer Anne, move to the colony. New Athens consists of two beautiful islands in the South Pacific and is inhabited by approximately fifty thousand people (cf. *CE*, p. 135). The exotic setting is a parallel between Clarke's novel and classic romances of Empire. In the nineteenth century, the term 'South Sea' signified the Pacific Ocean with its numerous islands.[215] Nevertheless, in literature and films, the South Sea is not only a geographical expanse. Many stereotypes are associated with the region. For instance, the South Sea is regarded as an Eden-like, timeless and melancholic place. Nature is fertile and provides for the islanders' needs. Furthermore, Judeo-Christian notions of virtue and vice are not valid in the South Sea; it can serve as a venue for cannibals and pirates, and the islanders are frequently portrayed as idle, promiscuous and wild. The indigenous inhabitants can either be noble and innocent or bloodthirsty and ignoble savages. On the one hand, the intrusion of Europeans, for instance traders and missionaries, might be seen as corruptive to the paradise and its population. On the other hand, though, anthropophagy and savagery can be redeemed by the conversion to Christianity. To come back to *Childhood's End*, the aim of the settlement is to produce new works of art, and for the people to live in a more traditional way than those who embrace the technological gadgets of the Overlords. For example, the New Athens people prepare their meals themselves instead of dialling "Food Central" (cf. *CE*, pp. 134ff.).

New Athens was founded by the Jew Ben Solomon, and it started as an "open conspiracy against the Overlords" (*CE*, p. 138). Solomon understands that there has not been any significant work of art since the arrival of the aliens on Earth:

> Was it possible, he [Ben Solomon] sometimes said to himself, that despite all their enormous intelligence the Overlords did not really understand mankind, and were making a terrible mistake from the best of motives? Suppose, in their altruistic passion for justice

[215] Cf. *OED Online*, s.v. 'South Sea'.

> and order, they had determined to reform the world, but had not realized that they were destroying the soul of man? (*CE*, p. 137)

When Solomon raises the idea of the "soul of man", he unfolds an interesting dichotomy: the human beings represent art, spiritualism and maybe even Nature, whereas the aliens stand for science, rationality and culture. This recalls the confrontation of European civilizers with indigenous peoples. Especially in early colonial literature, the latter are mainly described as being more 'natural', wild and pristine than the former. In contrast, the Europeans are associated with reason and technological progress.

The Overlords eventually send an inspector to the colony. During a discussion with some teachers, the topic of imperialism is directly mentioned. The alien inspector explains that there are similarities between bringing up children and 'educating' indigenous peoples (cf. *CE*, p. 154). Nevertheless, he simultaneously makes clear that the purpose of the Overlords is much more 'reasonable' than the motivations of the European colonizers. As an example, he refers to the British in India:

> [An] analogy can be found in the history of your colonial powers. The Romans and British Empires, for that reason, have always been of considerable interest to us. The case of India is particularly instructive. The main difference between us and the British in India was that they had no real motives for going there – no conscious objectives, that is, except such trivial and temporary ones as trade or hostility to other European powers. They found themselves possessors of an empire before they knew what to do with it, and were never really happy until they had got rid of it again. (*ibid.*)

Thus, we learn by implication that the aliens dominate Earth for a special reason. However, at this stage, their motives are not yet understood by mankind or by the reader. What is striking is the fact that the Overlords would "get rid of [their] empire […] without the slightest hesitation" (*ibid.*). This implies that the aliens are not emotionally attached to Earth and its inhabitants; they simply fulfil their task.

Childhood's End then develops into a novel of prophetic eschatology. The prospect of a violent disruption of the world as we know it is a common topic in science-fiction novels, and it serves as a tool to create suspense. From the point of view of George and Jean Greggson, the reader learns that the children in New Athens slowly transform. For example, they begin to exhibit superhuman faculties such as telekinesis (cf. *CE*, pp. 171f.) and spiritual vision, i.e. Jeffrey can see the Overlords' planet in his dreams (cf. *CE*, pp. 163f.). In general, this metamorphosis signifies "the end of civilization, the end of all that man had striven for since the beginnings of time" (*CE*, p. 173). Exactly one century after the arrival of the aliens, Karellen reveals to the people why the children undergo these changes: the human race is about to "jump to the next stage" (*CE*, p. 176) of evolution; man will finally become part of an immaterial entity, the Overmind.[216] The Overmind is the power that generates the changes in the children and makes use of the Overlords as man's "guardians" (*CE*, p. 177). Yet, Karellen cannot (or refuses to) explain what this entity is since it is perfectly ungraspable. Thus, in accordance with the theories of apophatic or negative theology, it rather becomes clear what the Overmind is *not*: material, intelligible, predictable and controllable. With regard to colonial encounters, the Overmind is as incomprehensible to human beings as the concept of the omnipresent God in Judeo-Christian belief might have been for pagan indigenous peoples. Despite his intelligence, the Overlord seems to struggle to find the appropriate words during his speech (cf. *CE*, pp. 177f.). What the reader along with the characters in the novel understands is that mankind is destined to serve a higher purpose. After some words of comfort,

---

[216] As the Overmind is immaterial and some future kind of intelligence, it is comparable to Vanamonde in Clarke's novel *The City and the Stars* (1956, Cf. Arthur C. Clarke, *The City and the Stars* [London: Gollancz, [3]2003]). However, the latter is generated by man himself, i.e. by scientific experiments in the far future. Cf. Russell Blackford, "Technological Meliorism and the Posthuman Vision: Arthur C. Clarke and the Ultimate Future of Intelligence," in: *The New York Review of Science Fiction* 14:3 (2001), 11.

the Overlords eventually collect and evacuate all children to their spaceships (cf. *CE*, pp. 178ff.).

What is striking is the fact that the Overlords cannot become part of the Overmind. Karellen explains that the alien race has already reached the apex of its evolution:

> Despite all their powers and their brilliance, the Overlords were trapped in some evolutionary cul-de-sac. Here was a great and noble race, in almost every way superior to mankind; yet it had no future, and it was aware of it. (*CE*, p. 169)

This is one of the differences between man and the aliens. The children of man can undergo a metamorphosis and reach a higher stage of evolution, whereas the Overlords remain what they are. Likewise, there is no hint in the novel that the Overlords have children. Therefore, they can never join the more abstract entity, the Overmind. When Karellen sees the children ascend to the Overmind, he recalls his own function: the Overlords only serve the superior form of being. He even compares his race to a tribe living on a plain:

> [H]is people were no better than a tribe that has passed its whole existence upon some flat and dusty plain. Far off were the mountains, where power and duty dwelt, where the thunder sported above the glaciers and the air was clear and keen. There the sun still walked, transfiguring the peaks with glory, when all the land below was wrapped in darkness. And they could only watch and wonder; they could never scale those heights. (*CE*, p. 211)

Ironically, the melancholic overtone of Karellen's thoughts as well as his envy makes the alien appear human.

After the evacuation of the children, the perspective of the novel changes: we are with the scientist Jan Rodricks on the Overlords' planet. Jan describes the planet as an "enormous wafer-thin crescent reaching up in the sky like a great bow placed beside the sun" (*CE*, p. 185). He learns that the Overlords "had evolved on a much smaller world and then conquered this one, changing not only its atmosphere but even its gravity" (*CE*, p. 187). This tells us that the Overlords are superior to other civilizations due to their technology and their intelligence. They conquered a new territory and changed it according to their needs, much like the Europeans who established trading posts and infrastructure in the colonies. What is striking is that the world of the Overlords – the ruby light, the functional architecture and the Satan-like creatures flying around – reminds Jan of medieval depictions of Hell (cf. *CE*, p. 187). Due to the Jungean concept of a racial memory, this evokes "terror" in the scientist (cf. *ibid.*). Moreover, it implies that human beings and Overlords could never live together on the same planet; there cannot be a futuristic 'multiethnic' society. Their worlds are utterly different, and the Overlords' planet is incomprehensible to Jan. This reminds the reader of a 'savage' confronted with a highly-developed Western society. The most ungraspable phenomenon Jan observes is some sort of volcano that changes colours and releases streams and rings of light (cf. *CE*, p. 192). From the fact that this phenomenon is the only thing Jan is not allowed to photograph, and since Jan suddenly feels that "the Overlords had masters, too" (*CE*, p. 193), we might guess that the scientist catches a glimpse of the Overmind. Therefore, we can conclude that the Overmind represents some kind of omnipotent deity for the Overlords. Even though the latter cannot become part of it, they have to serve their 'God'. This might be interpreted as a science-fictional version of religion.

On Earth, the Overmind generates the metamorphosis of the children of man. They greatly enhance their powers, for example they change the flow of rivers (cf. *CE*, p. 197) and alter the spin of the moon (cf. *CE*, p. 205). Yet, their increase in power is accompanied by a process of dehumanization. Jan, the last survivor of mankind, witnesses the changes. The narrator tells us that the children remind him of some primitive race: "They might have been savages, engaged in some complex ritual dance. They were naked and filthy, with matted hair obscuring their eyes" (*CE*, p. 196). They also appear to be de-individualized. Apart from their wild outward appearance, the children are morally depraved. For example, they destroy "all the trees and grass, all the living creatures" (*CE*, p. 198). Their "complex ritual dance" (*CE*, p. 196) is a stereotype of primitivism. In addition, the Overlords seem to be scared of them and withdraw: "It is no longer safe for us to stay. They may ignore us still, but we cannot take the risk" (*CE*, p. 205). Thus, the emotionless children might murder again. The depiction of the children at this stage of evolution is the portrayal of the ignoble savage in colonial literature *par excellence*. For instance, Robert Michael Ballantyne (1825-1894) writes about a cannibal in *The Coral Island* (1857):

> His hair was frizzed out to an enormous extent, so that it resembled a large turban. […] Altogether, with his yellow turban-like hair, his Herculean black frame, his glittering eyes, and white teeth, he seemed the most terrible monster I ever beheld.[217]

The depiction of the children can also be compared to the way Charles Darwin describes the indigenous population of Tierra del Fuego:

> I could not have believed how wide was the difference between savage and civilized man: it is greater than between a wild and domesticated animal, inasmuch as in man there is a greater power of improvement. The chief spokesman was old, and appeared to be the head of the family; the three others were powerful young men, about six feet high. […]
>
> The old man had a fillet of white feathers tied round his head, which partly confined his black, coarse, and entangled hair. His face was crossed by two broad transverse bars; one, painted bright red, reached from ear to ear and included the upper lip; the other, white

---

[217] Robert Michael Ballantyne, *The Coral Island* (Ware: Wordsworth Classics, 1993), pp. 138f.

> like chalk, extended above and parallel to the first, so that even his eyelids were thus coloured.[218]

The children of man are predestined to join the Overmind, and it becomes obvious that all achievements of civilization and of the Golden Age on Earth do not matter any more. What was important for the generation of their parents (a comfortable lifestyle, entertainment and education) has become irrelevant. In addition, the children – or savages respectively – are characterized by moral depravity and thus inferior to the colonizer, i.e. the Overlords in Clarke's novel. Ironically, their savage features even evoke a shift in sympathy from the inhuman descendents of man to the 'devilish' alien race.

However, the transformation of the children is not yet complete. Several years later, the children's faces have become uniform, just like an "average face" (*CE*, p. 197). This recalls H.G. Wells' depiction of the Eloi in *The Time Machine* (1895): the Eloi, who are also a future stage of human evolution, all look alike, even the sexes are not distinguishable.[219] The children of man are deprived of their human qualities. In general, we might say that the loss of individuality is due to the fact that the children are destined to become part of one entity. Jan learns that the human beings of his generation are dead, i.e. "*Homo sapiens* was extinct" (*CE*, p. 201, italics by A. C. Clarke). People in their final days committed suicide or died in fierce and dangerous leisure activities (cf. *CE*, p. 202). In addition, the last men were characterized by "savagery and selfishness" (*ibid.*), much like the degenerate human beings Max Nordau describes in *Degeneration*.

Eventually, the children join the Overmind, ascending to the sky in "a great burning column, like a tree of fire [...]" (*CE*, p. 208). In Judeo-Christian belief, an equivalent might be found in the idea that the souls of the dead ascend to God in Heaven. In order to be absorbed into the ultimate form of being, the descendents of man must be structurally identical: "The creation of a thoroughly

---

[218] Charles Darwin, *The Voyage of the Beagle. Journal of Researches into the Natural History and Geology of the Countries Visited during the Voyage of HMS Beagle round the World, under the Command of Captain Fitz Roy, RN.*, p. 196.
[219] Cf. H.G. Wells, *The Time Machine*, p. 26.

new transcendent of understanding of humanity's future treats the isomorphism as an opportunity of interpolating a new form of experience."[220] The planet is then destroyed in a cataclysmic shock (cf. *CE*, p. 210), and we might even say that the 'volcano' Jan observes on the planet of the Overlords eventually 'erupts' on Earth.[221] In remembering the human beings he knew (cf. *CE*, p. 212), Karellen's melancholic thoughts make Karellen and the other aliens appear human, whereas the children have lost all their human qualities.

It is interesting to note that, again, Clarke hints at a nuclear holocaust on Earth: the children feed on the planet's energy (cf. *CE*, p. 197), and their metamorphosis involves the annihilation of the entire planet. Terence Hold makes clear that the choice of children as agents of destruction is not arbitrary. He states that after 1948, approximately two-thirds of the most popular science-fiction stories feature children that are associated with the loss of adult control.[222] In times of the Cold War (*Childhood's End* was published in 1953), this might be linked to the threat of nuclear weapons and their implicit imagery of childhood. For example, the nuclear bombs were called "Little Boy" and "Fat Boy", and the plane that dropped them had a female name, "Enola Gay". Similarly, just as the consequences of a-bombs were largely unknown to the public before the airdrops over Japan, the superhuman powers of the children in *Childhood's End* are incomprehensible to both their parents and the Overlords. The children are far more powerful than their parents and feed upon the achievements of former generations. Neither humans nor the Overlords can control these beings that finally bring about the apocalypse.

Nonetheless, the act of destruction can also be interpreted as constructive or nutritious, as John Hollow suggests.[223] The last generation of human beings finally becomes part of something

---

[220] Peter Stockwell, *The Poetics of Science Fiction* (London *et al.*: Pearson, 2000), p. 218.

[221] Cf. John Hollow, *Against the Night, the Stars. The Fiction of Arthur C. Clarke* (London *et al.*: Ohio University Press, 1983), p. 82.

[222] Cf. Terence Holt, "The Bomb and the Baby Boom," in: *Tri Quarterly* 80 (1990), 208.

[223] Cf. John Hollow, *Against the Night, the Stars. The Fiction of Arthur C. Clarke*, p. 82.

greater. After their transformation, the children leave their material state behind and live as part of the Overmind. Hence, the immaterial entity stands for unity and harmony of different species, and it appears as if they are more powerful together than separately. The change from diversity to homogeneity that the Overmind generates might be comparable to biological isomorphism, i.e. to "[a] similarity of appearance displayed by organisms having different genotypes."[224] Moreover, the transformation of the children of man resembles the Judeo-Christian concept of life culminating in Paradise. This implies that the Overmind is more than a colonizer that exploits (transforms) Earth and its inhabitants. Ungraspable and of virtually unlimited intelligence and authority, this immaterial entity has more similarities with a spiritual being like God than with an imperial power. What is more, the idea that Earth is annihilated unfolds a paradigmatic shift in alien-encounter science fiction. In most other works, victory over the invaders from outer space is followed by a decolonization process. *Childhood's End*, though, does not portray a futuristic postimperial situation on Earth, in which people are either proud of being liberated from the oppressor or deplore the loss of their alien idols. Instead, Earth after the Overlords is irrelevant. What counts for the human race is access to the universe – a precious gift that can only become reality through joining the Overmind. Ultimately, humans have changed from 'suicidal lemmings' into a higher form of life, higher even than their minders, the Overlords.

In conclusion, the Overlords are the race that bears most parallels to an imperial ruler; the aliens conquer the planet with the help of technological and intellectual superiority, impose new laws on human beings, 'educate' and look after mankind like a midwife takes care of a child, and finally leave Earth behind after having fulfilled their task. Naturally, this idealized portrayal of a colonizer does not allow for any notions of postcolonial guilt. The aliens lead mankind to a heteronomous destiny. In addition, various orientalist paradigms are treated: the depiction of the natives as children or pygmies, their ritual dancing and their inferior moral values. The aliens' use of the English language, of indirect rule and their pater-

[224] *OED Online*, s.v. 'isomorphism'.

nalistic relationship with humans recall distinctly British imperial practices. As to the future of man, Clarke presents the metamorphosis in an ambiguous way: in undergoing the transformation, "the human race has both gained (access to a transcendent universe) and lost (its own soul, its individuality)."[225] However, as the Overlords regret the fact that they cannot become part of this superior entity, we tend to believe that isomorphism is a chance for mankind. The success of *Childhood's End* is due to Clarke's vivid way of story-telling as well as to his close references to history and colonialism.

[225] Cf. Bruce A. Beatie, "Arthur C. Clarke and the Alien Encounter: The Background of *Childhood's End*," 63.

2.2 Intervention from Outer Space: Fred Hoyle and John Elliot, The *Andromeda* Novels

A for Andromeda (1962) and its sequel, *Andromeda Breakthrough* (1964), are based on the eponymous BBC series and were written by Fred Hoyle and John Eliot. Just like *Childhood's End*, the *Andromeda* novels portray benevolent aliens. In these works, the extraterrestrial perform some sort of social engineering: they intervene into the lives of a lower civilization (mankind) in order to change humanity for the better. Alien influence is entirely rejected by man. Yet, all events have been calculated and are ultimately beneficial. What is different in the *Andromeda* novels is that an invasion is stirred up but never happens. Instead, the aliens indirectly rule man with the help of 'tools' on Earth – a supercomputer and an artificially created woman, called "Andromeda". Hoyle's and Eliot's novels also treat the crucial role of human scientists who are determined to make contact with outer space and eventually become agents of the aliens.

The authors of the novels combine scientific imagination and TV expertise. Sir Fred Hoyle FRS (1915-2001) was a mathematician, astronomer and science-fiction writer. Hoyle achieved an MA in physics at Emmanuel College in Cambridge and later became a fellow of St John's College. During World War II, Hoyle worked for a naval radar research establishment near Chichester, West Sussex. After the war, he and his family moved back to Cambridge. Hoyle became a lecturer of mathematics and a devoted astrophysicist. Incidentally, he received some criticism for advocating the Steady State theory of the creation of the Universe, a theory that is based on the idea that the Universe is always increasing but maintains a constant density since new stars and galaxies are created at the same rate that old matter becomes unobservable.[226] Meanwhile, however, the Steady State theory has been replaced by the Big Bang theory. Hoyle wrote about forty science-

---

[226] Cf. http://www.britannica.com/EBchecked/topic/564427/steady-state-theory (2012-05-28).

fiction novels, among them *Ossian's Ride*[227] (1959), *Seven Steps to the Sun* (1970) and *Comet Halley* (1985). Apart from fiction, he published autobiographical writings and popular books on mathematics and cosmology.[228]

Hoyle started his career as a writer of science fiction with the novel *The Black Cloud* (1957), of which the BBC intended to make a TV series. However, the rights for adaptation had already been sold so that Hoyle decided to create another science-fiction series. Together with the novelist, screenwriter and TV producer John Elliot, Hoyle developed the storyline for the series, and Eliot became the co-author of the *Andromeda* novels. John Elliot (1918-1997) had joined the BBC in 1949 and scripted TV plays such as *War in the Air* (1954) and *High Fidelity* (1959).[229] The two writers outlined the major characters of *A for Andromeda* and planned seven episodes of approximately forty-five minutes each. The series was filmed in June and July and broadcasted in October 1961, starring Julie Christie as Andromeda and Peter Halliday as Dr John Fleming. Due to the enormous success of the series (it attracted 12.9 million viewers), the BBC decided to produce a sequel in which the situation in Britain is contrasted to the one in a fictive country, called "Azaran", in the Middle East or Northern Africa. *Andromeda Breakthrough*, which consists of six episodes, was filmed in March and April 1962 and aired from June to August of the same year. Unfortunately, the BBC destroyed the video material of *A for Andromeda* in the late 1960s so that only one complete

---

[227] *Ossian's Ride* also treats benevolent aliens. In this novel, the extraterrestrials actually land on Earth (or more precisely in Ireland) and establish the "Industrial Corporation of Éire", from where they want to transform the planet into a high-tech utopia. However, the novel, which focuses on the adventures of the young scientist-protagonist Thomas Sherwood, is a thriller rather than a science-fiction novel. Cf. Fred Hoyle, *Ossian's Ride* (Portsmouth, NH *et al.*: Heinemann, 1959).

[228] Cf. Subodh Mahanti, "Fred Hoyle: The Most Versatile Physicist of the 20th Century," in: *Dream 2047* 11 (2008), 34-30 (pagination in reversed order).

[229] Cf. John Faulkner, "Remembering Fred Hoyle," Text of an After-Dinner Speech, in: *Astrophysics and Space Science* 285 (2003), 603. Interestingly, the BBC was planning to adapt John Wyndham's *The Kraken Wakes* (cf. chapter 3.2) at the same time. Nevertheless, *The Kraken Wakes* was dropped for *A for Andromeda*.

episode survived.[230] In order to provide "a more sophisticated adult alternative to *Doctor Who*," the BBC turned *A for Andromeda* into a standalone film of about ninety minutes in 2006.[231] Since the novels do not differ significantly from the original TV series, I intend to discuss the written works together with the series in this chapter.

In *A for Andromeda*, an English radio telescope receives a message from outer space, which is decoded as the blueprint of a supercomputer. The computer enables a team of scientists to create an alien girl of immense intelligence whom they give the name Andromeda, and later André. Even though Andromeda claims that she has been sent to save humanity from itself, the military soon recognizes the potential of the computer and the girl and misuses them to design powerful missiles. After some of the staff become severely ill from a bacterium produced with the instructions of the computer, Andromeda and Dr John Fleming, a physicist who deeply distrusts the alien machine and the girl, destroy the invention and escape to a small island where Andromeda disappears. *Andromeda Breakthrough* directly follows up on *A for Andromeda*. André is found alive and, together with Fleming, she is taken to Azaran, where the multinational cartel, Intel, and an ambitious dictator have a copy of the supercomputer built. Alien bacteria spread through the oceans, which leads to natural disasters and a decrease in oxygen. The Western scientists finally succeed in creating anti-bacteria to save the world, and the computer is switched off. The novels are told from the point of view of an omniscient

---

230 Cf. Andrew Pixley, "Viewing Notes," in: *The Andromeda Anthology: A for Andromeda &The Andromeda Breakthrough. 3 DVD Box Set* (UK: 2 Entertain Video, 2006), 29ff.

231 Cf. Markus Hearn, "Viewing Notes," in: *A for Andromeda* (UK: BBC, 2006). Generally speaking, the viewer receives the impression that the main focus of the film differs from the one of the original series: it tells the story of Dr Fleming instead of laying emphasis on the fate of mankind confronted with aliens of superior intelligence. The first half of the film narrates the love story between Fleming and the mathematician Christine, an element which does not exist in the 1961 series. Subsequently, it centres around Fleming's distrust in André. The ending of the film remains open: the lab with the supercomputer burns down and André is liberated from the extraterrestrials, but it is not clear whether she will live on Earth like a human being, if she builds another computer, or if she becomes the object of medical research.

narrator, mostly through the eyes of the scientists and officials involved in the events. Strikingly, we do not hear André's voice; the girl is not self-determined but controlled by alien powers and characterized by the people around her.

With regard to the topic of imperialism, the *Andromeda* novels and other works of alien-encounter science fiction treat their subject matter in a similar way. For example, they raise questions about what constitutes a human being, and they illustrate that a position of hegemony is reached through superior intelligence and fire power. What is original here is the idea that the aliens never appear on Earth, and that only two humans are ever granted the opportunity to see them. Nevertheless, people fear an invasion after an intellectually superior creature and a computer that far exceeds human technology are 'sent' to Earth from another galaxy. For example, Fleming explains: "I can foresee a time when we create a higher form of intelligence to which, in the end, we'll hand over."[232] The politician Michael Osborne supports Fleming's pessimistic view:

> Given that an intelligence in some recess of space sends us a stream of technical data which enables us obediently to make an anthropomorphic creature to run its machine, who's honestly going to believe that the whole business is for our benefit and not theirs?[233]

Even André herself warns Fleming of a take-over: "I can see the difference between our intelligence and yours. I can see that ours is going to take over and yours is going to die. [...] [Y]ou'll go down with the dinosaurs" (*AFA*, p. 152). Therefore, various characters fuel anxieties of an imminent invasion which eventually does not happen. The reader receives the impression that the invasion element is insufficiently developed, and he or she might be disappointed. A reason that makes the *Andromeda* novels an interesting object of study is that the aliens turn out to be benevolent and use

---

232 Fred Hoyle and John Elliot, *A for Andromeda* (London: Souvenir Press, 2011), p. 144. All subsequent references to this edition are in brackets in the text.
233 Fred Hoyle and John Elliot, *Andromeda Breakthrough* (London: Corgi Books, 1966), p. 15. All subsequent references to this edition are in brackets in the text.

humans themselves as agents to save Earth. In addition, the novels reflect topics that are still discussed fifty years after their publication: genetic engineering and the responsibility of scientists, computer-controlled weaponry and political unrests in the Middle East.

As to the alien Other, the novels feature various extraterrestrials: aliens from the Andromeda Galaxy, a supercomputer, an artificially created monster, called "Cyclops", and the female human-alien hybrid who is the protagonist of the works. Especially throughout the course of *A for Andromeda*, not only the extraterrestrials but also their 'tools' on Earth are perceived as alien Others. The plot starts with the recording of a message at a radio-telescope station near Bouldershaw, Yorkshire. The message is sent from the Andromeda Nebula [234] and transmitted by an alien life form.[235] In contrast to the other works discussed in this paper, Earth does not face an invasion but the scientists are determined to make contact with outer space. Information about the aliens is scarce; instead of describing the creatures' biological and social traits, their intentions, *et cetera*, the authors only allow the reader a short glimpse of the alien planet at the end of *Andromeda Breakthrough*:

> An enormous plain stretched into the background where it merged with the dark sky. In the foreground stood monstrous elongated shapes, placed haphazardly and apparently half buried in the level, soft-looking surface. (*AB*, p. 185)

---

[234] The Andromeda Nebula is also called Andromeda Galaxy or, technically, Messier 31. At a distance of 248,000 light years (not two hundred light years, as mentioned in *A for Andromeda*), it is the closest galaxy to the Milky Way, where Earth is located. The Andromeda Nebula can be viewed without the aid of telescopes. Cf. http://www.britannica.com/EBchecked/topic/24105 /Andromeda-Galaxy (2011-12-28).

[235] The message from the Andromeda Galaxy recalls the so-called "Wow Signal", even though the latter was recorded in 1977, i.e. long after the publication of the novels. The Wow Signal was recorded by the Big Ear radio telescope in Ohio, and the scientist who detected it, Professor Jerry Ehman, wrote "wow" next to the signal printout since it was the most striking radio signal ever recorded by SETI (the Search for Extra-Terrestrial Intelligence). Cf. http://planetary.org/explore /topics/search_for_life/seti/alien_signal.html (2011-12-28).

The long, immobile aliens recall giant sand eels. Moreover, we learn that they are "big brains" whose "senses are different" from ours (cf. *ibid.*). As to their intentions, Andromeda explains that they try to break with the circular recurrence of history of the less evolved species in the universe. The idea of circular recurrence of history is also evaluated in a negative way in Stephen Baxter's *Timelike Infinity* (cf. chapter 1.3). The *Andromeda* novels seem to purport the same message: the species are trapped in their fate, and it is impossible for them to reach a better status without external influence. Thus, the aliens from the Andromeda Nebula are benevolent towards man; unlike those aliens of superior intelligence depicted in other works, they offer assistance. They basically help the human brain develop more quickly:

> [The human race] lives and reproduces and works and struggles by animal instincts. That's all human beings are – animals who spend their time competing for existence, keeping their bodies alive. And when the earth gets too crowded there is a holocaust and the survivors begin the cycle over again, and the brain never develops. (*AB*, p. 186)

This implies that, in order to improve the species as such and its living-conditions, man ought to gain more knowledge and evolve more quickly – an idea that recalls renaissance or enlightenment after an era of darkness and ignorance. Here, the aliens seem to offer tutelage on the way to civilization, a parallel to the Judeo-Christian *mission civilisatrice*. The question arises why the aliens should choose to control events from their planet instead of appearing on Earth, as is the case in numerous other works of alien-encounter science fiction. The reader could speculate that the immobile creatures cannot travel, and that a personal encounter would perhaps be unnecessary since the aliens are highly intelligent mind machines that influence other species through their elaborate plans. Incidentally, when the series was developed, the BBC would have faced difficulties in showing aliens in action as there were no computer-animated effects (in the original series, the extraterrestrials look as if they were made from a row of staples and some sort of glass tubes). In the novels and in the series, humans decide to reject alien influence and destroy the supercomputer (cf. *AB*, p. 190) so that the fate of man will not be altered further. In contrast, for example, to the Overlords in Arthur C. Clarke's *Childhood's End* (cf. chapter 2.1), the extraterrestrials from the Andromeda Nebula do not force their will upon man (the Overlords make use of violence). Humans themselves remain responsible for their destiny, and this actually has a positive overtone in Hoyle's and Elliot's novels.

The supercomputer is considered an alien Other as well. Strikingly, the machine shares some features with a biological creature: it is referred to as "he" (cf. *AFA*, pp. 52ff.), and it learns by way of educated guessing (cf. *AFA*, pp. 70, 108f.) and by electrocuting the data-processing assistant, Christine (cf. *AFA*, pp. 102f.). The computer punishes those people that prevent the aliens from fulfilling their mission. For instance, when Fleming sabotages it, the machine creates a formula for a fatal "anti-enzyme" or "cell destructor" (cf. *AFA*, p. 147). Moreover, due to the fact that André does not kill Fleming, the computer gives her an electric shock, a method that recalls torture (cf. *AFA*, p. 157). The most severe punishment for Fleming's resistance is the creation of bacteria that almost make Earth uninhabitable. This topic will be elaborated on later in the chapter. To sum up, the computer is perceived as an enigmatic hybrid being of creature and machine. It is incomprehensible, intellectually superior since it is controlled by the aliens, powerful, and both cruel and frightening.

Understandably, the scientists do not trust the supercomputer, especially when it instructs them to create a monster, "Cyclops" (cf. *AFA*, p. 89). The creature, which is taken care of by the biochemist Madeleine Dawnay, is harmless but exceedingly ugly:

> The creature was not unlike an elongated jellyfish, without limbs or tentacles but with a vague sort of bifurcation at one end and an enlargement that might be a head at the other. It floated in liquid, a twitching, quivering mass of protoplasm, its surface greeny-yellow, slimy and glistening. And in the middle of what might be its head was set – huge, lidless and colourless – an eye. (*ibid.*)

Due to its elongated shape, the creature looks like an amalgam of the aliens from the Andromeda Nebula and a human being. Cyclops divides the scientists: Dawnay is proud and fascinated by the fact that the computer enables her to create life (cf. *AFA*, p. 92), whereas Fleming, who decoded the message and built the computer, sees its dangerous potential. He compares the situation to encounters in colonial history: "The first explorers must have seemed harmless enough to the native tribes. [...] Kind old missionaries with ridiculous topees, but they finished up as their rulers" (*AFA*, p. 93). Fleming expects "some sort of take-over" (*ibid.*) from outer space, which generates suspense.

The creation of artificial life is one of the oldest and most popular topics in science fiction. The prototype of novels dealing with this trope is perhaps Mary Shelley's *Frankenstein or, The Modern Prometheus* (1818). It tells the story of the young and ambitious scientist Victor Frankenstein who wants to discover the secret of life. After several years of research and experiments, he animates a creature that is made of parts from dead bodies. Throughout the novel, it becomes evident that it is first and foremost his monstrous outward appearance that deprives the creature of compassion and community. His 'father' describes his physical traits as extremely horrible:

> His yellow skin scarcely covered the work of muscles and arteries beneath; his hair was of a lustrous black, and flowing; his teeth of pearly whiteness; but these luxuries only formed a more horrid contrast with his watery eyes, that seemed almost of the same colour as the dun-white sockets in which they were set, his shrivelled complexion and straight black lips. [...] Oh! No mortal could support the horror of that countenance. A mummy again endued with animation could not be so hideous as that wretch. I [Frankenstein] had gazed on him while unfinished; he was ugly then, but when those muscles and joints were rendered capable

> of motion, it became a thing such as even Dante could not have conceived.[236]

In addition, Frankenstein states that his creature is "gigantic", "deform[ed]" and "more hideous than belongs to humanity."[237] Thus, even though he created the wretch, Frankenstein perceives it as disgusting, scary and, to some extent, beyond understanding. He runs away from it so as not to be responsible for his own creation, and it becomes an alien Other after having been rejected by society for its repulsiveness. Cyclops in *A for Andromeda* is potentially dangerous. It becomes obvious that Dr Frankenstein as well as Dr Fleming distrust their creations – albeit for very different reasons. Cyclops clearly is an alien Other, and both scientists seem to regret their scientific achievements. Apart from that, both novels illustrate the risks that might accompany scientific ambition and 'playing God'.[238]

To come back to Hoyle's and Elliot's works, Cyclops is an imperfect attempt to build a human being. The computer learns about the anatomy of man by requiring a sacrifice, Christine. The next step in the making of a human being is a baby girl, modelled after Christine. The girl, whom they baptize "Andromeda" or "André" respectively, is beautiful, extremely intelligent and develops at an enormous pace. For instance, she reaches adulthood within four months and learns language and writing in a couple of weeks (cf. *AFA*, pp. 114f.). A theme that informs both *Andromeda* novels is the question of the girl's humanity or, more abstractly, what consti-

---

[236] Mary Shelley, *Frankenstein or, The Modern Prometheus* (London *et al.*: Penguin Popular Classics, 1994), pp. 55f.

[237] *Ibid.*, p. 73.

[238] Incidentally, what was romantic horror in Mary Shelley's times became a serious discussion about genetic engineering in the 1960s, when the *Andromeda* series was aired. After Francis Crick and James Watson had determined the structure of the DNA molecule in 1953, Edward Tatum foresaw in his Nobel Prize lecture of 1958 the changes biotechnologists could make to the function of a gene. Scientists also found methods of producing synthetic DNA. However, experiments in genetic engineering have been strictly regulated ever since, and discussions about the ethics of genetic engineering still concern us today. For more information on the history of genetic engineering and its application in the pharmaceutical industry, see Maureen D. McKelvey, *Evolutionary Innovations. The Business of Biotechnology* (Oxford *et al.*: Oxford University Press, 1996).

tutes a human being. Generally speaking, Andromeda is characterized through other characters: far from being self-determined, the girl is presented as what the scientists consider her to be. Directly after her creation, humans perceive her as clearly Other due to her alien characteristics. As to her relation to the supercomputer, Fleming makes clear that she is "an extension of the machine, like the other creature [i.e. Cyclops], only more sophisticated" (*AFA*, p. 110), which implies that Andromeda is something artificial or even mechanic. This view is corroborated by Andromeda's enormous brain capacity; she resembles an infallible "calculator" (cf. *AFA*, p. 115). Furthermore, her senses differ from those of human beings: she is able to communicate with the computer through its high-voltage panels (cf. *AFA*, p. 88). Concerning her origin, the lack of biological parents deprives her of humanness. She is 'sent' from outer space and 'assembled' on Earth with the help of the computer and genetic engineering. Above all, Andromeda has no free will: she obeys the computer's commands and is punished if she refuses to do so. However, the computer does not function as her "master" since it is the aliens that guide the computer – and indirectly the girl. They are therefore both "slaves" (cf. *AFA*, p. 152).

Andromeda's interface with the supercomputer evokes notions of technophobia in Fleming (ironically – since he is the scientist who built the machine). Just like the creation of life, technophobia has always been a popular trope in science fiction, especially in the early days of the genre, when a deep distrust in the consequences of scientific invention gave rise to numerous novels. An interesting example is Edward M. Forster's novella *The Machine Stops* (1909), in which the human race lives under ground. All their requirements are met by the omnipotent Machine. However, the Machine collapses and civilization is doomed to perish.[239] In more recent works, people dread the take-over and colonization of their world by mind machines (cyborgs, androids or robots) that have "incorporated the best survival characteristics of humanity [and] will create a new generation without human intervention."[240] The

[239] Cf. Edward M. Forster, *The Machine Stops* (London *et al.*: Penguin Classics, 2011).

[240] Daniel Dinello, *Technophobia! Science Fiction Visions of Posthuman Technology* (Austin, TX: University of Texas Press, 2005), p. 26.

activities of the mind machines might run counter to the ones of humans so that mankind may eventually face its extinction. These fears are illustrated in the *Terminator* tetralogy[241] (1984-2009), the *Matrix* films[242] (1999-2003) and, to a certain extent, in *I, Robot*[243] (2004).

Further characteristics of Andromeda's Otherness are her enhanced body and her lack of emotions. With regard to her body, Andromeda quickly recovers from severe illnesses (cf. *AB*, pp. 22, 53), which shows that she is physically stronger and tougher than human beings. Physical superpowers are, of course, a common trope in science fiction. Heroes with wonderful powers primarily permeate the comics, with Superman as their archetype. Like Andromeda, most of these heroes are social outcasts whom people treat with a mixture of fascination and distrust. As to Andromeda's psychological features, she appears to be rather withdrawn and callous: "Although she was alert and reasonably communicative, she might just as well have been walking and talking in her sleep, and that, in fact, is the impression which she gave" (*AB*, p. 115). Hence, Andromeda does not show her emotions as human beings would do, and this adds to her mysteriousness. It also seems that she is unable to tell right from wrong, which demonstrates that she has not undergone any process of socialization. For example, when the computer classifies Cyclops as "unwanted material", Andromeda ruthlessly kills the innocent creature (cf. *AFA*, p. 119), and she later tries to electrocute Fleming (cf. *AFA*, pp. 150f.). The reader generally receives the impression that Andromeda behaves like a programmed robot.

Yet, Andromeda changes tremendously in the course of the story, and this development influences the scientists' perception of

---

[241] Cf. *The Terminator* (USA and UK 1984, directed by James Cameron); *Terminator 2: Judgement Day* (USA and France 1991, directed by James Cameron); *Terminator 3: Rise of the Machines* (USA, UK and Germany 2003, directed by Jonathan Mostow); *Terminator Salvation* (USA, UK, Germany and Italy 2009, directed by McG).
[242] Cf. *Matrix* (USA and Australia 1999, directed by Andy and Lana Wachowski); *Matrix Reloaded* (USA and Australia 2003, directed by Andy and Lana Wachowski); *Matrix Revolutions* (USA and Australia 2003, directed by Andy and Lana Wachowski).
[243] Cf. *I, Robot* (USA and Germany 2004, directed by Alex Proyas).

the alien Other: Andromeda is more and more seen as human-like. Fleming teaches her senses and instincts by inflicting pain and pleasure (cf. *AFA*, pp. 127f.). The scientists also change her name to "André" (cf. AFA, pp. 144ff.), leaving the alien "Andromeda" behind and symbolically cutting her connection to the extraterrestrials. The most crucial step in her metamorphosis into a human being is that André stops setting herself off from the others and wants to liberate herself from the computer: "When I saw the computer all smashed I was so glad. [...] I felt free" (*AFA*, p. 164). In this situation, Fleming hints at Andromeda in Greek mythology, who was chained to a rock in order to be sacrificed, and who was then freed by Perseus. However, André is still Other, and the fact that she is repeatedly referred to as "goddess" illustrates that she somehow transcends mortal flesh (cf. *AFA*, p. 145; *AB*, p. 22). Perhaps the most significant proof of André's humanness – and the last step in her development from the Other into the Self – is Fleming's love: he eventually accepts her as a woman, protects her and shows affection. For instance, the narrator states:

> He did not move as she came close to him. Then very lightly he bent his head and kissed her, full on the mouth.
>
> As he felt her lips, warm and full against his, he sensed suddenly her full humanity. All the fear and strain of the past few months fell away from him and he was simply alone at last with the woman he wanted. (*AB*, p. 187)

Dr Fleming's desire for his creation and André's transformation seem to have found their origin in the Greek myth of Pygmalion. In Book X of *Metamorphoses* (AD 8), Ovid narrates the story of the sculptor Pygmalion who falls in love with one of his works of art, an ivory statue of a woman (called Galatea in later adaptations of the myth). Pygmalion begs Venus to animate his creation and, when he goes home to caress the statue, she eventually comes to life. The Pygmalion myth illustrates the artist's longing to ensoul a creation. Accordingly, Fleming's love completes André's change.

The ending of the *Andromeda* novels, however, might be disappointing for science-fiction fans. In fact, what could have been an alien-invasion plot develops into a soap-drama or romance. This ending bears parallels to numerous Hollywood films, and we can imagine that it is what the audience of the series would expect. With regard to the depiction of the alien Other, it is remarkable that a man should define André's womanhood; without Fleming, the artificially created girl would never be perceived as a human being.

To summarize, Andromeda undergoes a process of transformation that shapes the perception of the scientists who made her. First, she is the alien Other with an enhanced body and a close connection to a machine. Subsequently, she is perceived as some sort of hybrid or *simulacrum*[244] of a human, much like a beautiful female version of Frankenstein's monster. Finally, the love-story element obscures any non-human features and establishes André's "full humanity". André's increasing degree of humanness serves the purpose of making the love story between her and Fleming plausible and even desirable. In particular in the beginning, she might be perceived as an intruder, but is never characterized as an invader and, due to her beauty, the reader or audience expects one of the male characters to fall in love with her. Naturally, this element is more trivial than the complicated relationship of Self and Other in Gwyneth Jones' *Aleutians* trilogy, where humans seem to dread the blurring of boundaries between themselves and the aliens and where hybrid creatures become victims of discrimination and violence (cf. chapter 3.3).

---

[244] In his treatise *Simulacra and Simulation* (1981), the French philosopher Jean Baudrillard elaborates on symbols, signs and their reference to reality. Baudrillard claims that there is no such thing as reality since what we perceive as reality consists of references without referents (a hyperreality). Cf. Jean Baudrillard, *Simulacra and Simulation (Body: In Theory, Histories)*, translated by Sheila Glaser (Ann Arbour, MI: University of Michigan Press, 1994). In science fiction, the works of the American author Philip K. Dick treat *simulacra*. For instance, *Do Androids Dream of Electric Sheep?* (1968), which later became the film *Blade Runner* (1982), features artificial humans and animals (cf. Philip K. Dick, *Do Androids Dream of Electric Sheep?* [New York, NY: Del Rey, 1996] and *Blade Runner* [USA 1982, directed by Ridley Scott]). In the *Andromeda* novels as well as in *Frankenstein*, the artificially created beings are some sort of copy without an original: they are similar to human beings, but not the same.

Just like other works of alien-encounter science fiction, the *Andromeda* novels reflect the crucial role of science and reason as the basis of a hegemonic position in the universe. Scientific invention functions as an indicator of power and it determines the pride of a nation in its own achievements. With regard to Earth during the Cold War (when the novels where written), the omniscient narrator tells us that the world is divided between the USA and Asia, and that Britain is "something like the advanced headquarters of a besieged land", i.e. right in the middle of the opposing powers. America is seen as "a friendly but dominant occupying power to whom [Britain] was one square on a large chessboard" (*AFA*, p. 20). Thus, Britain is far from being self-determined and deprived of the prestige it enjoyed as an Empire.[245] Furthermore, unidentified missiles from the East pass over the UK – a threat that military officials interpret as "a new form of sabre-rattling" (*AFA*, p. 120). In order to avert the danger of the unknown missiles, the military makes use of André and the supercomputer, i.e. they develop highly advanced interception missiles, test them successfully and destroy the rockets from the East (cf. *AFA*, pp. 124-131).

This scientific achievement has various implications: it illustrates the superiority of alien intelligence as the 'wonderful' development of interception missiles would not have been possible without the girl and the computer, the military advantage uplifts Britain from its inferior position (the innovation is unique and more effective than American systems) and it generates national pride. It also demonstrates that fear and mistrusts of the alien Other are overcome as soon as its potential can be exploited for Britain's own purposes. In a speech on TV, the Prime Minister boasts:

> 'Not since the halcyon days of Queen Victoria [...] has this country held such a clear lead in the fields of in-

[245] Even though Britain under Winston Churchill was one of the victorious nations of World War II, it lost most of its overseas colonies in the aftermath, and the US superseded it as the world's foremost power. Throughout the Cold War, the foreign policy of the US was not only anti-communist but also anti-colonial. For example, after Dwight Eisenhower had forced Britain and France to end their military occupation of the Suez Canal Zone, they withdrew troops in 1957. Hence, the US contributed to the end of the age of colonialism.

> dustry, technology and – above all – security as that which we now have within our grasp.... (*AFA*, p. 142)

In fact, this bears parallels to the speech of the Prime Minister in Wyndham's *The Kraken Wakes* (cf. chapter 3.1); both politicians express national pride as well as notions of superiority and victory, and both announcements clearly have an imperial overtone. What is more, the officials understand that the supercomputer is of enormous economic value as further innovations could be sold. Michael Osborne, the Permanent Under-Secretary of State, explains: "It [the computer] means more to us, potentially, than the steam engine, or atomic power, or anything" (*AFA*, p. 154). Again, this shows that a hegemonic position in the world is reached through scientific achievements. Yet, supremacy is short-lived: after André has destroyed the computer, Britain is "relegated to a second-rate power; third-rate in fact" (*AB*, p. 15).

Another organization that understands the considerable value of the supercomputer is the multinational cartel, Intel. Basically, Intel is involved in "holding companies, secret understandings, private agreements, patent monopolies, [and it runs] offices in small and tolerant countries" (*AB*, p. 30). In addition, the cartel ruthlessly accumulates wealth – comparable to imperial nations in history – and it does not shy away from espionage and bribery (cf. *AB*, p. 59), abduction (cf. *AB*, pp. 70ff.) and murder (cf. *AB*, pp. 64, 71). Intel also manages to acquire copies of the supercomputer blueprint. To its own advantage, it has a second machine built in Azaran, a fictive country in the Middle East or Northern Africa (cf. *AB*, p. 59). Nevertheless, in the course of *Andromeda Breakthrough*, it becomes obvious that Intel only serves as an agent for the extraterrestrials from the Andromeda Galaxy: after the aliens' failure to gain power through the scientists (Fleming convinces André to destroy the computer), they secretly attempt to rule the world through an influential cartel,[246] a concept that might recall indirect rule in colonial history. Intel becomes increasingly powerful: it possesses a high-tech computer as well as the financial and

[246] The extraterrestrials' swift action after the destruction of the computer is an absurdity, of course, since the news would only reach the Andromeda Galaxy after 2.5 million years.

scientific prerequisites to make profitable inventions such as an enzyme that miraculously heals wounds (cf. *AFA*, p. 142).

Additionally, Intel takes advantage of the political instability in Azaran to further its projects. The cartel holds influence over Colonel Salim, Azaran's greedy and ruthless ambassador. Salim plans a *coup d'état* in order to become president of the country and break off ties with the Western nations (cf. *AB*, pp. 49ff.). Thus, his troops close all frontiers, take control of Azaran's capital and support Intel in establishing headquarters in the country (cf. *AB*, p. 103). The situation Salim envisages is comparable to company rule in the former colonies: a trading organization executes political power in order to gain profit (of which Salim expects to have his share). We can imagine that the setting of *Andromeda Breakthrough* is not arbitrary since the novel was written at a time of political revolutions in Northern Africa and the Middle East. For instance, Morocco and Tunisia regained independence from France and Spain respectively in 1956, and Algeria followed in 1962 after eight years of war.

In the *Andromeda* novels, Intel's rise to authority is part of the extraterrestrials' plan. They brainwash one of the cartel's directors, Janine Gamboul, and control her through the computer (cf. *AB*, pp. 110f.). Actually, brainwashing of terrestrial subjects is a popular trope in works that depict alien invasions. One of the most remarkable examples in literature is perhaps the *Tripods* trilogy, in which the alien Masters implant a "Cap" into the skull of every human adolescent and thereby turn him or her into a slave (cf. chapter 1.2). In film, brainwashed or extraneously determined human beings are portrayed in *Quatermass II*[247] (1957) and *Puppet Masters*[248] (1995). To come back to Hoyle's and Elliot's novel, the extraterrestrials from Andromeda intend to make use of Janine Gamboul's influential position to take over the world. Neverthe-

---

[247] *Quatermass 2* (US title: *Enemy from Space*, UK 1957, directed by Val Guest).

[248] *Puppet Masters* (USA 1995, directed by Stuart Orme). The film is an adaptation of Robert A. Heinlein's famous science-fiction novel *The Puppet Masters* (1951), in which parasites from outer space control human behaviour. Interestingly, the alien parasites bear striking parallels to the Russian Communists, which implies that Heinlein's novel reflects the Red Scare in the USA. Cf. Robert A. Heinlein, *The Puppet Masters* (New York, NY: Del Rey, Reissue 1986).

less, it seems that they fail a second time: Gamboul, who eventually becomes insane due to her obsession with power, is killed in a hurricane (cf. *AB*, pp. 163f.). This lets the reader assume that the highly intelligent aliens, who 'calculate' all events on Earth before they actually occur, are incapable of predicting a crucial variable, human behaviour – a theory that is to be falsified in the very end of the narrative.

As mentioned before, alien influence is rejected by several individuals. The key figure of resistance is John Fleming: he repeatedly revolts against the influence of the extraterrestrials on man, not knowing that their intentions are actually benevolent and that his rather crude actions were foreseen by the aliens and included in their plan. For instance, he sabotages the computer (cf. *AFA*, pp. 135f., 157), he tries to convince his colleagues to kill Cyclops (cf. *AFA*, p. 94) as well as the artificially created embryo (cf. *AFA*, pp. 110f.), and he persuades André to destroy the lab with the computer (cf. *AFA*, pp. 165ff.). The aliens punish his actions through the machine: the computer makes the scientists create life-threatening enzymes (cf. *AFA*, p. 146) and bacteria that almost wipe out the entire human species as they produce gales, hurricanes and a decline in oxygen (cf. *AB*, p. 135). The global weather change is similar to the one portrayed in *The Kraken Wakes*, where aliens apparently adjust Earth to their biological requirements and try to kill human beings (cf. chapter 3.1).

In the *Andromeda* novels, scientists play an ambiguous role since they create enzymes and bacteria that are not only fatal for humans but could end all life on Earth. Thus, they are subjected to and agents of the extraterrestrials at the same time. The President of Azaran calls Dawnay and her colleagues murderers:

> Hundreds of thousands of people have died because […] of these experiments of yours. […] The errors of politicians are sometimes expensive, and business men sometimes do their best to profit from them. But you scientists, you kill half the world. And the other half cannot live without you. (*AB*, p. 168)

This evokes feelings of "enormous guilt" (*ibid.*) in Dawnay, who actually wanted to work in Azaran for the benefit of the people (cf. *AB*, p. 48). What becomes obvious is that the scientist were unable to estimate the risks of their experiments; they appear to be naïve and 'backwards' compared to the aliens which initiated carrying out research. Eventually, the scientists have become servants of the extraterrestrials and vicariously punish disobedience. Therefore, rather than treating guilt in a postcolonial context, the novels emphasize the scientists' responsibility for the implications of their experiments and guilt for the harm they inflict on people and on the environment. As the scientists are agents of destruction instead of victims or helpless witnesses of what an alien oppressor does on Earth, the *Andromeda* novels differ from other narratives in a way that they highlight man's terrible complicity.

The ending of *Andromeda Breakthrough* appears paradoxical at first sight. On the one hand, the extraterrestrials actually succeed in interrupting the cyclical recurrence of history on Earth. When André and the scientists develop anti-bacteria, all nations cooperate in saving the planet and, unlike in John Christopher's *The Pool of Fire* (cf. chapter 1.2), Cold War paranoia and resentments seem to be overcome (cf. *AB*, p. 176). On the other hand, though, it appears that indirect rule fails since the aliens have no control over one crucial factor: human behaviour. The extraterrestrials lose the computer and the girl as their tools, and people break all ties with them, i.e. alien influence – albeit benevolent – is entirely rejected. However, André eventually reveals to Fleming that all events have been exactly foreseen by her 'masters'. Even the threat to human life had a purpose: the extraterrestrials wanted mankind itself to decide on its fate (cf. *AB*, p. 188), a final twist that appears rather implausible and inappropriate to the reader or viewer. We can imagine that many would have preferred human behaviour to be depicted as unforeseeable and as a decisive factor in the victory over the aliens.

To conclude, the *Andromeda* novels differ from other works of alien-encounter science fiction due to the fact that the fear of an invasion from outer space is kindled, but the invasion never actually happens. The highly advanced and benevolent aliens end the cyclical recurrence of history on Earth by influencing man from their planet in the Andromeda Galaxy. Human resistance plays a minor role. Alien interference is sabotaged by Dr Fleming, but even his behaviour is predicted and part of the aliens' mission, which is a rather disappointing twist in the story. Alien influence determines Britain's reputation in the world. Scientific achievements made with the help of the extraterrestrials uplift the country by restoring a hegemonic position and national pride. In Azaran, this process is interrupted by natural disasters – a punishment inflicted on man by human scientists themselves. Another theme of the novels is the depiction of the alien Other. Apart from the extraterrestrials, their tools or agents on Earth, i.e. the supercomputer, the artificially created monster and André, are considered Other. However, André undergoes a transformation: she develops from the Other into the Self and is ultimately seen as a human woman. The reader receives the impression that the love-story element is more important to the producers of the series or the authors respectively than the development of an invasion plot. Eventually, the aliens succeed in reuniting the human race – the ending we would expect from a TV series produced for a mass audience.

3. Close Encounters of the Third Kind: Different Invasions

3.1 Deep-Sea Aliens: John Wyndham, *The Kraken Wakes*

John Wyndham (John Wyndham Parkes Lucas Benyon Harris, 1903-1969) is considered one of the most widely read science-fiction authors of the United Kingdom. He was born in Knowle, Warwickshire on July 10, 1903, as the son of the barrister George Benyon Harris and of Gertrude Parkes, the daughter of an ironmaster from Birmingham. Wyndham made various unsuccessful attempts to earn a livelihood in farming, law, advertising and commercial art. In the 1930s, he sold science-fiction stories to periodicals such as *Amazing Stories* and *Wonder Stories*. During World War II, Wyndham joined the English civil service and later the British Army. After the war, he resumed his work as an author and published under various pseudonyms.[249] His major successes are, among others, *The Day of the Triffids* (1951), *The Kraken Wakes* (1953), *The Chrysalids* (1955), *The Midwich Cuckoos* (1957) and *Trouble with Lichen* (1960). He also wrote short stories, and his novel *The Web* was published posthumously in 1979. Film adaptations of his works are *Village of the Damned* (1960), *The Day of the Triffids* (1963), *Children of the Damned* (1963) and *Quest for Love* (1971).[250] *The Day of the Triffids* (1981) and *Choky* (1984-1986) have also been serialized by the BBC.[251] John Wyndham died on March 11, 1969, in London.

The Kraken Wakes (published under the title *Out of the Deeps* in the USA) is narrated by the journalist Mike Watson and subdi-

[249] Cf. Sam Moskowitz, *Seekers of Tomorrow: Masters of Modern Science Fiction* (Westport, CT: Hyperion Press, ²1974), pp. 118ff.
[250] Cf. Andy Sawyer, "'A Stiff Upper Lip and a Trembling Lower One': John Wyndham on Screen," in: I.Q. Hunter (ed.), *British Science Fiction Cinema*, 75.
[251] Cf. *ibid.* 87n1.

vided into a kind of foreword (the "rationale") and three "phases". Phase One starts off with the narrator and his wife witnessing the descent of fireballs into the sea. At first, they do not realize that this event is the beginning of an alien invasion. The aliens, called "xenobaths"[252] or "bathies"[253] in the course of the novel, establish themselves in the deep seas and, when observed or attacked, sink expedition boats, commercial ships and cruisers. The geographer Dr Alastair Bocker expects a global crisis, but nobody believes in his theories. Instead, the general public blames Cold War rivalries – or more precisely the Russians – for the strange incidents. In Phase Two, the imminent threat to mankind becomes obvious as so-called "sea-tanks" raid coastal towns and 'harvest' human beings, leaving only a putrid layer of organic jelly behind. Mike and his wife and co-worker, Phyllis, report about the events for the English Broadcasting Corporation (EBC), and the reader becomes gradually aware of the secrecy as well as manipulative potential of the media. The world as we know it does no longer exist in Phase Three of the novel. The aliens have changed the climate and caused the melting of the ice-caps. When large parts of England are flooded, the public order collapses. For some months, Mike and Phyllis carry on working for the EBC in London. Yet, as the sea-levels continue to rise, they set up residence in a cottage on a hill in Cornwall and live a self-sufficient life. Meanwhile, the global population has decreased to one-fifth or less of its original number. Scientists finally develop an ultrasonic weapon that destroys the aliens. However, neither the xenobaths' outward appearance nor their intentions are revealed. The novel ends with the authorities regaining control over the situation, and the couple decides to resume their profession in London.

The homodiegetic narrator, Mike Watson, is a journalist. On the one hand, the reader's knowledge about the strange incidents does not exceed Mike's. Mike's account is, generally speaking, a sequence of the events he experiences, interspersed with dialogues (especially with his wife Phyllis) and with reports of the media. It

---

[252] The name derives from the Greek prefix 'xeno', which signifies 'strange' or 'alien', and 'bathos', i.e. 'depth'. Cf. *OED Online*, s.v. 'xeno-' and 'bathos'.
[253] John Wyndham, *The Kraken Wakes* (London *et al.*: Penguin Books, 2008), p. 24. All subsequent references to this edition are in brackets in the text.

becomes obvious that Mike and Phyllis purport to gain as much information as possible, and they manage to receive details in rather unofficial ways. For instance, they have dinner with men from the military and are proficient in witty talk with journalist colleagues (cf. *KW*, pp. 17f., 23ff.). The dialogues frequently emphasize the couple's claim to the truth. Naturally, Mike and Phyllis have to respect censorship as the military's secrecy suppresses the publication of certain incidents (cf. *KW*, pp. 23f.). On the other hand, though, Mike frequently comments on the situation in a critical way. It becomes evident that his truth claims lead to a critical scrutiny of the public, of the English authorities, of the USA and of the Russians. He also illustrates that the media are largely influenced by the military and the government, and that the editorial opinion does not depend on the contents of the news but on the capacity for making profit; what matters is how many newspapers can be sold. It is striking that Mike begins his report with a "rationale" (cf. *KW*, pp. 7-9). When he and his wife watch icebergs from a hill in Cornwall in the fifth year of the invasion, Mike decides to write the report (that we read as the novel) since he feels that "it ought to be done" (*KW*, p. 7). This implies that the publication or sharing of knowledge is a major issue for the journalist, and Wyndham thereby creates his narrator's credibility.

In the beginning of the story, it does not immediately become evident that mankind is attacked by an alien organism. Much like in Wyndham's *The Day of the Triffids*, the catastrophe in *The Kraken Wakes* starts with fireballs falling from the sky into the sea. Mike remembers that he and his wife observed the strange phenomenon from aboard a cruiser ship during their honeymoon. Of course, the passengers recall stories of flying saucers (cf. *KW*, p. 13), because the flying-saucer mania flourished in the in 1950s. Mike obviously tries to be more objective about the unusual occurrences than the other passengers:

> Others besides ourselves were leaning over the rail, and in fairness I should perhaps mention that between them they appear to have seen cigar-shapes, cylinders, discs, ovoids, and, inevitably, saucers. We did not.

> What is more, we did not see eight, nine, or a dozen.
> We saw five. (*KW*, pp. 12f.)

This might be due to the fact that the events are narrated in retrospective, and that Mike, as a journalist, purports to give a factual account. As *The Kraken Wakes* is a science-fiction novel, the reader might accept *topoi* such as flying saucers and alien invasions. However, the narrator does not seem to believe in sensationalist or occult ideas and gives objectifiable details. As a consequence, he is reluctant to offer an explanation for the fireballs, which creates suspense and verisimilitude.

Having been eyewitnesses of the events, the couple becomes interested in turning them into a news story and decides to do some research. That is why they collect evidence of the red fireballs. For instance, Mike meets a Flight-Lieutenant of the Royal Air Force. The pilot says that he observed – and subsequently shot – some of the "miniature suns" during a flight operation (cf. *KW*, pp. 18f.). The lieutenant reported the incident, but the authorities consider it a hallucination. In addition, the lieutenant asks Mike not to publish his name since the hallucination might still be transformed into an "official secret" (*KW*, p. 17), i.e. a threat that is real. A military pilot that speaks of official secrets builds up suspense as this would imply that the red fireballs are more dangerous than people believe at this stage of the narration. Nevertheless, the reader is still uncertain. He or she hovers between considering the incidents a real danger and reducing them to another "Loch Ness monster" (*KW*, p. 18). This is also due to the reaction of the authorities; even for them it is not clear whether the fireballs are real or not. Maybe this is why they officially claim that the pilot suffers from hallucinations, even though he reports that he managed to shoot some of the red lights. With regard to an explanation of the phenomena, it is not surprising that the public as well as the heads of the government immediately draw a connection to the Cold War, and a rhetorical cut and thrust between the West and the East emerges. However, neither the Soviets nor the West try to investigate into the real nature of the fireballs; both sides seem to accept them as a menace and simply blow up as many as they can.

Undoubtedly, one of the predominant features of Wyndham's novel is uncertainty. People on Earth carry out research, but their results are scare. For instance, naval scientists geographically pinpoint the fireball descents: they ascertain that the incidents concentrate in deep-water areas (cf. *KW*, p. 24) and, according to some of them, this might even prove that the fireballs are somehow connected to an intelligent organism. In order to gain further information, the Admiralty makes an expedition to the Cayman Trench. An instrument called "bathyscope", i.e. a small chamber in which scientists can descend into deep water, is lowered into the sea. The scientists see "[s]omething big" (*KW*, p. 32) circling the chamber. We receive some information on its "monstrous" (*ibid.*) size, and the connection cuts off. For further investigation, an automatic submarine equipped with cameras, the "telebath", is lowered into the trench (cf. *KW*, pp. 33f.). What the scientists and the journalist detect on the screens is the following:

> A large, uncertain, oval shape at the extreme of visibility that moved from screen to screen as it circled round the descending instrument. For three or four minutes it continued to show on one screen or another, but always tantalizingly ill-defined, and never quite well enough illuminated for one to be quite certain even of its shape. Then, gradually, it drifted towards the upper edges of the screens, and presently it was left behind. (*KW*, p. 34)

Accordingly, the shape can neither be defined nor classified. It might be an animal, an undiscovered life form, a 'sea monster' of some sort, *et cetera*.

This scene is the moment of first contact between the Self and the Other, a moment that is shaped by an atmosphere of danger and precariousness. The scientists learn that something sabotaged their bathyscope (the cables are melted together, cf. *KW*, pp. 32f.) and killed the passengers. Thus, the scientists as well as the reader now understand that there is an – apparently hostile – organism or intelligence in the deep sea. At this point of the narrative, the idea of a second enemy materializes, i.e. both sensationalism and the Cold

War paranoia are replaced by marine monsters as agents of destruction. Allowedly, the image on the screens is exceedingly unclear, but it becomes obvious that mankind faces an enemy with a material existence.

Marine monstrosity is a popular topic in classical adventure stories. For example, the mere size of the white whale and of the squid in Herman Melville's *Moby Dick; or, The Whale*[254] (1851) renders the creatures monstrous. Furthermore, the krakens in Jules Verne's *Twenty Thousand Leagues under the Sea* (*Vingt milles lieues sous les mers*, 1869) are not only depicted as big and hideous, but they are clearly evil since they attack a submarine.[255] In science fiction, the octopoid Martians in H. G. Wells' *The War of the Worlds* (1898) and their 'descendents', the Tripods, bear characteristics of marine monsters. In *The Time Machine* (1895), the anonymous Time Traveller encounters shapeless marine invertebrates hopping about at a beach under the dying sun, and he grasps a glimpse of the end of life on Earth.[256] Another author whose works deal with deep-sea monstrosity is Howard Phillips Lovecraft (1890-1937). The Cthulhu Mythos, which contains approximately a dozen stories, portrays a race of supernatural beings (the "Old Ones") that lives in the lost city of R'lyeh somewhere in the Pacific Ocean. The statue of the priest, Cthulhu, is described as

> of vaguely anthropoid outline, but with an octopus-like head whose face [is] a mass of feelers, a scaly, rubbery-looking body, prodigious claws on hind and fore feet, and long, narrow wings behind.[257]

A more recent example is the film *Monsters* (2010), which features enormous octopoid extraterrestrials that have invaded Earth and

---

[254] Cf. Herman Melville, *Moby Dick; or, The Whale* (Ware: Wordsworth Classics, 1993).

[255] Cf. Jules Verne, *Twenty Thousand Leagues under the Sea*. Translated and with a Foreword by Mendor T. Brunetti (New York, NY: Signet Classic, 1969), pp. 385ff.

[256] Cf. Herbert G. Wells, *The Time Machine*, pp. 75f.

[257] Howard Phillips Lovecraft, *The Call of Cthulhu and Other Weird Stories* (London *et al.*: Penguin Books, 1999), p. 148.

inhabit an 'infected' zone in Mexico.[258] Some depictions of marine monstrosity are drawn from mythical creatures such as Leviathan and Scylla,[259] others make use of the grotesque features of marine organisms. In *Beowulf* (AD 700-1000), Grendel's mother is a sea monster.[260] Marine monsters also found their way into cartography. For instance, the "Carta Marina" (1539) by the Swedish bishop Olaus Magnus is illustrated with numerous sea-monsters.

With regard to marine monstrosity, *The Kraken Wakes* is preceded by a poem which determines the novel's title: "The Kraken" (1830) by Alfred Lord Tennyson (1808-1892).[261] With regard to the xenobaths, "The Kraken" shapes the image the reader constructs of the enemy of man: as the homodiegetic narrator does not provide sufficient information on the nature of the marine organisms in the novel, the reader might draw parallels to octopi or squids. Tennyson's poem centres upon a kraken that sleeps at the

---

[258] Cf. *Monsters* (UK 2010, directed by Gareth Edwards).

[259] Leviathan is a monster in Judeo-Christian mythology that combines features of a dragon, a crocodile, a snake and a whale. Scylla (in Greek mythology) was a beautiful naiad whom the jealous Amphitrite transformed into a ghastly sea-monster with tentacle-like legs and dog heads around her waist. In Homer's *Odyssey*, Scylla eats six sailors alive.

[260] Beowulf wounds his antagonist, Grendel, in a fight. He then defeats Grendel's vindictive mother in her murky lake.

[261] The poem reads:

> Below the thunders of the upper deep;
> Far, far beneath in the abysmal sea,
> His ancient, dreamless, uninvaded sleep
> The Kraken sleepeth: faintest sunlights flee
> About his shadowy sides: above him swell
> Huge sponges of millennial growth and height;
> And far away into the sickly light,
> From many a wondrous grot and secret cell
> Unnumbered and enormous polypi
> Winnow with giant arms the slumbering green.
> There hath he lain for ages and will lie
> Battening upon huge sea-worms in his sleep,
> Until the latter fire shall heat the deep;
> Then once by man and angels to be seen,
> In roaring he shall rise and on the surface die.

Alfred Lord Tennyson, "The Kraken" (1830), in: Armin Geraths and Kurt Herget (eds.), *Viktorianische Lyrik: Englisch – Deutsch* (Stuttgart: Reclam, 1985), pp. 136-137.

bottom of the sea. The sea is an alien landscape of "many a wondrous grot and secret cell", faintly illuminated by "sickly light". It is inhabited by "huge sponges", "enormous polypi […] with giant arms" and "huge sea-worms". The landscape and the massive organisms add to the atmosphere of mystery and danger on the one hand, and to the notion of grandeur on the other. Eventually, "the latter fire shall heat the deep", so that the kraken "shall rise and on the surface die". The rise of the kraken constitutes its transgression of the natural and ideological border, as well as its death: the monstrous must not exist in the world of normality outside the deep sea. What is more, Phyllis' account of a dream appears closely modelled on the poem: "Sometimes I dream of them lying down in those deep dark valleys, and sometimes they look like monstrous squids or huge slugs, other times as if they were great clouds of luminous cells hanging there in rocky chasms" (*KW*, p. 229). Thus, the image of the enemy is stamped by non-factual allusions such as poems and dream scenes.

The xenobaths as sea-monsters embody two functions: they are agents of fear and destruction as well as colonial intruders. Generally speaking, 'monstrous' is defined as "deviating from the natural or conventional order".[262] In Wyndham's novel, the people are perfectly ignorant about the nature of the xenobaths. The impossibility to classify and catalogue the aliens poses a threat to the stable world order as well as to its claim to absoluteness, which consequently evokes fear. As to their function for society, monsters constitute a projection screen for individually or collectively suppressed instincts and potentials; they are a manifestation of what has no place in society, what cannot be described within the norm, and what is therefore ostracized.[263] As to suppression, the invasion by monsters in Wyndham's novel shows what happens when the Cold War turns into a war of aggression; it seems that the author demonstrates an alternative future scenario. Moreover, the xenobaths develop into an ideological enemy as they do not correspond to the culturally shaped normality, which dictates what must and

[262] *OED Online*, s.v. 'monstrous'.

[263] Cf. Eckhard Pabst, "Das Monster als genrekonstituierende Größe im Horrorfilm," in: *Enzykopädie des Phantastischen Films. Vol. 3*, ed. by Norbert Stresau and Heinrich Wimmer (Meitingen: Corian, 1986-1998), p. 2.

what must not exist. Since these aliens live in the deep sea, the water surface serves as a natural border between the normal and the monstrous. However, this border becomes unstable: it is transgressed by man (sea-travel, exploration and bomb launches) and by the xenobaths (raids of coastal towns). What follows is that the author establishes an imperial scenario. The transgression of a border leads to war and maybe even extinction of one species. This is what finally constitutes the aliens' status of an enemy.

In addition, it becomes more and more obvious that the aliens are colonizers of Earth, and those who already believe in this idea at that point of the narrative theorize on how to deal with a new – and apparently intelligent – species at the bottom of the sea. The oceanographer Alastair Bocker, for example, claims that it is necessary to establish communication with the new life form. As they require an entirely different environment (the deep sea), he sees the possibility of a "compromise", i.e. co-existence on Earth (cf. *KW*, p. 107). Both humans and aliens could "live peacefully in their separate spheres" (*ibid.*). Wyndham never mentions the origin of the xenobaths in his novel. Yet, we know that they inhabit deep-water areas with a high pressure and might therefore speculate that the aliens are from Jupiter. Under its cloudy surface, the main bulk of Jupiter consists of liquid metallic hydrogen – which requires a pressure of more than four million bars and a low temperature.[264] The xenobaths might also have come from another galaxy or another solar system in our galaxy. However, these options are rather unlikely since the distance to Earth would be too great. Eventually, Bocker's idea of co-existence does not receive any support. It seems that human beings are more willing to kill the new species than to communicate with it. Naturally, this is due to the fact that the xenobaths are dangerous; they sink ships, raid towns and kill people, as we find out in the course of the novel.

Just like invaders in colonial history, the xenobaths must have certain forms of technology. For instance, they can melt metals (cf. *KW*, p. 33), and they possess weapons of some sort to sink ships. One of these weapons sets up intense vibrations, the other one cuts the bottoms of ships open. Thus, the aliens have established colo-

[264] http://nineplanets.org/jupiter.html (2012-06-17).

nies in the deep sea and defend their territories. About half a dozen vessels sink, among them a Russian ship, a US cruiser and a destroyer (cf. *KW*, p. 42). The scientists do not understand the alien devices (cf. *KW*, p. 104), which recalls the idea of savages being unable to understand firearms or nautical instruments, and it implies that the aliens might be superior to man. In a colonial context, technology has various implications: it establishes a means of dominating the environment and society, serves as a tool for exploitation and enrichment, and it has the potential of fuelling both innovation and social conflict.[265] These aspects illustrate that the aliens can become highly dangerous for mankind if their level of technology is advanced enough to take over the planet.

Given the idea that there are two intelligent life forms on Earth, a natural struggle for domination will emerge. Bocker makes clear that

> [t]he most powerful of all weapons is intelligence; any intelligent form dominates by, and therefore survives by, its intelligence: a rival form of intelligence must, by its very existence, threaten to dominate, and therefore threaten extinction. Any intelligent form is its own absolute; and there cannot be two absolutes. (*KW*, p. 180)

The thesis that "there cannot be two absolutes" implies that either the xenobaths or man will eventually survive. This is due to the fact that the two different species need entirely different ecological requirements. Just like the Masters in John Christopher's *Tripods* trilogy (cf. chapter 1.2), the xenobaths eventually alter the planet according to their needs, which would be the end of the human race. Bocker's ideas are heavily influenced by Charles Darwin's evolutionary theory. In *The Descent of Man*, Darwin states:

> Extinction follows chiefly from the competition of tribe with tribe, and race with race. [...] [W]hen of two adjoining tribes one becomes less numerous and less

[265] Cf. Istvan Csicsery-Ronay, "Science Fiction and Empire," 233.

> powerful than the other, the contest is soon settled by war, slaughter, cannibalism, slavery, and absorption. Even when a weaker tribe is not thus abruptly swept away, if it once begins to decrease, it generally goes on decreasing until it becomes extinct.[266]

Darwin continues with the thesis that the more civilized race, i.e. the mentally and technologically superior one, finally defeats the more savage race.[267] In *The Kraken Wakes*, the military strikes back with nuclear weapons: under the pretence of testing new weapon systems, the Americans drop deep-water atomic bombs near the Marianas, where the destroyer went down (cf. *KW*, p. 43), and further launches follow. However, some bombs do not go off and others cause an ecological disaster (cf. *KW*, pp. 52ff.). Therefore, it is questionable which species will be superior, the humans or the xenobaths. Yet, due to the lack of information about the aliens, the reader cannot come to a conclusion at this point.

Bocker eventually introduces the concept of empire. He seems to be more farsighted than the general public and the media since he claims that the intentions of the xenobaths are the ones of colonists, i.e. they establish an empire in the deep sea. Explaining the aliens' *modus operandi*, Bocker retraces the steps of colonization in history. These steps are settlement, exploitation of the territory, defence against intruders and communication infrastructure. Bocker claims that,

> [...] having settled into the environment best suited to them, these creatures' next thought would be to develop that environment in accordance with their ideas of what constitutes a convenient, orderly, and, eventually, civilized condition. They are, you see, in the position of – well, no, they are *actually* pioneers, colonists. Once they have safely arrived they set about improving and exploiting their new territory. (*KW*, p. 63, italics by J. Wyndham)

---

[266] Charles Darwin, *The Descent of Man, and Selection in Relation to Sex*, pp. 211f.

[267] Cf. *ibid*., p. 212.

It is striking that the scientist, after a short moment of hesitation, calls the aliens "pioneers" and "colonists" that intend to live on Earth in "civilized" conditions. This appears much like the description of European settlers in America, Canada, Australia, *et cetera*. For example in *The Romance of Empire* (1924), Philip Gibbs (1877-1962) praises the pioneers' courage and endurance, and he tells us how they established settlement: "The adventurers quickly got to work. They cleared the ground and, as a protection against the savages, built a rough kind of fort with palisades in the form of a triangle, guarded by guns at each corner."[268] To come back to Bocker's theory, the adjective "civilized" initially appears inapt when thinking about an alien settlement at the bottom of the ocean. However, Bocker speaks about developing an "environment in accordance with their ideas of what constitutes a […] civilized condition." Here, he admits to the fact that the xenobaths live and think very differently from human beings. In fact, the oceanographer seems to be objective since he does not judge them. In this respect, Bocker differs from, for example, the Victorian scientists that would see the colonial Other through English eyes and frequently spoke of indigenous peoples in derogative terms. His objective depiction of the aliens renders Bocker more reliable than the public thinks he is. Nevertheless, the people still consider him a "Cassandra" (*KW*, p. 107), i.e. a prophet of bad tidings that nobody believes.

What is more, the oceanographer claims that the aliens carry out mining operations in the ocean. This is due to the idea that they require metals for defence mechanisms (cf. *KW*, p. 64). He also explains that the xenobaths might have developed technology for working metals in the conditions of the deep sea, i.e. the immense pressure, the cold and the darkness (cf. *ibid.*). In fact, this kind of technology would render the aliens much more intelligent than the people think they are. In the course of the novel, we learn that the xenobaths actually build "sea-tanks" with which they attack coastal towns (cf. *KW*, pp. 137, 169, 176ff.). As to communication, Bocker makes clear that the aliens might build a tunnel from the Caribbean to the west of Guatemala, connecting the Pacific and the Atlantic

---

[268] Philip Gibbs, *The Romance of Empire* (London: Hutchinson, 1924), p. 54.

Ocean like the Panama Canal (cf. *KW*, pp. 65f.). Hence, in the 'hands' of the aliens, science as a saviour turns into science as a tool for the extinction of the human race.

In contrast to other works about alien invasions, there is no reversal of the colonial gaze (cf. Introduction) in *The Kraken Wakes*, i.e. the Western world, which used to study its subject peoples, does not become the object of study for the aliens, as we assume (allegedly, though, nobody knows about their actual intentions). Instead, Dr Bocker theorizes about the intruders. It is evident that Bocker anthropomorphizes the xenobaths and characterizes them as 'civilized': the oceanographer thinks they behave just like colonists, they can work metals, and their intelligence and technological faculties are considerable. Incidentally, in the mid-nineteenth century, marine organisms in rock pools and aquariums were sometimes anthropomorphized. Authors of aquarium manuals depicted sea creatures as primitive beings living in pool colonies, and the language of the manuals clearly had a colonial and paternalistic overtone. For example, John Harper states: "Most animals, especially simple ones such as those of which I write, have a sweet will of their own, and will not be forced, even in the slightest degrees to do what their masters wish."[269] This illustrates that marine organisms might bear parallels to exotic tribes that cannot only be observed but also ruled to a certain extent. However, Wyndham reverses this idea: in *The Kraken Wakes*, human beings are actually the ones who appear primitive when compared to the xenobaths. To put it in a nutshell, according to the theories of Alastair Bocker, the aliens are depicted as extraterrestrial pioneers that open up new territories. This implies that they are characterized by courage, a sense of adventure and intelligence. Moreover, human beings correspond to an indigenous people that faces intrusion into its realm.

In Phase Two of the novel, the public is mainly manipulated by the media and by the government. First of all, the official explanation for the loss of the ships is "metal fatigue" (*KW*, p. 88), i.e. a

---

[269] John Harper, *The Sea-Side and Aquarium or Anecdote and Gossip on Marine Zoology* (Edinburgh: William P. Nimmo, 1858), p. 111. For more examples of colonial language in rock-pool manuals, see Rebecca Stott, "Through a Glass Darkly: Aquarium Colonies and Nineteenth-Century Narratives of Marine Monstrosity," in: *Gothic Studies* 2/3 (2000), 305-327.

reason that can be scientifically proved and thus appears credible to the public. However, when the English cruiser, Queen Anne, sinks (cf. *KW*, p. 89), the journalists are forced to present another explanation since few would believe that the famous and new ship was manufactured with brittle material. As a consequence, the media manipulates the public a second time. Freddie Whittier, the EBC's Director of Talks & Features, asks Mike to convince the people of a threat from the deep sea: "Make 'em really believe there is something down there" (*KW*, p. 90). Whittier's demand for a feature story about the xenobaths builds up on the fact that the people claim the Russians sank the Queen Anne, and we can imagine that they expect a counterstrike. Yet, when they are persuaded that some organism in the water caused the incident, the Cold War paranoia will "cool off" (*KW*, p. 105), and they will 'switch' to the image of the other enemy again. In order to enquire into the opinion of the public, Mike decides to do some research in the local pubs, and he learns that the beliefs of the people diverge considerably: some still make the communists responsible for the loss of the cruiser; others now accept the danger from the deep and demand swift action (cf. *KW*, pp. 94ff.).

Deeply embedded in the ideology of the Cold War, the public and the authorities believe in science as their saviour. In fact, swift action is taken by the USA. The Americans send a flotilla of ten vessels equipped with high-explosive and atomic bombs to the Cayman Trench. Nonetheless, before they can actually drop any bombs, four of the ships explode and disappear in the water, and the remaining six flee (cf. *KW*, pp. 96f.). Again, the dropping of bombs and the media spectacle that accompanies it does not provide any results, let alone destroy the xenobaths. Instead, more ships are lost and people are killed. However, the military does not give up. The Royal Navy and their scientists, ironically called "boffins" by a young lieutenant (cf. *KW*, p. 109), develop mechanical "dolphins" that swim in front of a ship and automatically spot and destroy anything unusual at the bottom of the sea (cf. *KW*, pp. 108ff.). The dolphins are successfully tested and can be attached to any vessel that has to cross the territory of the xenobaths. This would make sea-travel safe again. In fact, despite the failures, the public still believes that science can save mankind.

What follows is a speech of the Prime Minister to the House. The speech indirectly characterizes the authorities. Just like the media, the politicians manipulate the public and blind them for the real threat. Moreover, the Prime Minister's speech bears traits of propaganda when he proudly announces:

> The Battle of the Deeps has been won. Our ships, which we had to divert, are able once more to ply upon their usual courses.
>
> But we have seen before, and we must remember, that to win a battle is not of necessity to win a war. [...] To us, here in the sunlight, these creatures of the darkness and the depths, are still, anonymously and amorphously, "those things down there."
>
> When we know more about them, their nature, their strengths, and, most importantly, their weaknesses: when, in fact, we have a full view of what we are about, then we shall be able to launch our attack upon this pestilence so that, with its utter destruction, our ships and our seamen shall be free to sail upon the high seas of the world facing only such perils as their gallant fathers faced before them. (*KW*, p. 111)

Here, the reader feels reminded of the fight against National Socialist Germany. In addition, the rhetoric of the Prime Minister is imperialistic. The fact that he talks about the Battle of the Deeps places the fight against the aliens into a tradition of colonial warfare. What comes to the reader's mind is, for instance, the Battle of Arcot (1751), the Battle of Bunker Hill (1775) or the Battle of Ladysmith (1899). The subtext of the speech is a notion of victory, pride and prestige. Even though he also makes clear that the true nature of the menace is still opaque, he seems to be confident that man will soon understand the aliens' weaknesses and be able to eradicate them. At first sight, this idea might give hope to the public, but it actually masks ignorance. We realize that the authorities are helpless in their fight against the unknown enemy. Despite the new technology, a dozen ships sink shortly after the speech (cf. *KW*, p. 112). This emphasizes the unreliability of the authorities.

The Cold War, the temporal setting of *The Kraken Wakes*, is presented as ridiculous. For instance, Mike explains with a mocking overtone:

> Since it was axiomatic that any Soviet misadventure must be attributable in some way to capitalist jackals or reactionary fascist hyenas, [the sinking of the Russian ship] assumed an importance which quite eclipsed the more serious American loss [...]. (*ibid.*)

The narrator then comments: "[I]n quite a short time, the *status quo ante bellum hypotheticum* was restored, and we were back on the familiarly comprehensible basis of international suspicion" (*KW*, p. 53, italics by J. Wyndham). Just like after the descent of the red fireballs, the people oscillate between the belief in xenobaths and Cold War paranoia.[270] Due to their ignorance, they construct two different images of an enemy and 'swap' between the two in an apparently random way. The Russians also take the role of scapegoats.

The question arises which qualities are projected on the Cold-War enemy, i.e. the Russians. At first sight, they are depicted in an exaggerated and sarcastic way. For instance, a captain of the Royal Navy claims that "[s]uspicion of capitalists [is] part of their moth-

[270] The Red Scare is also expressed – albeit in a more subtle way – in Wyndham's *The Midwich Cuckoos* (1957). In this novel, the inhabitants of a small town in England become unconscious for one day (the "Dayout") and, subsequently, all women of childbearing age are pregnant. The children, i.e. the "cuckoos" of the title, might be interpreted as allegorical Russians that infiltrate the country. This thesis is corroborated by their social and mental traits: they are uniform, emotionally cold, cruel and of cunning intelligence – stereotypical features of the "Ivans", as one of the characters in the novel calls the Russians. Moreover, their 'parents' fear an invasion from within, an idea that raises notions of the 'Communist fifth columns' mentioned by Winston Churchill in his Iron Curtain speech of 1946. However, in the second part of *The Midwich Cuckoos*, the reader learns that the infiltrations by extraterrestrials have taken place all over the world, i.e. in Russia as well. Finally, human beings kill all alien children. Cf. John Wyndham, *The Midwich Cuckoos* (London *et al.*: Penguin, 1960). For more information on the influence of the Cold War on British fiction, see Andrew Hammond, "'The Twilight of Utopia': British Dystopian Fiction and the Cold War," in: *Modern Language Review* 106 (2011): 622-681.

er's milk" (cf. *KW*, p. 25). This sounds like an *idée réçue*. In addition, Bocker says that the Russians would even cooperate with an alien intelligence if they could:

> In the middle of all this the Muscovite, who seems to be constitutionally incapable of understanding anything to do with the sea, started making trouble. The sea, he appeared to be arguing, was causing a great deal of inconvenience to the West; therefore it must be acting on good dialectically materialistic principles, and I have no doubt that if he could contact the Deeps he would like to make a pact with their inhabitants for a brief period of dialectical opportunism. (*KW*, p. 202)

Naturally, Bocker is sarcastic. Still, the quote demonstrates that the Russians might go out of their way to be somehow superior to the West. Hence, the enemy is represented as ideological and stupid.

In the course of the novel, we eventually realize that the narrator criticizes the lack of cooperation between the nations. This becomes apparent in a dialogue between the journalist couple and their friend Tuny, or Petunia. Tuny serves as a spokesperson for the public in expressing Cold War paranoia. She is sure that the threat from the deep sea "was thought up in Moscow" (*KW*, p. 84): the Russians sink ships with "midget submarines", and the West does not interfere as they are reluctant to attack the communists (cf. *KW*, p. 85). Tuny also makes clear that many people share her opinion. As they cannot imagine a new intelligent life form in the ocean, they blame the Russians for the incidents. Mike and Phyllis, who have carried out more research into the matter than others, do not believe in Tuny's theories. The journalists are portrayed as more competent and maybe even more intelligent than average people. The fact that they do not share the opinion of the public implies that the author of the novel distances himself from oversimplified accusations. The Cold War also complicates the fight against the xenobaths as the nations do not cooperate. Instead, they get involved into a science race, i.e. the Russians and the West quarrel over the question who first invented remote control for missiles. They accuse each other of espionage, theft, *et cetera* (cf.

KW, p. 106). This situation clearly demonstrates that, despite the common danger, national resentments cannot be overcome. It seems as if Wyndham purports to prove that the authorities are unable to solve problems as long as they do not collaborate. What is more, the narrator ironically comments that national resentments appease the public since they distract from the real danger: "This action, with its reassuring ring of normality, exerted a valuable tranquillizing influence" (*ibid.*). Eventually, the public refuses to believe in extraterrestrial fireballs and xenobaths until it is too late.

In the meantime, the xenobaths have become a vital threat to everybody who lives near the sea. Apart from sinking ships, they go on shore and kill human beings. According to Bocker's theory, the aliens – or colonists respectively – exploit the resources of Earth after having set up settlement. Exploitation takes place in the form of raiding coastal towns and "shrimping" (*KW*, p. 145) human beings. Bocker, the journalist couple and their team decide to fly to Escondida in the Caribbean in order to investigate into the raids. After some days of idleness in the tropical sun, the expedition team actually gets the chance to experience an attack. At the beach of the island, three "sea-tanks" appear and drive to the Square of the town. Mike reports that a sea-tank resembles "an elongated egg which has been halved down its length and set flat side to the ground, with the pointed end foremost" (*KW*, p. 138). Moreover, it is "between thirty and thirty-five feet long" (*ibid.*), and the people are unable to figure out by which mechanism the machine moves. Naturally, they are scared of the unknown and shoot at the sea-tanks, but the machines remain unharmed. What then happens is extraordinary and hideous at the same time: the sea-tanks pop, producing jelly bubbles with sticky cilia. Mike narrates:

> In a lurching amoebic way [the excrescence] ascended for ten feet or so. There it vacillated, steadying into a more stable sphere. Then, suddenly, something happened to it. It did not exactly explode. Nor was there any sound. Rather, it seemed to split open, as if it had been burst into instantaneous bloom by a vast number of white cilia which rayed out in all directions. [...]

> Four or five of the cilia, like long white whiplashes, flicked in through the window and dropped to the floor. Almost as they touched it they began to contract and withdraw. (*KW*, pp. 139f.)

The depiction of what is inside the sea-tanks arouses fear and disgust. The bubble organism with its cilia is so alien that people perceive it as monstrous and grotesque. What we generally associate with slimy bubbles is illness, stench and decay. In addition, slime emphasizes the Thing-ness of the aliens[271] as well as their disturbingly abnormal features. The cilia seem to be like tentacles, and the people do not know what these 'arms' are about to catch. Thus, this enemy is repulsive and not controllable. Subsequently, Mike makes clear that the sticky cilia only grab animate objects such as human beings and drag them into the Square. The victims are utterly helpless since they are enmeshed with the cilia "like flies on a fly-paper" (*KW*, p. 141). The organisms bind them up in 'bundles' and return to the sea. Numerous inhabitants of the town are dead or injured after the raid (cf. *KW*, pp. 141ff.). We can only speculate why the xenobaths 'shrimp' human beings. They might eat the corpses or use them as a breeding material for their offspring. Nonetheless, nobody knows what their intentions are as there is no communications between aliens and humans.

The raids have various consequences. First, the public now accepts that there are 'monsters' in the deep sea. They cease to blame the Soviets for any occurrences they cannot explain. Therefore, by the end of Phase Two of the novel, humans become aware of the fact that extraterrestrials have invaded their planet. Second, the people painfully learn that human beings are not the apex of evolution. Mike admits that he feels frightened about being confronted with something utterly new:

> I should be tempted to think that God proposed to teach me a lesson. That He said: '[…] You think you rule the world, and possibly heaven, too. Very well,

[271] Cf. Kelly Hurley, *The Gothic Body. Sexuality, Materialism, and Degeneration at the* Fin de Siècle, pp. 34f.

> you conceited little mites, there's a lot about life and nature that you don't know'. (*KW*, p. 148)

We can imagine that many people would feel like Mike. They are scared of anything they cannot scientifically explain or even predict. Additionally, the fact that the bombs have not yet destroyed the threat makes them desperate. Third, it becomes evident that the scientists are unable to classify the jelly bubbles. Dr Bocker terms them "pseudo-coelenterata" (*KW*, p. 151), saying that they are neither coelenterata (such as anemones, corals or jellyfish) nor animals, maybe not even living creatures (cf. *KW*, p. 153). The lack of classification renders the 'objects' monstrous and unknowable. Bocker continues speculating that the pseudo-coelenterata "may well be artificial organic constructions *built* for a specialized purpose" (*ibid.*, italics by J. Wyndham), i.e. for 'harvesting' human beings. Yet, the narrator never ascertains the true nature of the aliens and their sea-tanks.

Human resistance in *The Kraken Wakes* takes the form of counterattacks during alien raids, i.e. the natives of Earth fight back when the invaders 'land' on their shores. The beach as the *locus* of encounters between the Self and the Other is emblematic: numerous travel reports and adventure narratives feature similar settings. As to the geographical distribution of the alien attacks in Wyndham's novel, the reader learns that the raids happen all over the world, for example on the April Islands (cf. *KW*, pp. 114ff.), on the Cayman Islands (cf. *KW*, p. 129), in the Caribbean (cf. *KW*, p. 160), on Hokkaido and Honshu (cf. *ibid.*), *et cetera*. Initially, this gives the Europeans the impression that the terrible events occur far away: "*Ex Africa semper aliquid novi* may be translated, with a touch of freedom, as 'Funny things happen in other places', conveying that Europe [...] is the customary seat of stability" (*KW*, p. 168, italics by J. Wyndham). However, this attitude turns out to be a dangerous mistake: the xenobaths soon approach Europe as well. For instance, a little Irish village is attacked by six sea-tanks (cf. *KW*, pp. 176f.). As a consequence, the authorities in Ireland, England and Scotland organize men laying mine-fields and defending the coasts with bazookas and mortars (cf. *KW*, p. 177). Here, the Cold-War mentality transpires again; the population believes that the build-up of arms provides advantages over the enemy. In the course of the story, raids and counterattacks develop into a global war that determines the structures of power. In fact, the weapons destroy large numbers of sea-tanks and the raids finally stop (cf. *KW*, pp. 178f.).

Nevertheless, the success of the counterattacks is deceiving. At this point of the narrative, man does not yet bring about the final victory over the extraterrestrials, as is the case in other works of science fiction. Instead, active resistance by humans might leverage alien attacks: Bocker publicly announces that the aliens might make further assaults, which would then be more efficient since they could have learnt something about human beings. The images he uses in his speech are interesting:

> [W]hen the cannibal's fire is not quite hot enough to boil the pot, the intended meal may feel some relief, but he has *not*, in the generally accepted sense of the phrase, scored a victory. In fact, if he does not do something before the cannibal has time to build a better and bigger fire, he is not going to be any better off. (*KW*, p. 179, italics by J. Wyndham)

Talking about cannibals (the aliens) and their meal (man) implies that the former are the less 'civilized' but, in this situation, more powerful than the latter; barbarity and brute force seem to win over reason. Obviously, the oceanographer takes the possibility of the aliens' superiority over man into consideration, i.e. he already has a premonition of the future structures of power on Earth. This is why he comes to the conclusion that the xenobaths must eventually be exterminated (cf. *KW*, pp. 180f.).

Phase Three of *The Kraken Wakes* is set approximately five years after the arrival of the aliens on Earth (cf. *KW*, p. 197). The raids have stopped for some years, and the public seems to have forgotten the xenobaths. Scientists still work on an effective weapon to destroy the aliens, but they have not yet developed a solution (cf. *ibid.*). The fact that society has undergone tremendous changes is narrated *in medias res*: we accompany Mike and Phyllis on a boat journey from London to Cornwall. Gradually, Mike hints at a different world order: food supplies are scarce, houses are deserted, people live on farming, boats have become a very precious possession and cities such as London are considered a "trap" (cf. *KW*, pp. 184ff.).

The narrator also gives insights into the events of the past years, i.e. into the aliens' means of changing Earth into a habitable planet for xenobaths: as they are marine 'organisms', they cause floods in order to take over the planet and alter it according to their biological requirements. At first, scientists detect unusually dense fogs over the Atlantic and the Pacific Ocean (cf. *ibid.*). Meteorologists and oceanographers explain the fogs by increased currents of cold water and lower temperatures (cf. *KW*, pp. 190ff.). Then, massive icebergs appear in the Arctic, and the reader learns that the formation of icebergs is part of the aliens' new means of attack. After having produced ice, they melt it and thereby cause disastrous global floods (cf. *KW*, p. 199). In the USA, for example, the Everglades and the swamps expand over the country, and vast areas in Texas, Louisiana and the Mississippi Delta disappear beneath the water (cf. *KW*, p. 211). In England, people raise levees and walls in order to keep the rivers in their beds (cf. *ibid.*). However, as the water continues to rise, it puts an enormous pressure on the walls, and the cities are flooded (cf. *KW*, pp. 214f.). The floods lead to an exodus: all over the world, people flee to higher regions in order to escape from the water. For instance, the Dutch withdraw from their country and settle in Belgium and in the south of Germany, the Danish move to Sweden, and the Londoners of Lea Valley, Westminster, Chelsea and Hammersmith flee to the heights of Hampstead and Highgate. Parliament now resides in Harrogate, Yorkshire (cf. *KW*, pp. 215ff.). Apart from the floods, the population faces icy cold weather and gales. Thus, the streets are mostly deserted (cf. *KW*, pp. 227f.). Eventually, the xenobaths' interference with the climate system and the water levels destroys the world as we know it: people lose their homes, their jobs and their security.[272] In order to describe the situation, Phyllis quotes Kipling:

---

[272] The drastic change of climate in *The Kraken Wakes* recalls Hollywood movies such as *The Day after Tomorrow*, *Deep Impact* and *2012*. In *The Day after Tomorrow* (2004), the world is taken over by a new ice age, and the population of the USA flees to the warmer regions of the south. Interestingly, the film reverts

"Lo! All our pomp of yesterday is one with Nineveh and Tyre" (*KW*, p. 222). This quote is taken from the poem "Recessional" (1897), which makes clear that dominion can be fragile.[273] In Wyndham's novel, the Empire has fallen, and it is evident that the aliens' form of attack is much more efficient than any kind of weapon; man seems to have lost the battle. Nevertheless, the intention of the xenobaths still remains unclear.

The idea of England under water is not original. Richard Jefferies' (1848-1887) post-apocalyptic novel *After London; or Wild England* (1885) illustrates the consequences of a non-specified catastrophe and society's return into medieval conditions. The first of the two parts of the novel is the more interesting one. It tells us what England looks like thirty years after the terrible event: the island is to a major part sunk in water, and the scarce population settles around a big inland lake (the former Thames). The omniscient narrator impressively describes the pastoral landscape, for example the "endless forest and marsh", "vast quantities of fern" and "fir and beech and nut tree covers".[274] This portrayal poses a stark contrast to the industrialized cities in England. In addition, domestic animals have died out and only a few wild breeds remain. As to the races of man, we learn that there are 'savages' such as bloodthirsty Bushmen, nomadic gipsies and half-bred "foot-

---

immigration history as the Americans desperately try to make their way over the Mexican border (cf. *The Day after Tomorrow* [USA 2004, directed by Roland Emmerich]). In *Deep Impact* (1998), a comet is about to collide with Earth. In order to ensure the survival of the human race, 800,000 people are selected and allowed into the shelters. In the end, though, the spaceship Messiah destroys the comet and saves Earth (cf. *Deep Impact* [USA 1998, directed by Mimi Leder]). *Deep Impact* is thus similar to *Armageddon* (cf. *Armageddon* [USA 1998, directed by Michael Bay]). In the most recent of the films mentioned, *2012* (2009), the world is threatened by an impending cataclysm caused by the rays of the sun. Worldwide tsunamis are followed by floods, and those who can afford it escape in ships that suggest Noah's Ark. At the end of the film, the water recedes and all continents have moved together (cf. *2012* [USA 2009, directed by Roland Emmerich]). Just like in Wyndham's novel, the global catastrophes in the films diminish the population and worsen the conditions of life for those who survive.

[273] Cf. Eileen Gillooly (ed.), *Rudyard Kipling* (New York, NY: Sterling Publishing, 2000), p. 46.

[274] Richard Jefferies, *After London; or Wild England* (Cirencester: Echo Library, 2005), p. 7. All subsequent references to this edition are in brackets in the text.

gipsies". The men in the towns are descendents of the ancients and form some sort of medieval nobility (cf. *AL*, pp. 16ff.). However, it soon becomes obvious that they are morally corrupted tyrants that hold slaves and fight wars with other provinces. In quasi-Rousseauian terms, the narrator muses over the disgraceful nature of man:

> Men for ever trample upon men, each pushing to the front, nor is there safety in remaining in retirement, since such are accused of biding their time and of occult designs. Though the population of these cities all counted together is not equal to the population that once dwelt in a single second-rate city of the ancients, yet how much greater are the bitterness and the struggle! (*AL*, p. 20)

Here transpires a notion of degeneration. All the knowledge of the ancients is lost as well, and only the nobles are literate, a skill that they use in order to oppress their subjects (cf. *AL*, p. 24). Generally speaking, the splendid Empire has fallen into ruins.

The second part of Jefferies' novel tells the story of a baron's impoverished son, Felix of Aquila. Felix is an ambitious and intelligent young man who decides to go on a circumnavigation of the inland lake. His incentives appear imperial:

> What was there behind the immense and untraversed belt of forest which extended to the south, to the east, and west? Where did the Great Lake end? Were the stories of the gold and silver mines of Devon and Cornwall true? And where were the iron mines, from which the ancients drew their stores of metal? (*AL*, p. 5).

The reader draws the conclusion that Felix travels for reasons of curiosity and wealth, just like the explorers of the preceding centuries. During his voyage, Felix faces many dangers: the primitive Bushmen, the gales on the lake and the "black waters" – the putrid and poisonous swamp that was once London (cf. *AL*, pp. 132ff.).

Eventually, Felix helps a tribe of shepherds to defend themselves against the attacks of gypsies and is nominated their king. Felix intends to set up a feudal utopia in the idyllic landscape and travels back to his home province for his love, Lady Aurora (cf. *AL*, pp. 145ff.). Thus, despite the catastrophe that shapes the geography of England as well as society, the novel ends on a hopeful note. Contemporary critics praised *After London* for its realistic depiction of the future landscape, its exact use of ecological science, its minute details and its underlying romance.[275] Moreover, Jefferies' novel might be considered a landmark in science fiction since it builds up on inverted notions of empire: the post-apocalyptic setting, man's relapse into barbarism and the loss of knowledge and science that accompanies it. We can imagine that *After London* influenced works such as Wyndham's *The Kraken Wakes* or J. G. Ballard's *The Drowned World*[276] (1962).

Man's relapse into barbarism is a central topic in Phase Three of *The Kraken Wakes*. Due to the floods, people flee to fortified heights. They defend their territories with weapons since provisions are scarce. Gangs raid food stores and epidemics spread from a lack of hygiene (cf. *KW*, p. 220). People live without any of the modern amenities such as electricity and fresh water. Accordingly, after the xenobaths have taken control over Nature, mankind leads a 'savage' life. People also deteriorate morally: they develop a 'kill-or-be-killed' mentality, which renders Wyndham's portrayal of human nature rather negative. Furthermore, England has fallen into anarchy. For example, the districts that surround London "have formed themselves into miniature independent states" (*KW*, p. 227) that do not allow anyone to enter their territories. Travellers are shot at (cf. *ibid.*). Mike's rhetoric reminds the reader of those travellers that enter the realms of a certain tribe in classical adventure literature:

> The natives of the districts had banded together and turned out the refugees and the useless on to lower ground where they had to shift for themselves. […] Any stranger who did manage to sneak in could not

[275] Cf. John Rieder, *Colonialism and the Emergence of Science Fiction*, p. 127.
[276] J. G. Ballard, *The Drowned World* (London: Orion, ³2001).

> hope to remain unnoticed for long, and his treatment was ruthless when he was discovered – survival demanded it. (*KW*, p. 231)

This recalls the situation of Henry Rider Haggard's heroes in *King Solomon's Mines*[277] (1885) and *She*[278] (1887), for example. In both novels, the protagonists enter forbidden territories in 'savage' Africa and are confronted with numerous dangers. Nevertheless, their courage is rewarded in the end. They receive priceless treasures, and Africa provides the opportunity to restore qualities such as masculinity and chivalry. This 'good' side of Africa as well as the rich natural resources justify European imperialism. The dwellers of the independent states in *The Kraken Wakes* are comparable to natives, which characterizes them as less 'civilized' than their enemy, the xenobaths.

In Wyndham's novel, the journalist couple desperately tries to survive in a disintegrated society and, simultaneously, continue their work as journalists. They volunteer to stay with the EBC in London instead of giving up their jobs. The EBC sets up headquarters in the top floors of a building in Marble Arch and continues broadcasting the news (cf. *KW*, p. 212). The journalists live and work in a self-supporting station supplied with food, diesel-oil and petrol (cf. *KW*, p. 228). However, as the state of the country gradually declines, it is obvious that the reporters become depressed with their work. Mike sarcastically comments on their broadcasts:

> Our task of composing never-say-die material on the theme that we spoke from, and for, the heart of an empire bloody but still unbowed was supposed, we knew, to have a stabilizing value even now, but we doubted it. (*KW*, p. 223)

Hence, the purpose of the news is to keep up morale, but the journalists know that their work is in vain. As long as man lives under primitive and even life-threatening conditions, people are unlikely to believe encouraging news. We can also imagine that the radio

---

[277] Cf. Henry Rider Haggard, *King Solomon's Mines*.

[278] Cf. Henry Rider Haggard, *She* (London *et al.*: Penguin Classics, 2001).

has lost a major part of the influence it still had during World War II.

Finally, the climate changes transform society as they generate insularity and isolation. When the radio signal in the UK breaks off completely, Mike and Phyllis do not see any reason to stay in London and prepare for a voyage to Cornwall. They plan to live in the cottage where they used to spend their holidays as it is built on a hill (cf. *KW*, pp. 232ff.). After a dangerous boat journey of approximately one month, Mike and Phyllis arrive at Rose Cottage. Due to the rise of the sea-level, the estate has become an island. Generally speaking, the couple leads a self-sufficient and secluded life on the island. They are well-provisioned and need not fear the guerrilla wars and starvation that takes place around them (cf. *KW*, p. 235). Therefore, at first sight, the island might be the safe haven Mike and Phyllis were hoping to find when they were still in London. However, just like in Defoe's *Robinson Crusoe*[279] (1719) or in the film *Cast Away*[280] (2000), the couple desperately suffers from loneliness. Moreover, the winters are freezing cold and many people die of pneumonia; only one-eighth to one-fifth of the population survives (cf. *KW*, pp. 231ff.). We can also imagine that the journalists miss their work and the rather fast pace of life that accompanies it. As a conclusion, the situation in Rose Cottage inverts various clichés of desert island fiction, for example the beautiful landscape, the hot climate and living on what Nature provides. Instead, the couple's life deteriorates and they make plans to move further south, where it might be easier to grow crops (cf. *ibid.*).

The end of the novel appears rather abrupt but meaningful with regard to cooperation, victory and the question of guilt. Mike and Phyllis learn from one of the locals that the xenobaths have been defeated since the Japanese have developed an ultrasonic weapon that kills the aliens in the deeps. Thus, more advanced technology is decisive for the resistance against and the victory over the aliens; science eventually saves humanity and, in imperial terms, Earth is instantly decolonized. What is more, the Japanese are willing to share their technology with the Americans (cf. *KW*, p. 239). Hence,

---

[279] Cf. Daniel Defoe, *The Life and Adventures of Robinson Crusoe,* ed. by Angus Ross (London *et al.*: Penguin Books, 1965).
[280] *Cast Away* (USA 2000, directed by Robert Zemeckis).

the science race and the notions of competition between the different nations have ceased. Under the threat of extinction, they cooperate in order to defeat the alien enemy. Unlike in Wells' *The War of the Worlds*, human beings themselves fight off alien rule. On the whole, the depiction of human resistance in *The Kraken Wakes* appears to be an appeal to actively rise against oppressors. Humans take the role of natives in colonial encounters, but they strike back and eventually become the winners of the arms race against the invaders. The reader receives the impression that they deserve freedom and happiness after having averted the take-over of their planet. What is more, guilt is denied in Wyndham's novel: the apparently evil nature of the aliens constitutes man's innocence, and blasting all xenobaths up appears right and glorious.

What is striking is that, even after their death, the nature of the xenobaths remains a mystery. The reader might expect human scientists to do research on dead extraterrestrials, as is the case in relevant Hollywood movies. Yet, this is impossible due to the fact that the xenobaths' bodies have adapted to a very high pressure. Bocker explains on the radio that, after the attack with ultrasonic weapons, "a lot of jelly stuff came up, and went bad quickly in the sunlight. No shape to it. Not the pressure to hold the things together [...]" (*ibid.*). Therefore, people are still ignorant about the outward appearance of the aliens, their intentions, their origin, *et cetera*. Incidentally, Tennyson's poem, "The Kraken", can be seen as *prolepsis* since the shapeless dead kraken corresponds to what remains of the xenobaths on the surface of the water. Thus, due to the poem, the reader might have contemplated the death of the aliens *ab initio*.

Interestingly, John Wyndham authored two different endings for *The Kraken Wakes*. In the published edition, which is analyzed in this chapter, the authorities set up a Council for Reconstruction. The Council asks Mike and Phyllis to resume their work for the EBC in London. The couple finally agrees to the plan (cf. *KW*, p. 240). This ending implies a new start for the population and illustrates that, despite the tremendous losses and the hostile ecological conditions, there is hope for man. Due to scientific invention, the end of the human race is averted. The original ending[281] of the novel differs from the one that was eventually published in a way that it is much more pessimistic. First of all, the protagonist couple is apparently killed by sea-tanks. Second, the original version does not feature any ultrasonic weapons which kill the invaders. The xenobaths suddenly stop doing whatever they did in the deep sea. Just like their arrival on Earth, their outward appearance or their intentions, the end of "xenobathic activity" is a mystery. Bocker considers different possibilities:

> [T]he decline in xenobathic activity [...] may be due to failure to adapt, to breed, to resist disease, or any of the other causes to which it is popularly ascribed, and we may, in consequence be able to continue the work of reconstruction without further troubles from the Deeps. Nevertheless, there are dangers in easy optimism. It must be pointed out that we still know little or nothing of the natures of these xenobathic entities, and it would be unwise to overlook the possibility that they might from time to time require periods of regeneration analogous with our own need for sleep, or that of other types of creatures for hibernation. This could well be such a period of quiescence.[282]

Accordingly, the xenobaths might have died of natural causes (a scenario which closely resembles the death of the Martians in *The War of the Worlds*), or they might still inhabit the oceans and will perhaps attack humans again in the future. In this version, mankind does not succeed in liberating itself from the invaders, which implies that active resistance has been more or less in vain and that human science and technology cannot defeat the xenobaths. To a certain extent, the victory of the alien Other recalls Arthur C.

[281] The John Wyndham Archive of the Sidney Jones Library, University of Liverpool, holds the original holograph manuscript of *The Kraken Wakes*.

[282] Cf. John Wyndham, Holograph Manuscript of *The Kraken Wakes*, pp. 293f. Quoted in: Michael Douglas Green, "Social Critique in the Major Novels of John Wyndham: Civilization's Secrets and Nature's Truths," available on http://spectrum.library.concordia.ca/1011/ (2012-06-17).

Clarke's *Childhood's End* (cf. chapter 2.1). Clarke's work, however, ends on an optimistic note whereas Wyndham's original version would have been rather disappointing for mainstream readers. This might be a reason why Wyndham rewrote the ending. In addition, it appears as if the first version simply owes too much to Wells' famous work.

To conclude, John Wyndham's *The Kraken Wakes* depicts the struggle of the human race to avert its extinction. Mankind is attacked by alien xenobaths that establish colonies in the deep sea. The rhetoric is frequently imperial: the aliens invade and colonize the oceans, exploit coastal towns and defend themselves against counterstrike. The xenobaths are generally characterized as monstrous and indefinable; they remain unseen throughout the whole novel. However, as the novel is set during the Cold War, the general public does not believe in extraterrestrials or sea-monsters, but the Western states blame the communists for the events and *vice versa*. The Cold War is depicted as ridiculous and, at best, the Russians take the role of scapegoats since alien invaders are beyond human belief. The xenobaths as monsters embody suppressed emotions in favour of a war of aggression. What is more, the success of the monsters actually determines if the 'normal' world order collapses or not. Due to the climate change and the floods, society relapses into barbarism, and the Empire is in ruins. Human beings undergo typical experiences of a subject people, for instance the loss of territories, fear, violence, privations, the transformation of society and death. Science and cooperation between the nations eventually bring about the victory over the xenobaths. Even though *The Kraken Wakes* never became as famous as *The Day of the Triffids*, it is a well-told alien-invasion story that fascinates the reader through its rise of suspense and its underlying criticism of the media and of the Red Scare.

3.2 The Native Other: Brian W. Aldiss, *Non-Stop*

Non-Stop (1958, published under the title *Starship* in the USA) is Brian Aldiss' first novel, and it is definitely not exemplary of alien-encounter narratives. In fact, it differs from his later work, *The Interpreter* (cf. chapter 1.1), in various respects. First and foremost, *Non-Stop* lacks the popular invasion plot; the novel does not feature any extraterrestrials as alien Others at all. Hence, the "colonial gaze", i.e. the view of the colonizer upon the colonized (cf. Introduction), is not reversed – a major paradigmatic shift. Since there are no aliens that alter Earth and enslave the population, Aldiss treats the topic of exploitation in an original way. However, *Non-Stop* was written in the middle of the decolonization process and its political subtext should not be denied. It discusses central aspects of imperialism such as paternalism and responsibility for a subject people. The novel also raises complex questions with regard to a conqueror's right of intervention into a 'lower' culture. What is most striking, though, is that the Others in *Non-Stop*, i.e. the so-called "dizzies" which inhabit a multigenerational spaceship, are blatantly 'savage', a portrayal that typically justified domination and exploitation in colonial encounters. They take the role of natives that are exploited by humans from Earth.

Scholars praise *Non-Stop* for its treatment of tropes such as 'generation starship' and 'conceptual breakthrough'.[283] The novel is divided into four parts of approximately equal length: "Quarters", "Deadways", "Forwards" and "The Big Something". The action of the novel is woven around two conceptual breakthroughs, i.e. the protagonist discovers the truth about the world around him in two different situations: it becomes obvious that the characters in the novel do not live on Earth but in an immense spaceship orbiting Earth. The lives of the inhabitants are characterized by the struggle for survival and the desperate mood their religion, the "Teaching", creates. The plot is narrated through the eyes of Roy Complain, a hunter and member of the Greene tribe. Complain and

---

[283] Cf. John Clute and Peter Nicholls (eds.), *The Encyclopedia of Science Fiction*, s.v. 'Brian W. Aldiss'.

three other men of the same tribe are recruited by the priest, Marapper, who reveals that they are onboard a spaceship. Marapper decides to make his way to the control room since he thinks that the ship is lost in space. During their journey through the Deadways – the corridors between the numerous decks of the ship – the five men fight evolved rats, encounter "Giants" and ghost-like "Outsiders" (who turn out to be human beings from Earth), experience zero gravity and discover a swimming-pool which they mistake for the sea.

After several days, they arrive at the quarters of the relatively civilized tribe of Forwards, and Complain falls in love with one of the political leaders, Laur Vyann. From the diaries of the original captain of the spaceship, the couple receives some fragmented information about the crew that inhabited the ship more than twenty generations ago: a group of settlers established colonies on the planet Procyon V, called "New Earth".[284] However, a virus in the water of the planet paralyzed and killed most of the colonists, and the ship crew was affected as well. They tried to return to Earth but never arrived. The different tribes onboard the ship are the remote ancestors of the survivors. In the last part of the novel, the protagonist and his band experience the second conceptual breakthrough. The "Giants" explain that the spaceship is not off course but in orbit around Earth. "Little Dog", their research institute, secretly studies the tribes in their closed environment. The ending of *Non-Stop* remains ambiguous: the energy supplies of the control room are cut off, the spaceship breaks up, and Vyann and Complain hope to be taken back to Earth.

The novel depicts two different scenarios of imperialism: colonization and intervention into 'lower' cultures in a paternalistic context. Generally speaking, colonization serves as the background of the plot. The starship was originally designed to take settlers to

---

[284] Procyon (Alpha Canis Minoris) is the eighth brightest star in the sky. Its distance from Earth is approximately eleven light years, and its radius is about two times bigger than that of the sun. The Greek name means "before the dog" since Procyon is located before Sirius, the "Dog Star". The giant star is hotter than the sun, which would make human settlements impossible, but scientists expect it to cool down due to decreased core hydrogen fusion.
Cf. http://stars.astro.illinois.edu/sow/procyon.html (2011-03-13).

"New Earth" and to collect information and samples from the planet.[285] The beginning of its return journey is set in the year 2221. Yet, the details the captain's diaries reveal are scarce. Reading the entries, Complain and Vyann learn that the journey to the planet took about seven generations, that scientists had tested the environment of the planet before any settlement plans were carried out, and that the colonists brought cattle and birds to "New Earth" (cf. *NS*, pp. 160-172). The diaries leave numerous gaps, though. First of all, the captain does not explain why human beings decided to colonize Procyon V. Potential reasons are their spirit of adventure or the desire for a utopia, which is closely connected to the trope of the Eden myth. "New Earth" also echoes the pastoral in science fiction, i.e. a tale in which life in harmony with Nature is opposed to the urban, the industrial and the technological. Incidentally, Aldiss' *Helliconia* trilogy (1982-1985) can be interpreted as pastoral. It narrates the experiences of the dwellers of the planet Helliconia in the different seasons. The seasons are centuries long, and many people die during the harsh winters. In the course of the story, the reader realizes that Helliconia is monitored and controlled from the space station Avernus. One major theme of the trilogy is the question of intervention into Helliconian affairs.[286] Intervention in *Non-Stop* will be elaborated on later in this chapter.

The pastoral can also portray a post-holocaust world, which leads us to negative reasons why the colonists in *Non-Stop* might have decided to leave Earth. We can imagine that they saw themselves confronted with overpopulation, starvation and natural disasters. A recent example of this theme in film is *Cargo*: after the ecological breakdown of the Earth, people live under inhumane conditions in space stations. Many of them dream of escaping to the paradisiacal planet of Rhea. However, the protagonist, Laura Portmann, finds out that Rhea is an illusion and that people only experience it in virtual reality.[287] In *Non-Stop*, there is no hint

[285] Cf. Brian W. Aldiss, *Non-Stop* (London: Orion, 2000), p. 137. All subsequent references to this edition are in brackets in the text.
[286] Cf. Brian W. Aldiss, *The Helliconia Trilogy. The Classic Epic Trilogy in One Volume* (New York, NY: Voyager/Harcourt, 1996).
[287] Studying some recent examples, a thematic shift becomes evident. The 'generation starship' trope of the 1950s and 1960s has become 'generation cyber-

whether Procyon V is an Eden-like place. The reader does not learn how they discovered the planet or if they made any adjustments to its environment. Terraforming is a commonplace topic with regard to colonization of other worlds. Examples are depicted in Olaf Stapledon's *Last and First Men*[288] (1930), Robert A. Heinlein's *Farmer in the Sky*[289] (1950) and Arthur C. Clarke's *The Sands of Mars*[290] (1951). Brian Stableford coined the term 'Earth-Clones' for planets that have been altered to be hospitable to human life.[291]

The colonists in Aldiss' novel and in other works of new empires are comparable to the pioneers and early settlers of the Americas, South Africa, Australia, *et cetera*. In science fiction, the ship becomes a spaceship, the unmapped territories in remote corners of the world turn into faraway planets in different solar systems, and indigenous peoples are extraterrestrials. The colonists of new empires probably face the same hardships and privations as the settlers in history. In *The Romance of Empire* (1924), Philip Gibbs elaborates on the crucial role the colonists played in the making of the British Empire:

> [The] Empire was not so much gained by fighting and bloodshed as by courage of a quiet kind – the courage of endurance, of industry, of honesty, of long patience, and sober character. Soldiers and sailors, naturally, have most of the popular homage, but no less honour should be given to those farmers and merchants and

---

space', i.e. human beings are unaware of the fact that everything they experience is a product of computer networks. Admittedly, the term 'generation' might not be appropriate since family is mostly a product of virtual reality in those works. The Platonic question of 'generation starship', i.e. what constitutes reality, remains, though. Examples of what I have called 'generation cyberspace' works are the *Matrix* trilogy (USA 1999-2003, directed by Andy and Larry Wachowsky) and *Cargo* (Switzerland 2009, directed by Ivan Engler and Ralph Etter).

288 Olaf Stapledon, *Last and First Man* (London: Gollancz, ^{4}2003).

289 Robert A. Heinlein, *Farmer in the Sky*, introduction by William H. Patterson Jr. (Riverdale, NY: Baen, 2008).

290 Arthur C. Clarke, *The Space Trilogy: Islands in the Sky, The Sands of Mars, Earthlight* (London: Gollancz, 2001).

291 Cf. Brian Stableford, *The Dictionary of Science Fiction Places* (New York: Wonderland, 1999), s.v. 'Earth-Clones'.

> thrifty traders who dared greatly and suffered much, for no higher aim than a prosperous home and a peaceful life. This is the true glory of the Empire.[292]

Accordingly, it is not only due to explorers and the military that the British Empire was the largest in the world in the nineteenth century. As to Aldiss' novel, human settlements on "New Earth" could have been accompanied by the extension of human territories and an improvement of living-standards.

Nonetheless, the diaries of the captain reveal that the establishment of settlements on Procyon V eventually proved to be a failure. At first sight, the reason for the failure was not hostile extraterrestrials as in Ray Bradbury's *The Martian Chronicles*[293] (1950), for example. In fact, it was an overlooked detail that rendered the planet uninhabitable for humans: the water of Procyon V was infested by viral proteins that cause an illness called "Nine Day Ague" (cf. *NS*, pp. 164-166). The majority of the crew died, and it is assumed that the disease was also fatal for the settlers on the planet. Therefore, despite thorough scientific tests, people had been unaware of this danger until it was too late. In addition, it becomes obvious that the expectations of the colonists were not fulfilled: they had intended to create "New Earth" but the planet remained alien and, to a certain extent, hostile.

The alien protein, christened "bestine" by the young scientist June Besti (cf. *NS*, p. 167), plays a crucial role in the creation of a new race of man. What is striking is that, according to June, the less complex organisms quickly adapt to the alien substance in the water: "It looks as if the more complex the organism, the more difficulty it has in rejecting to the new proteins and viruses. Bad luck on man [...]" (*NS*, p. 168). As a consequence, humans, horses and cows die, whereas pigs, dogs and rodents recover from the

---

292 Philip Gibbs, *The Romance of Empire*, p. 5.

293 Cf. Ray Bradbury, *The Martian Chronicles* (New York, NY: Simon & Schuster, 2012). Incidentally, fighting hostile extraterrestrials on other planets is a common topic of video games. *StarCraft* (Blizzard Entertainment, 1998), *Half-Life* (Valve, 1998) and its sequel *Half-Life 2* (Valve, 2004), the *Halo* series (Bungie, 2002-2009), *Dawn of War* (THQ, 2004) and its sequel *Dawn of War II* (THQ, 2009) or *James Cameron's Avatar: The Game* (Ubisoft Lightstorm Entertainment, 2009) are only some of numerous examples.

illness. She calls the survivors "low-level mutations" (cf. *NS*, p. 164). The plants, or "hydroponics", thrive as well, and they soon invade the decks and corridors of the spaceship (cf. *NS*, p. 170). The hydroponics create the jungle the different tribes inhabit more than twenty generations later. The tendency towards 'simplicity' is finally the reason why the remote ancestors of the crew have developed into less complex organisms or underwent a process of degeneration.[294] They have adapted to the alien protein in the water. To sum up, the colonization of "New Earth" did not fail due to hostile extraterrestrials. Rather, it was an alien influence that killed most of the crew and created a new race of man.

The encounter between "Giants" (humans from Earth) and the new human race, called "dizzies" by the "Giants", recalls alien encounter on the one hand, and an encounter between the 'savage' and the 'civilized' on the other hand. First, the "dizzies" can be interpreted as alien since alienness or otherness depends on the point of view. In the context of science fiction, 'alien' signifies "of or pertaining to an (intelligent) being or beings from another planet; that derives from another world".[295] We can conclude that the "dizzies" come from another world, i.e. the ship, as they have never set foot on Earth. Moreover, they have evolved under the influence of an alien protein; their bodies differ from the ones of humans on Earth. They appear alien to the "Giants" from Earth since they are physically smaller, their lives are shorter, and they have lost much of the knowledge of former generations. The closed environment of the spaceship is a 'pocket universe'.[296] Fermour, a scientist from Earth, explains to Complain and his band:

---

[294] The *Oxford English Dictionary* defines 'degeneration' as "a change of structure by which an organism, or some particular organ, becomes less elaborately developed and assumes the form of a lower type" (*OED Online*, s.v. 'degeneration', b.). A 'degenerate' is thus "[o]ne who has lost, or has become deficient in, the qualities considered proper to the race or kind [...]" (*ibid.*, s.v. 'degenerate'). With regard to *Non-Stop*, the "dizzies" might be interpreted as degenerates since this new race of man has regressed to a simpler organism under the influence of the alien protein from Procyon V. I will elaborate on the differences vis-à-vis human beings from Earth in the course of this chapter.

[295] *OED Online*, s.v. 'alien'.

[296] The *Encyclopedia of Science Fiction* offers two different definitions of 'pocket universe'. Broadly defined, the term describes "an actual miniature universe pocketed within a larger explanatory frame or device [...]." In a narrower usage of

> That's why we proper Earthmen call you "dizzies": you live so fast, it makes us dizzy. But that isn't all that is wrong with you! Imagine this great ship, still automatically functioning despite the lack of anyone to control it. It supplied everything: except the things which, by its nature, it could not supply, fresh vitamins, fresh air, fresh sunlight. Each of your succeeding generations becomes smaller; Nature survives how she may, and that was her way of doing it, by cutting down on the required materials. Other factors, such as inbreeding, have changed you until – well, it was decided you were virtually a separate race. In fact, you had adapted so well to your environment, it was doubtful if you would be able to survive if transferred down to Earth. (*NS*, pp. 234f.)

Thus, the alien protein from Procyon V and the closed environment have manipulated evolution and created 'aliens'. Second, the expression "it was decided" shows us that the human beings on Earth have taken control over the new race; they rule the "dizzies" like colonial subjects. Complain is apparently traumatized by the epiphany and reacts by confirming his otherness:

> So we're not human beings at all [...]. All that we've suffered, hoped, done, loved ... it's not been real. We're just funny little mechanical things, twitching in a frenzy, dolls activated by chemicals ... Oh, my God! (*NS*, p. 234)

He is suddenly aware of his own alienness, which must be shocking since the "dizzies" have apparently considered themselves 'proper' human beings. Moreover, he likens his own people to "mechanical things" and "dolls", which implies that someone else

---

the term, it implies that "the world initially perceived seems to be the entire world, and the web of taboos prevent[s] the truth about its partial nature [...]." Cf. John Clute and Peter Nicholls (eds.), *The Encyclopedia of Science Fiction*, s.v. 'pocket universe'. Since most of the inhabitants of the spaceship in *Non-Stop* are ignorant of the true nature of their habitat, the narrower definition applies.

plans and controls their lives. On the one hand, this could open up a discussion about the ethics of genetic engineering.[297] On the other hand, it is comparable to a scenario in colonial history since the "dizzies" are not a free race. They are comparable to a 'primitive' people being patronized by a 'civilized' one.

In contrast to other works of alien-encounter science fiction, *Non-Stop* does not depict advanced technology as a basis for dominance. Instead, the superior position of the humans on Earth is gained through knowledge: they conduct research on the inhabitants of the spaceship without them being aware of the situation. Thus, a 'higher' culture exploits a 'lower' culture for the acquisition of knowledge. The "dizzies" have become objects of an experiment designed "to discover the effects of a closed environment on man […]" (*NS*, p. 237). Fermour explains that the human government on Earth found out about the lost spaceship ("Big Dog"), had it towed into Earth's orbit and set up a research institute, "Little Dog":

> When "Big Dog" was towed into orbit, we – Earth – fully realized our grave responsibility to you all. Doctors and teachers were your especial need. Holy men were required, to counter the vile irreligion of the Teaching – which, vile though it was, undoubtedly assisted your survival in some measure. But there were snags: the doctors and people could not just creep into the air locks and mingle with you, easy though that was, with the inspection way system and the hydroponic tangles to shelter them. They had to be trained at Little Dog Institute to move and speak as quickly as possible, to sleep in catnaps, to – oh, in short to act

[297] Genetic engineering, or something very similar, was already treated in the early works of science fiction, such as Herbert G. Wells' *The Island of Doctor Moreau* (1896), Olaf Stapledon's *Last and First Man* (1930) and Aldous Huxley's *Brave New World* (1932, cf. Aldous Huxley, *Brave New World* [New York, NY: HarperCollins, 2004]). More recent examples are Octavia Butler's *Dawn (Xenogenesis)* (1987, cf. Octavia E. Butler, *Dawn [Xenogenesis]* [London: Gollancz, 1988]), Storm Constantine's *Hermetech* (1991, cf. Storm Constantine, *Hermetech*. Revised Edition [Stafford, UK: Immanion Press, 2004]) and Peter Watts' *Starfish* (cf. Peter Watts, *Starfish* [New York, NY: Tor, 1999]).

> like dizzies. And to bear the horrible stench in the ship. And, of course, they had to be abnormally small men, since none of you are above five feet high. (*NS*, p. 236)

Thus, the scientists have 'infiltrated' the environment of the "dizzies" and studied them like animals in a zoo or maybe even like animals in an aquarium; the spaceship is like a cosmos in a glass. Apart from the fact that they take control, these scientists are comparable to numerous nineteenth-century ethnologists who studied the life and customs of indigenous peoples, for instance Edward John Eyre (1815-1901), Edward Burnett Tylor (1832-1917) and Alfred L. Kroeber (1876-1960). Nonetheless, the "Giants" do not reveal any details with regard to the results of the experiment. Fermour's comment remains ambiguous: "[The experiment] has taught us more about man and society than we have been able to learn on Earth for centuries" (cf. *NS*, p. 237). The scientist might allude to the transformations generated by the alien protein, he could talk about the notable influence religion has on man, or he might hint at the idea that interference from a 'superior' culture can be beneficial, which would justify the "Giants'" manipulation of the "dizzies".

Classifying the Greene tribe as 'primitive' or 'savage' is a consequence of the way they are depicted. The portrayal works on two levels: ethnology and politics. With regard to the ethnological level, Aldiss takes pains to describe the culture and the religion of the Greene tribe. Along with the scientists from Earth, the reader adopts the viewpoint of an outsider observing the "dizzies". First of all, we receive information about the lifestyle of the Greene tribe: they are semi-nomadic (cf. *NS*, p. 5), go hunting with bow and arrow (cf. *NS*, p. 18) and chop down the hydroponics for various purposes, for instance for food, for medical use and for the production of basic commodities (cf. *NS*, p. 6). The tribe is unable to maintain crops and cattle (cf. *NS*, p. 5). On the one hand, this depiction recalls adventure stories from the nineteenth century. A prominent example is Herman Melville's novel *Typee. A Peep at*

Polynesian Life[298] (1846). The narrator Tommo and his friend Toby flee from a whaling ship in order to live an idyllic life on the island of Nukuheva. It is inhabited by two native tribes, the Typees and the Happar. The two sailors eventually live among the Typees and describe their customs in detail: their leisure activities, their tattoos, their taboo religion, polygamy, their ignorance of money and their cannibalistic rites. In the sequel, *Omoo. A Narrative of the South Seas* (1847), the protagonist Tommo explores the lifestyle of the indigenous peoples of Tahiti, interspersed with comments on missionary work.[299]

On the other hand, the portrayal of the tribe bears similarities to certain ethnological texts. In *Pre-Historic Times as Illustrated by Ancient Remains and the Manners and Customs of Modern Savages*[300] (1865), which enjoyed a considerable audience and attention in the nineteenth century, John Lubbock (1834-1913) elaborates on pre-historic archaeology and portrays those cultures he considers "modern savages", for example Hottentots, Tasmanians, Fijians, Tahitians, Eskimos, North American Indians, and many more. Lubbock purports that the "modern savages" are crucial for the understanding of ancient Europe[301] and thoroughly describes their dresses, food, housing, weapons, languages, religious ceremonies, *et cetera*. Eventually, this serves the purpose of making the natives appear barbarous.[302] About the Bushmen, for example, he writes the following:

---

[298] Herman Melville, *Typee. A Peep at Polynesian Life* (London *et al.*: Penguin, 1996).
[299] Cf. Herman Melville, *Omoo. A Narrative of Adventures in the South Seas* (London *et al.*: Penguin, 2007).
[300] John Lubbock, *Pre-Historic Times as Illustrated by Ancient Remains and the Manners and Customs of Modern Savages* (London: Williams and Norgate, [3]1872). Lubbock's work quickly became a classic in its field. Between 1865 and 1913, seven editions of *Pre-Historic Times* were published.
[301] *Ibid.*, p. 428.
[302] Obviously, Lubbock sees the natives 'through English eyes'. He defends his viewpoint by stating: "It must not be supposed that in the preceding chapter I have selected from various works all the passages most unfavourable to savages, and that the picture I have drawn of them is unfair. In reality, the very reverse is the case. Their real condition is even worse and more abject than that which I have endeavoured to depict." *Ibid.*, p. 538.

> The Bushmen resembled the Hottentots in many things, but were even more uncivilized. They had no knowledge of metallurgy, no domestic animals, and no canoes. They frequently stole the cattle of their more advanced neighbours, but always killed and ate them as quickly as possible. Their principal weapons were bows and poisoned arrows. Lichtenstein asserts that they had no names, but this was probably an error. Bleek regards them as the lowest of human races, and Haeckel even goes so far as to assert that they seem 'to the unprejudiced comparative student of nature, to manifest a closer connexion with the gorilla and chimpanzee than with a Kant or a Goëthe [*sic*].'"[303]

On the whole, the depictions of the various peoples do not differ significantly and, apart from emphasizing their Otherness, Lubbock gives 'evidence' of the natives' inferiority to Europeans. With regard to the Bushmen, he adopts the viewpoint of Haeckel and even likens them to animals. The indigenous peoples serve as the mirror image of the European.

In *Non-Stop*, the Greene tribe is characterized by cultural and moral inferiority. The rites and customs of the "dizzies" can be classified as stereotypical. For instance, "barbaric outbreaks of festivity" alternate with "inertia" (cf. *NS*, p. 39). One event is particularly illustrating with regard to an exuberant atmosphere. After having found bags of dye, the people of the Greene tribe celebrate their colourful clothes:

> Everyone seemed to be here, dancing senselessly in an orgy of enjoyment. […] Several groups, divided from the main one in biparous fashion, jigged rapturously to the sound of stringed instruments. The noise was incessant, and the frenetic movements of the dancers – heads jerking, fingers twitching – an onlooker might have found cause for alarm. But there were few nonparticipants. (*NS*, p. 24)

---

[303] *Ibid.*, pp. 434f.

This "orgy" of "senseless" actions, "incessant" music, cheering and "frenetic movements" recalls depictions of savage rites in colonial literature, for example the witch-hunt in the fictive African kingdom of Kukuanaland that Sir Henry Rider Haggard writes about in *King Solomon's Mines* (1885). The evil prophet Gagool, an embodiment of superstition, holds pseudo-religious ceremonies such as the "witch-hunt". The atmosphere in the eponymous chapter is simultaneously fantastic and realistic: it is dark, thousands of natives stamp their feet and sing a "war chant" or "death-dirge", and the "witch doctresses" wildly dance and yell. Eventually, they randomly appoint opponents of the regime and slaughter them.[304] The graphic description illustrates that the culture of the Kukuanas is exotic and mysterious. Chaos, magic and violence dominate the scene, and the native culture can therefore be seen as antithetical to Victorian English culture. The reader perceives the witch-hunt as irrational and barbarous. Accordingly, the "barbaric outbreaks of festivity" make the "dizzies" in *Non-Stop* appear savage and culturally inferior to the human beings from Earth. Incidentally, they also perform witch-hunts in order to catch the vampire-like Outsiders (which turn out to be human beings from Earth) (cf. *NS*, p. 29).

Among the Greene tribe, inventions and knowledge of former generations have long been forgotten. This situation is comparable to the one in John Christopher's *Tripods* trilogy (cf. chapter 1.2). Cameras, electric fans, vases, books, fire extinguishers, shampoo, watches and other "totems of a more varied and advanced civilization" are unknown to the members of the Greene tribe (cf. *NS*, p. 49). When Complain and his band find these items in a storeroom of the spaceship, they look at them helplessly (cf. *ibid.*). The fact that they do not even try to find out what the items are made for or how they work implies a lack of curiosity, maybe it even proves incapacity of advancement. As to progress, Lubbock claimed that the technologically advanced civilizations of the future would be more intelligent, happier and also more moral than his contemporary ones.[305] It is striking that, according to Lubbock, progress is accompanied by virtue. In return, this characterizes 'primitive'

---

304 Cf. Henry Rider Haggard, *King Solomon's Mines*, pp. 102f.

305 Cf. John Lubbock, *Pre-Historic Times as Illustrated by Ancient Remains and the Manners and Customs of Modern Savages*, pp. 602f.

peoples such as the "dizzies" as morally inferior to the humans from Earth.

In Aldiss' novel, savagery and alienness are also expressed by superstition and cruelty. The novel reveals numerous details about the religion of the "dizzies". The reader learns that the "Teaching", formulated in the "Litany" (cf. *NS*, pp. 23, 40), has turned the history of the spaceship into a myth. For instance, death is referred to as the "Long Journey" (cf. *NS*, p. 14), and the Litany ends with the words "And the ship brought home" (*NS*, p. 140). What is more, the Teaching generates callousness: the "dizzies" are indoctrinated to believe in unattainable felicity (cf. *NS*, p. 27), in the idea that they are descendents of cowards (cf. *NS*, p. 43) and in the advantages of acting out anger and rage (cf. *NS*, p. 184). This seems to be the opposite of Judeo-Christian belief; it is 'savage' since a 'civilized' society would not accept a religion that teaches hopelessness and suppresses affection and kindness. Above all, the "dizzies" believe in supernatural beings, the so-called "Outsiders":

> They had no hearts or lungs, but exactly resembled other men, so that they could live undetected among mortals, gathering power, and syphoning off the powers of men, like vampires drawing blood. Periodically among the tribes witch-hunts were held; but the suspects, when carved up for examination, always had hearts and lungs. (*NS*, p. 29)

Naturally, ghosts or vampires are emblems of superstition, and witch-hunts are a common topic in works of fiction that narrate encounters with indigenous peoples. Scenes like the witch-hunt in *King Solomon's Mines* illustrate that 'European reason' reigns over 'savage ignorance'. Ironically, Complain and his friends later find out that the "Outsiders" are human beings from Earth (cf. *NS*, p. 212).

Furthermore, the Teaching is informed with elements of psychoanalysis. For example, the holy trinity is formed by "Froyd, Yung and Bassitt"[306] who have "gone alone through the terrible

[306] In contrast to Sigmund Freud (1856-1939) and Carl Gustav Jung (1875-1961), Bassitt is a fictional character. He was an Aviarist Second Class on board the

barriers of sleep [where] they found [...] but grottoes and subterranean labyrinths full of ghouls and evil treasure, leeches, and the lust that burns like acid" (*NS*, p. 88). "Conscious" signifies God, and "Unconscious" stands for the devil (cf. *NS*, p. 63). Thus, the priests of the Greene tribe perform religious rites and some sort of degenerate psychoanalysis at the same time.[307] The result is that the tribesmen are considered naïve and ridiculous by the "Giants". Obviously, the theories about the Conscious and the Subconscious are taken from psychology textbooks, or "lookers" as the "dizzies" call them (cf. *NS*, p. 45). Their pseudo-religion originates in the fact that the aviarist Bassitt "turned to put faith in psycho-analysis" (*NS*, p. 170) instead of believing in God when he saw himself confronted with the Nine Day Ague and the miserable situation onboard the spaceship. Bassitt "evolved a dismal religion of his own" (*NS*, p. 162) and preached it to his fellow men. Nevertheless, this has long been forgotten; the "dizzies" mistake Freud, Jung and Bassitt for supernatural beings. Their pseudo-religion seems to be a 'savage' trait they must be liberated from.

Apart from superstitious, the members of the Greene tribe are depicted as cruel and callous. They grow up in an environment where "[v]iolence and death [are] pandemic" (*NS*, p. 5). Moreover, children that are born with deformities are killed, "only the knife await[s] them" (*NS*, p. 4). Cruelty towards innocent children appears barbaric and repulsive to the reader. The idea that this is considered normal among the people of the Greene tribe characterizes them as Other. With regard to violence against women, Complain's wife, Gwenny, is abducted by two men and Complain is unable to save her (cf. *NS*, p. 19). Thus, he is publicly punished for his shortcoming: the Guard captain strikes him six times with a whip (cf. *NS*, pp. 24f.). Due to a female shortage, the men of the Greene tribe act out mating duels (cf. *NS*, p. 22). The reader also learns that the laws of the Greene tribe prohibit affection. For example, parents

---

spaceship, i.e. he was responsible for the birds the colonists shipped to Procyon V (cf. *NS*, p. 162).

[307] However, the influence of the Teaching on man is more powerful in similar works of science fiction, for instance in Heinlein's *Orphans of the Sky* (1941, cf. Robert A. Heinlein, *Orphans of the Sky* [London: Gollancz, 1963]) or in H. G. Wells' *The Island of Doctor Moreau* (1896).

are not allowed to take care of their children anymore when the latter are waist high (cf. *NS*, p. 32). Generally speaking, "sentiment [is] one of the weaknesses the Greene tribe [strive] to eradicate" (*ibid.*). To put it in a nutshell, cruelty and the lack of affection emphasize the moral inferiority of the "dizzies". Again, they appear alien when compared to human beings from Earth. In fact, the "dizzies" resemble ignoble savages[308] in nineteenth-century novels of adventure, and this depiction might serve as a justification for oppression and exploitation. Consequently, "the white man's burden"[309] appears to be a noble endeavour.

The environment the "dizzies" live in is a futuristic counterpart of the jungle in colonial literature. Nature and culture blend as the dense ponics (the plants that thrive on board the ship) seem to have adapted perfectly to their surroundings:

> [T]he interlacing root structure [...] lay like a mesh under the grit, its lower tendrils biting deep into the deck. [...] [H]ere the humus was particularly deep, almost two feet of it covering the deck: evidence that these were unexplored parts, across which no other tribe had ever worked. (*NS*, p. 6)

The "ubiquitous" plants are the habitat of previously domestic animals such as dogs and pigs that have become wild again (cf. *NS*, pp. 18, 72). Complain and his band frequently struggle to get through the tangle (cf. *NS*, p. 71). Other *topoi* of the jungle are the hot climate (cf. *NS*, p. 10) and the "plague of flies" (*NS*, p. 72). The artificiality of the jungle reminds the reader of the humid green living-space inside the cities of the Tripods in John Christopher's

---

[308] The 'ignoble savage' is a manifestation of cruelty, ignorance and brutishness and thus the mirror image of the 'noble savage'. The term 'noble savage' first appeared in the play "The Conquest of Granada" (1672) by John Dryden (1631-1700), and it referred to a Native American. Generally speaking, a noble savage is an innocent and pristine man who lives according to natural law, i.e. "an idealized concept of uncivilized man, who symbolizes the innate goodness of one not exposed to the corrupting influences of civilization." Cf. http://www.britannica.com/EBchecked/topic /416988/noble-savage (2011-03-22).

[309] Rudyard Kipling (1865-1936) coined the term "the white man's burden" in his eponymous poem (cf. Introduction).

novels (cf. chapter 1.2). The jungle also recalls classic narratives of adventure. The most popular example might be the Congolese jungle in Joseph Conrad's *Heart of Darkness* (1899). The European ivory traders experience it as extremely hot, impenetrable and full of hidden dangers. Through their eyes, the jungle is the venue of madness and 'savage' customs such as cannibalism. Nonetheless, they also see the potential for exploitation. Likewise, the jungle in Aldiss' *Non-Stop* is 'uncharted territory' for the Greene tribe and challenges them to expand their territories, the "Quarters". They chop down the ponics in order to gain land for agriculture and settlement (cf. *NS*, p. 6). Hence, the nomadic "dizzies" temporarily colonize various decks and rooms of the spaceship. The notion of taking possession of uncharted territory permeates desert island fiction. For instance, Robert Michael Ballantyne's *The Coral Island* (1857) narrates the tale of three castaway boys from England who 'colonize' an island in the South Sea by giving English names to the various areas;[310] the white man taking possession seems to come naturally, which is racist propaganda. In both Aldiss' novel and in colonial literature, the jungle is the *locus* of savagery that must be colonized and transformed into a civilized place. This is frequently accompanied by exploitation.

In contrast to the Greene tribe, the people of Forwards are portrayed as more civilized (cf. *NS*, pp. 9, 114). The former seem to be scared of the more advanced tribe: "[T]he men [of Forwards] had alien ways and weapons, and powers unknown. They were slowly advancing through the tangle and would eventually wipe out all the smaller tribes [...]" (*NS*, p. 29). When Complain enters the territory of Forwards, he experiences the people as well-organized (cf. *NS*, p. 107), clean (cf. *NS*, p. 119), neatly dressed (cf. *ibid.*) and skilled in agriculture (cf. *NS*, p. 141). Furthermore, he falls in love with one of their political leaders, Laur Vyann (cf. *NS*, pp. 141ff.). The question arises why the Forwards tribe has reached a higher step on the ladder of civilization. First of all, we might speculate that those people have regained more knowledge of their ancestors, that their environment might be advantageous for the maintenance of crops and cattle, and that they have developed a rigid govern-

[310] Cf. Robert Michael Ballantyne, *The Coral Island*, pp. 50, 63.

mental structure. Moreover, we can conclude that they are less superstitious than the Greene tribe. Vyann remarks to Complain: "You take the Teaching too seriously – it's what I might expect from someone out of a provincial tribe!" (*NS*, p. 144). The complex question why some nations are more 'civilized' than others was widely debated in the nineteenth century. The most famous anthropologist who elaborated on the topic is Charles Darwin. In *The Descent of Man, and Selection in Relation to Sex* (1871), Darwin claims that nomadic habits are detrimental to progress, whereas "a fixed abode, and the union of many families under a chief, [are] the indispensable requisites for civilization."[311] He also emphasizes the influence of natural selection: a nation that produces intelligent, brave, patriotic and energetic offspring over a considerable period of time will eventually advance.[312] With regard to the people of Forwards, Darwin's theories might apply. In the course of the novel, another reason for progress is revealed: one of the human scientists from Earth, Zac Deight, lives *incognito* among the Forwards tribe and influences the tribesmen's culture, especially with regard to religion. We learn that he reduces the impact of the Teaching and, consequently, of superstition, cold-heartedness and ignorance (cf. *NS*, p. 237). Nonetheless, intervention into a culture will be discussed later in this chapter. On the whole, the Greene tribe appears 'backwards' and more alien to us than the Forwards tribe.

Apart from Deight, other scientists involved in the experiment secretly manipulate the lives of the 'savages'. "Little Dog" controls the ship (cf. *NS*, p. 231), and the "Giants" govern the habitat as well as the lifestyle of their objects of study. For example, the lights onboard the ship are switched off from midnight to six o'clock in the morning (cf. *NS*, p. 234), the humans maintain and repair the ship (cf. *ibid.*), they kill rats (cf. *NS*, p. 238), they mitigate the strict laws of the Teaching (cf. *NS*, p. 237) and they destroy any evidence of manipulation (cf. *ibid.*). Their physical transformation of the environment of the "dizzies" corresponds to 'ecological imperialism' according to Alfred Crosby'.[313] The scientist

---

[311] Charles Darwin, *The Descent of Man, and Selection in Relation to Sex*, p. 158.
[312] Cf. *ibid.*, p. 168.
[313] Cf. Alfred Crosby, *Ecological Imperialism: The Biological Expansion of Europe, 900-1900* (Cambridge *et al.*: Cambridge University Press, 1986).

Fermour even compares himself to Albert Schweitzer (1875-1965) and to Turnball.[314] It is striking that they define their role as caretakers of the "dizzies", much like the Overlords who 'nurse' mankind in Arthur C. Clarke's *Childhood's End* (cf. chapter 2.1). This means that the scientists as creators of the habitat and agents of the "dizzies'" well-being treat the latter like a father who takes care of his children. We learn that the humanist scientist, Zac Deight, "loved dizzies" (*ibid.*). However, he never reveals the truth about the experiment to them; they remain his 'guinea pigs'. He does not liberate them from the poor and desperate conditions onboard the ship, either. Therefore, Deight does not assume full responsibility for the creatures he is in charge of, and he fails as their metaphorical father, however artificial the situation may be.

Frederic Jameson elaborates on the political implications of the experiment in Aldiss' novel. He holds that "the inauguratory act of the launchers of the spaceship implies a terrible and godlike responsibility which is not without serious political overtones [...]."[315] Here, Jameson hints at paternalism in a colonial context. Basically, paternalism is responsible for the fact that the "dizzies" have been confined to the spaceship for a considerably long time;[316] unlike the human beings from Earth, they are not free to make their own decisions. It also leads to manipulation and exploitation, as I have stated above. In addition, the situation resembles paternalistic practices of the British in colonial India, for example. Numerous aspects reveal that indirect rule is a double-edged sword. In India, the British provided 'improving benefits' such as military defence, infrastructure, education and the abolition of cultural evils like *sati* (widow burning). However, the foundation of schools and colleges that propagated Western thinking stressed the superiority of European knowledge. The native dynasties remained, but they ruled under British supervision. The majority of the Indian engineers who constructed railways, bridges and canals were officers of the Royal Engineers, i.e. British military person-

[314] Turnball is a fictional character who, according to Fermour's account, lived / will live in the twenty-first century.
[315] Frederic Jameson, "Generic Discontinuities in SF: Brian Aldiss' *Starship*," in: *Science Fiction Studies* 1:2 (1973), 58.
[316] Cf. *ibid.*, 63.

nel. This form of "technocratic paternalism" implies that "[m]anaging the land and managing the labour went hand in hand."[317] Likewise, indirect rule was carried out in African and North American countries. Retrospectively, it becomes obvious that the imperial rulers were generally driven by their own political and material interests.

In contrast to real colonial subjects, the "dizzies'" attempts of resistance are scarce. Unlike in the other works discussed in this thesis, the subject race does not bond together to fight the oppressors; there is no independence movement in Aldiss' novel. The only individual who actively revolts against the scheming of the scientists is the priest, Marapper. His thirst for knowledge generates the first conceptual breakthrough (cf. *NS*, pp. 68ff.), and he wants to kill Fermour in a fit of rage (cf. *NS*, p. 235). The other members of the Greene tribe seem to be desperate, helpless and naïve; they do not try to improve their situation. The "dizzies" might even resemble children. The theory that savages are childlike was indeed widely discussed in Victorian England and people believed that "ontogeny recapitulates phylogeny".[318] Depicting the "dizzies" as children implies that they are intellectually inferior to the "Giants", and it might provide a justification for paternalistic practices.

To come back to the political notions of the experiment in Aldiss' novel, the manipulation of the "dizzies" raises ethical concerns about the intervention of 'civilized' into 'savage' cultures. Even though *Non-Stop* is a work of fiction, the debate has its source in history or, more specifically, "in the relations between industrialized and so-called underdeveloped societies of our own planet."[319] Since the Renaissance era, when the establishment of overseas colonies and trading posts led to encounters between the Europeans and indigenous peoples in remote countries, there have been various ways of intervention. They all had in common that the Europe-

---

[317] David Arnold, *The New Cambridge History of India. Science, Technology and Medicine in Colonial India, Vol. 3* (Cambridge *et al.*: Cambridge University Press, 2000), p. 119.

[318] Ernst Haeckel's (1834-1919) famous statement implies that evolution is replicated in the development from foetus to adulthood.

[319] Frederic Jameson, "Generic Discontinuities in SF: Brian Aldiss' *Starship*," 66.

ans saw it as their obligation to educate the 'savages'. Education according to Judeo-Christian standards was intended to improve the moral and intellectual faculties of the 'primitives' and consequently advance progress in the country. For instance, one way of intervention was to take 'savages' to Europe and teach them the Bible as well as Western lifestyle. The French philosopher Michel Eyquem de Montaigne (1533-1592) narrates an autobiographical anecdote in his essay "Des cannibales" ("On Cannibals", 1588). In 1562, the twelve-year old King Charles IX (1550-1574) was introduced to three members of the Brazilian Tupinamba tribe who were 'exhibited' at his court in Rouen and, after an interview, the two parties marvelled at each other's customs.[320] Columbus also brought several native Americans back to Spain in order to teach them Spanish and Catholic religion,[321] and Darwin presents a similar story in his *Journal of Researches* (1839): for the same reasons as Columbus, Captain Fitz Roy had taken three natives of Tierra del Fuego to England and brought them back to their country of origin after three years (cf. chapter 2.1).

Another way of intervention was to establish missionaries in the colonies and spread the Gospel among the natives. In Victorian England, the "white man's burden" was propagated by the Church and fixed in the popular imagination through adventure fiction such as Ballantyne's *The Coral Island*. The novel is informed with comments about the benefits of Christian missions in the South Sea. For instance, one of the castaway boys repeatedly exclaims: "God save the missionaries!"[322] as he thinks they suppress the natives' cruelty and thus render the islands safer for Europeans. Whenever natives are educated in English and acquainted with the Holy Scripture, their Otherness is perceived as less dangerous and objectionable. Naturally, this depiction is one-sided as it does not imply any discomfort about Christianization. Yet, in reality, spiri-

[320] Cf. Michel de Montaigne, *The Essays of Michael Lord of Montaigne*, translated by John Florio, available on: https://faculty.washington.edu/ellingsn/MntgCnbl.pdf (2011-03-27). The quintessence of Montaigne's essay, i.e. his concept of what 'barbarous' and 'savage' signify, is unusual for the sixteenth century and worth reading. However, the reliability of his accounts has often been questioned.

[321] Tzvetan Todorov, *The Conquest of America. The Question of the Other*, p. 43.

[322] Robert Michael Ballantyne, *The Coral Island*, p. 183.

tual education soon developed into material exploitation, as a letter from the Dominican friar Bartolomé de Las Casas (1484-1566) in Venezuela to the Spanish Crown exemplarily reveals:

> We declare ourselves ready to pacify them [the natives] and to reduce them to the service of our lord the king, and to convert them and instruct them in the knowledge of their Creator; after which we shall cause these populations to pay, each year, tributes and services to their Majesties, according to the possibilities granted them by their resources: all for the best advantage of the king of Spain and of these countries."[323]

Hence, the "white man's burden" is closely connected to financial interests, and the transition to politics is smooth.

Generally speaking, political intervention and development aid have positive and negative implications. It is undeniable that some development programmes of the Western world have been beneficial for people in other countries. Recently, the United Nations have intervened into various less developed countries. One reason for this was to stop ethnic tensions and genocide. In Chad and the Republic of Congo, for example, the political environment has become more stable. Intervention also took place after natural disasters such as the earthquakes in Haiti or the tsunamis in India and Japan. The UN rebuilt houses, schools and hospitals, secured vital structures (power and water supplies, policing bodies, *et cetera*) and provided food and healthcare for the locals. Moreover, we tend to believe that financial aid and business investment improve the quality of life for the indigenous population and accelerate progress in Third-World countries.

Nevertheless, in some cases political intervention is not only philanthropic. Frederic Jameson explains:

> The real questions – whether "progress" is desirable and if so which kind of progress, whether a country

[323] Bartolomé de Las Casas, "Letter to a Dignitary of the Court," 1535-10-15, quoted in: Tzvetan Todorov, *The Conquest of America. The Question of the Other*, p. 170.

> has the right to opt out of the international circuit, whether a more advanced country has the right to intervene, even benignly, in the historical evolution of a less advanced country; in sum, the general relationship between indigenous culture and industrialization – are historical and political in character.[324]

Especially when wars are fought over resources in formerly colonized countries (Iraq, Afghanistan, Nigeria, Angola), the historical and political nature of intervention is evident. What is more, foreign involvement might eventually destroy indigenous cultures. For instance in Renaissance Mesoamerica, seventy million natives were killed due to massacres, enslavement, inhumane labour conditions and diseases (notably smallpox and measles).[325] In addition, native religion, language and philosophy have perished due to the adoption of European customs, a phenomenon that is referred to as 'Westernization' or 'Occidentalization'. The loss of culture and customs is commonly considered negative. On the whole, though, the evaluation of intervention schemes and development aid is too complex to be discussed in its full scope here.

In Aldiss' novel, intervention into a 'lower' culture in the form of an experiment is depicted as ruthless and cruel. Complain's brother, Gregg, makes clear that life onboard the spaceship is like "going through hell" and "suffering […] tortures" (cf. *NS*, pp. 238f.). Complain adds that his people would "rather die there [on Earth] than live here [on board the ship]" (*NS*, p. 240). It is evident that they desperately want to be taken to Earth, and that they consider the "Giants" 'enlightened saviours' that can liberate them from the 'Dark Ages' of the ship. Hence, the loss of their culture or lifestyle is exactly what the "dizzies" desire; in terms of colonial politics, they demand assimilation instead of paternalism. This is impossible, though, since the "dizzies" are too 'alien' for life on Earth; due to the mutated proteins in their bodies they would not survive. Indeed, what humans do to the "dizzies" makes the reader think of animal experiments or maybe even stem cell research, i.e.

---

[324] Frederic Jameson, "Generic Discontinuities in SF: Brian Aldiss' *Starship*," 67.

[325] Cf. Tzvetan Todorov, *The Conquest of America. The Question of the Other*, pp. 133-142.

research that is highly debatable from an ethical point of view, and the reader receives the impression that the humans from Earth ought to feel guilt and shame for their exploitative means of gaining knowledge. The ending of the novel leaves the fate of the "dizzies" unknown. A swarm of moths activate the "Ultimate Emergency Stop", the ship breaks up, and each of the numerous decks floats into space, "buoyant as a cork in a fathomless sea" (cf. *NS*, p. 241).

To conclude, *Non-Stop* treats two different aspects of imperialism. First, the spaceship was originally designed to the take colonists to the Earth-Clone Procyon V. This scenario recalls settlement in the New World; the ship is replaced by a spaceship, new territories are on faraway planets, and indigenous peoples might bear parallels to extraterrestrials in science fiction. However, the project fails, and many humans die. Second, Aldiss' novel depicts intervention into a less civilized culture. The human beings from Earth, who study the development of a new race of man in a confined environment, observe the "dizzies" like ethnologists and exploit them for the acquisition of knowledge, which implies that the alien Other takes the role of the native – a major difference to the other novels discussed in this paper. Characterizing the inhabitants of the spaceship as 'savages' due to superstition, ignorance and cruelty emphasizes their Otherness, implies that they are inferior to Earthmen and serves as a justification for intervention. On a political level, the "Giants" rule the "dizzies" like colonial subjects in a paternalistic context.

The preface to the novel can be read as criticism of intervention. Aldiss states that "[a]n idea, which is man-conceived, unlike most of the myriad effects which comprise our universe, is seldom perfectly balanced. Instead, it bears the imprints of man's own frailty [...]" (*NS*, n. pag.). In addition, the preface reveals his concept of 'civilized' and 'primitive' since he asserts that "[a] community which cannot or will not realize how insignificant a part of the universe it occupies is not truly civilized" (*ibid.*). We might deduce that "community" refers to the "Giants" or mankind respectively. Hence, their 'playing God' in an exploitative experiment renders them 'uncivilized' like the "dizzies" and they ought to feel guilty for what they have done. Furthermore, due to the fact that they are technologically and intellectually superior to the inmates of the spaceship, they have a certain duty to improve the living-conditions onboard the ship, i.e. take full responsibility for their 'subjects'. Eventually, the humans from Earth fail in fulfilling their obligations.

3.3 Imperial Pop Stars: Gwyneth Jones, The *Aleutians* Trilogy

Gwyneth Jones (* February 14th, 1952, in Manchester, UK) is a British writer of science fiction and a feminist critic.[326] She has published more than twenty novels for children and young adults under the pseudonym Ann Halam. Jones' first novel was *Water in the Air* (1977). The *Inland* series, i.e. *The Daymaker* (1987), *Transformations* (1988) and *The Skybreaker* (1990), is considered the best among her works for young adults. It explores the tension between magic and observable reality in a far-future England. Apart from children's and juvenile literature, Jones has written about twenty adult science-fiction novels, some of which received notable rewards. For example, *Bold as Love* (2001) won the Arthur C. Clarke Award, and *Life* (2004) was awarded the Philip K. Dick Award. Most of Jones' adult works deal with sex and gender roles, and her depiction of aliens can be read as a trope for the construction of human identity. Gwyneth Jones also published two non-fiction titles, *Deconstructing the Starship: Science, Fiction and Reality* (1999) and *Imagination / Space* (2009).

The *Aleutians* trilogy consists of *White Queen* (1991), which won the James Tiptree Jr. Award, *North Wind* (1994) and *Phoenix Café* (1997). Altogether, the trilogy spans three hundred years, from the landing of the aliens on Earth in 2038 to their departure in 2338. The aliens are called "Aleutians" as they first appear on the eponymous island chain.[327] Interestingly, the narrative perspective of the novels constantly shifts: the story is told from the points of view of humans, aliens and hybrid creatures. This offers the reader a complex picture of both human and alien identity and society. Here, Jones illustrates that categories such as man-alien or male-female are not stable but *in flux*, a major *sujet* in her works. In fact,

---

326 For a detailed biography and full bibliography, see Mark Bould, "Gwyneth Jones: An Introduction," in: *FEMSPEC: An Interdisciplinary Feminist Journal Dedicated to Critical and Creative Work in the Realms of Science Fiction, Fantasy, Magical Realism, Surrealism, Myth, Folklore, and Other Supernatural Genres* 5:1 (2004): 190-196.

327 In this chapter, the name "Aleutians" refers to the aliens in the novels, not to the inhabitants of the Aleutian Islands.

various scholars have analyzed the treatment of identity – especially sexual identity – in the *Aleutians* trilogy.[328] In contrast to them, I intend to focus on postcolonial aspects since Gwyneth Jones deals with these issues in an original and interesting way. The three novels of the trilogy mirror the three phases of Aleutian colonization of Earth: *White Queen* narrates the first contact and the development of the invaders into a colonizing species, *North Wind* depicts the height of the Aleutian empire on Earth, and *Phoenix Café* deals with the decline of the empire and the departure of the aliens. Nevertheless, the novels will not be analyzed individually in this chapter. Instead, I am going to explore the following topics: the introduction of colonial rule, Earth under the rule of the Aleutians and disengagement of the colonizers from their subject race. Incidentally, Jones also published several short stories that feature the characters of the *Aleutians* trilogy. *The Buonarotti Quartet* (2009) contains four stories: "Saving Tiamaat", "The Fulcrum", "The Voyage Out" and "The Tomb Wife".[329] "Identifying the Object" (1990), "Blue Clay Blues" (1992), "The Universe of Things" (1993) and "Collision" (2009) are collected in *The Universe of Things* (2011).[330]

It generally seems that the Aleutians introduce colonial rule on Earth without ever having planned to do so. In the beginning of *White Queen*, the reader learns that they come from an unnamed planet with "blue suns", "tiny moons", "parklands", "cities", "protected wilderness", "climate control" and "no population problem," a world where "everyone was free to live exactly as they pleased;

---

[328] Cf. Sherryl Vint, "Why Have There Been No Great Women Scientists? Gender and Genetics in Gwyneth Jones's Life," in: *New York Review of Science Fiction* 22:2 (2009): 1, 8-13; Sherryl Vint, "Double Identity: Interpellation in Gwyneth Jones's Aleutian Trilogy," in: *Science Fiction Studies* 28:3 (2001): 399-425; Istvan Csicsery-Ronay, "The Lost Child: Notes on *White Queen*," in: *FEMSPEC: An Interdisciplinary Feminist Journal Dedicated to Critical and Creative Work in the Realms of Science Fiction, Fantasy, Magical Realism, Surrealism, Myth, Folklore, and Other Supernatural Genres* 5:1 (2004): 234-253.

[329] Cf. Gwyneth Jones, *The Buonarotti Quartet* (Seattle, WA: Aqueduct Press, 2009).

[330] Cf. Gwyneth Jones, *The Universe of Things* (Seattle, WA: Aqueduct Press, 2011).

and yet tenderly protected."[331] Despite this apparently utopian home planet, three to five million Aleutians live in a spaceship, the so-called "shipworld" (*NW*, p. 9), that travels through space with the aim of finding other habitable planets. When they accidentally approach Earth, nobody wants to land; they all want to go back home instead. Eventually, three Aleutian captains, Clavel, Rajath and Kumbva, decide to go to Earth within the context of a private expedition in order to establish trade relations with the 'natives'.[332] Nevertheless, even though the aliens land on Earth as private traders, there is no doubt that they are actually invaders. In her essay "Aliens in the Fourth Dimension" (2000), Gwyneth Jones makes clear that she intended to write an alien-invasion narrative:

> Colonial adventure has been a significant factor in the shaping of my own, European, twentieth-century, culture. I wanted to think about this topic. I wanted to study the truly extraordinary imbalance in wealth, power, and per capita human comfort, from the south to the north, that came into being over three hundred years or so of European rule in Africa, Asia and the Indian subcontinent: an imbalance which did not exist when the Portuguese reached China, when the first British and French trading posts were established on the coasts of India, when European explorers arrived in the gold-empire cities of West Africa.[333]

The central question is how the Aleutians mutate from shipwrecked traders into rulers of Earth. In the first novel of the trilogy, certain characteristics of a colonizing power are discernible or, put in another way, the Aleutians fulfil various prerequisites of colo-

---

[331] Gwyneth Jones, *White Queen* (London: VGSF, 1992), p. 68. All subsequent references to this edition are in brackets in the text.
[332] Cf. Gwyneth Jones, *Phoenix Café* (London: Vista, 1998), p. 48. All subsequent references to this edition are in brackets in the text.
[333] Gwyneth Jones, "Aliens in the Fourth Dimension," in: *Speaking Science Fiction. Dialogues and Interpretations*, ed. by Andy Sawyer (Liverpool: Liverpool University Press, 2000), 202. The essay is also available on Gwyneth Jones' homepage: http://homepage.ntlworld.com/gwynethann/ESSAYS.htm (2011-07-18).

nial domination. First, the reader receives the impression that the captains are fascinated with the idea of travel, exploration and the extension of trade networks. This is a parallel to the Europeans from the Renaissance onwards. The mere idea of discovering unknown territories and exotic peoples excited many scientists, mariners and the nobility. Discovery meant prestige, and it was almost always accompanied by material gain. Even the propagation of the Gospel among the 'savages' served this purpose. Accordingly, the three captains travel to faraway planets and explore the possibilities of making profit. Nevertheless, it is never specified whether the Aleutians prefer certain goods or money from Earth. Moreover, as they are able to create what they need from their own body cells,[334] it is questionable if they require terrestrial goods or capital anyway. This might be a slight flaw in the narrative.

Another distinct feature of colonialism is settlement, i.e. presence in the invaded territory. The Aleutians settle in a villa, called "Uji"[335], in Thailand. Their patron is a Japanese billionaire, Kaoru, who hosts them since he believes that the Aleutians are those aliens that saved some people from an earthquake in Japan, according to a legend (cf. *WQ*, p. 102). The Aleutians appear like 'superbeings' to him, similar to the Europeans and their 'miraculous' technology in the colonies. The people who dwell in the area accept Kaoru's hospitality as long as they are safe from alien contamination. Hence, they prevent contact by establishing a quarantine shield: "The valley was roofed over with the membrane the locals had agreed to accept as quarantine" (*NW*, p. 143). Basically, humans and aliens live next to each other without ever having any contact. It is striking that the Aleutians live in the luxurious mansion of a billionaire, whereas the local Thai population dwells in much simpler houses, as we can assume. This characterizes the aliens as superior beings, and it might remind the reader of plantation owners in nineteenth-century Africa or South America, for example. To conclude, Kaoru paves the way for permanent settlement of the Aleutians on Earth and contributes to their superior position. With

---

[334] Cf. Gwyneth Jones, *North Wind* (London: Vista, 1998), p. 235. All subsequent references to this edition are in brackets in the text.

[335] Uji is a city near Kyoto in Japan. The Japanese owner of the villa might have called the place "Uji" in remembrance of his former home town.

regard to the future, the Aleutians are sure that "[e]ventually, all of earth will be like the Uji valley" (*NW*, p. 253).

Uji also becomes the first Aleutian trading post on the planet. As stated before, the landing party consists of "private adventurers" taking part in a "marginal" expedition (*WQ*, p. 139), whose objective is "planetfall and plunder" (*WQ*, p. 213). Consequently, their reason for the invasion of Earth is clearly an economic one; the aliens are not interested in studying human biology, culture or society. Moreover, "plunder" sounds reckless and greedy, as if the aliens intend to take what they can get, no matter if there is a fair or legal basis. They seem to have a 'seek-and-destroy' attitude in a commercial context. This theory is corroborated by one of the Aleutians, Rajath. While talking to his band about how to make profit on Earth, he suggests cheating the natives:

> <[…] We have generated some excitement, people will pay extra to buy what we have owned. We have only to trade our goods for land, wait, sell; and take our profit home along with enough curios to dine out on for a lifetime.>[336] (*WQ*, p. 91)

This requires a superior status of the aliens: Rajath assumes that the people will buy what belonged to the Aleutians for ideological reasons, like religious devotional objects. In fact, his strategy implies manipulation and exploitation. However, as the aliens hold that "time is cheap" (*ibid.*) due to their concept of reincarnation, they do not immediately start trading. Therefore, people remain ignorant about Aleutian goods. Rumours spread about "exciting waste-disposal techniques, genetic material for superefficient food plants" (*WQ*, p. 100), which illustrates that the humans consider Aleutian technology far advanced, but they actually do not know. It is only in the second novel of the trilogy that some products are mentioned. For example, the Aleutians launch "water tablets", "cleeno" (antibacterial cloth), miniature animals as toys and

---

[336] The Aleutians communicate non-verbally, in the so-called "Common Tongue" (cf. *WQ*, p. 56). Their silent dialogues are printed in triangular brackets (< and >) in the novels. In my quotations, I keep this notation in order to indicate statements in the Common Tongue.

"shado" (heat-absorbing material) on the terrestrial market (cf. *NW*, pp. 96-99).

Ironically, there is no discernible purpose for any sort of trade relationship, though: the Aleutians seem to desire profit for profit's sake. As stated above, the aliens can effortlessly produce whatever they require from their body cells. What they cannot 'grow' themselves is "dead" and eerie to them (cf. *PC*, p. 37). Hence, it is questionable if the Aleutians need money or goods from Earth. Furthermore, trade relationships with aliens from other planets are never mentioned. Thus, their depiction differs crucially from the one of the nuls in Brian W. Aldiss' *The Interpreter* (cf. chapter 1.1). The Aleutians' apparently purposeless interest in profit might criticize consumer society or, on a more abstract level, human nature: people are driven by the idea to accumulate wealth and property although they already have everything they need in life. In a colonial context, the greed of the Aleutians – their mission of "planetfall and plunder" – reflects the attitude of colonial rulers in history.

The third prerequisite of colonial domination that the Aleutians fulfil is superiority over the natives. This is generated through their technology as well as through their status as 'angelic superbeings' or even saviours of mankind. As to Aleutian technology, the aliens possess "insectoid flyers" (*NW*, p. 264) that enable them to travel in space and land on other planets. In contrast to the xenobaths in John Wyndham's *The Kraken Wakes* (cf. chapter 3.1) and to the Masters in John Christopher's *Tripods* trilogy (cf. chapter 1.2), the Aleutians do not require any technology that adjusts terrestrial pressure and atmosphere to their biological needs. The microorganisms and devices they introduce, for instance water-purification bacteria (cf. *WQ*, p. 254), "stone-devouring commensals" (*NW*, p. 267) and the pipelines they build on Earth (cf. *NW*, p. 14), appear miraculous to human scientists:

> [...] Aleutian gadgets were the symbol of Aleutia's presence. Their function could be identified through human analogy: camcorder, computer, food processor, musical instrument. But nobody had any idea how they worked. (*WQ*, p. 254)

Thus, human beings cannot understand, let alone copy, the technology of the Aleutians, which consolidates the dominant position of the aliens. Just like in historical colonial encounters, it highlights the inequality in power between the natives and the invaders.

The depiction of the aliens usually plays a crucial role in the establishment of their position as rulers of Earth. This is the case in various works of alien-encounter science fiction, for instance in the *Tripods* trilogy or in *The Interpreter*. However, the Aleutians are not depicted as truly superior to man. Their portrayal evades clear-cut categories. Instead, it is made up of two main antitheses: alien and humanoid as well as atavistic and 'superhuman'. As to the first pair of binary opposites, there are certain features that constitute the Aleutians' alienness or Otherness. Due to their slender bodies (cf. *WQ*, p. 52), greyish or pale skin colour (cf. *WQ*, p. 51), dark eyes and the lack of eyebrows and noses (cf. *WQ*, pp. 111, 52), the Aleutians resemble the greys, a common trope in science-fiction literature and films.[337] This image generally evokes fear as the greys are implemented in popular imagination as aliens that abduct human beings, take them to their spaceships and perform medical experiments.[338] Moreover, the knees of the Aleutians are reversed (cf. *WQ*, p. 19) and they sometimes run on all fours (cf. *NW*, p. 41).

---

[337] In Herbert G. Wells' *The First Men in the Moon* (1901), the Selenites – native inhabitants of the Moon – are greys. Cf. Herbert G. Wells, *The First Men in the Moon* (Rockville, MD: Arc Manor, 2008). Examples in films are *Close Encounter of the Third Kind* (USA 1977, directed by Steven Spielberg), *Communion* (UK and USA 1989, directed by Philippe Mora), *Intruders* (USA 1992, directed by Dan Curtis) and *Fire in the Sky* (USA 1993, directed by Robert Lieberman). Nevertheless, more recent science-fiction films do not portray this type of alien any more.

[338] Every year, thousands of individuals claim that they spotted UFOs or were abducted by aliens. The cases can be reported to the National UFO Reporting Centre, an independent organization in Davenport, Washington. Cf. http://www.nuforc.org/ (2011-09-03). Furthermore, the SETI (Search for Extra-Terrestrial Intelligence) Institute, that used to be funded by the NASA, searches for evidence of life in the universe. Their way of spotting signals is taken up in Hollywood movies such as *Contact* (USA 1997, directed by Robert Zemeckis). Cf. http://www.seti.org/page.aspx? pid=584 (2011-09-20).

Another feature that distinguishes them from humans is that they are hermaphrodites (cf. *NW*, p. 17).[339]

Perhaps the most striking feature of the Aleutians' Otherness is the so-called "wanderers", particles secreted from glands that carry a 'biochemical cocktail' of information about the individual. The wanderers are a crucial part of Aleutian social interaction:

> Those louse-like red bugs are cell colonies which are *sentient*, in that they replicate not only the individual's whole genetic identity, but also his current emotional status, his current skills: his whole life-status, condensed into chemical signals. (*NW*, p. 92, italics by G. Jones)

The aliens exchange wanderers by eating them (cf. *WQ*, p. 86) and during sexual intercourse. To conclude, the physical appearance and the conscious biochemical interaction of the Aleutians are alien characteristics. Yet, these features appear random since the alienness of the Aleutians is already constituted by their non-terrestrial origin.

What is more interesting is that the Aleutians are simultaneously characterized as humanoid. Clementina Steward, a scientist from Earth, carries out research on alien DNA, or "aDNA". Her results have two implications: she detects astonishing similarities to human DNA (cf. *PC*, p. 129) and makes clear that aDNA is more advanced. The latter thesis is based on the observation that the cells of the aliens are "mobile factories" that can develop into

---

[339] More than twenty years before the publication of Jones' trilogy, the US-American author Ursula Le Guin explored a post-gender society in *The Left Hand of Darkness* (1969). Apart form the fact that both the Aleutians and the Gethenians in Le Guin's novel are hermaphrodites, there are various similarities between two alien species. For instance, both species are humanoid, less aggressive and less technically orientated. Furthermore, both challenge the sex/gender system of man as well as the Self/Other dichotomy (cf. Ursula Le K. Guin, *The Left Hand of Darkness* [London: Hachette Digital, 1969]). For a detailed comparison of the works, see Wendy Gay Pearson, "Postcolonialism/s, Gender/s, Sexuality/ies and the Legacy of *The Left Hand of Darkness*: Gwyneth Jones's Aleutians Talk Back," in: *The Yearbook of English Studies* 37:2, Science Fiction (2007), 182-196.

anything, for instance tools or food (cf. *WQ*, p. 164). Furthermore, some of the aliens on Earth behave strikingly human. One of them is the poet and captain of the landing party, Clavel. Clavel feels passion and falls in love with Johnny Guglioli. Johnny is sexually attracted to Clavel, who he thinks is a young woman. This shows that he does not perceive the aliens as of a different species; Clavel is different but not alien. Accordingly, Catherine, the protagonist of *Phoenix Café* and a hybrid creature of human and Aleutian, exclaims: "How little divides us" (*PC*, p. 291).

The depiction of humanoid aliens generally has various effects. First, it influences our reception of the novels: the reader can create distance, empathy and sympathy vis-à-vis the aliens. The Aleutians are not incomprehensible or monstrous (like the xenobaths or the Masters in their tripods), and they do not evoke repulsion. Instead, the Aleutians might bear similarities to the attractive André in the *Andromeda* novels (cf. chapter 2.2). Hence, humanoid aliens challenge the stability of the two, strictly separate, categories 'Self' and 'Other' since the boundaries between them are permeable. This is a contrast to the depictions of colonial encounters in nineteenth-century literature, in which the relationship between the European colonizer (Self) and the subject race (Other) is almost always clear-cut. The white man is usually civilized, dominant and active, whereas the native is savage, childlike and passive.[340] The idea that the boundaries are permeable, i.e. that there is a 'common humanity' between the European and the 'savage' is not original, though. In fact, it recalls the insights of Marlow, a riverboat captain in the Congo, in Joseph Conrad's *Heart of Darkness* (1899). Marlow's idea of a 'common humanity' with the Congolese natives can be read as man's terror of the disintegration of boundaries between human and alien:

> No, they were not inhuman. Well, you know, that was the worst of it – this suspicion of their not being inhu-

[340] Naturally, there are exceptions to this rather simple opposition. Apart from Joseph Conrad's *Heart of Darkness*, which will be further elaborated on, an exception can be found in Sir Henry Rider Haggard's *King Solomon's Mines* (1885), in which a black African, Umbopa, has noble and gentlemanly qualities. Cf. Henry Rider Haggard, *King Solomon's Mines*.

> man. It would come slowly to one. They howled and leaped, and spun, and made horrid faces; but what thrilled you was just the thought of their humanity – like yours – the thought of your remote kinship with this wild and passionate uproar. Ugly. Yes, it was ugly enough […].[341]

The question is which feelings the disintegration of the boundaries between Self and Other evokes. Marlow considers this entirely negative, or "ugly" respectively.

Analogously, most of the human beings in Gwyneth Jones' trilogy are terrified of the similarities between themselves and the aliens. However, the trilogy also offers a different view with regard to a 'common humanity' of humans and Aleutians, a view that undermines Marlow's fears in Conrad's novella. Ellen Kershaw, spokesperson of the fake "government of the world" that deals with alien affairs, considers the possibility of co-existence with the Aleutians on Earth: "The two races might be good for each other, in the long run. Some kind of fruitful union might be achieved" (*WQ*, p. 310). Moreover, the relationship between Earth and Aleutia is referred to as an "unconsummated wedding, the irremediable almost-matching of two worlds" (*ibid.*) and as "just out of sync" (*WQ*, p. 309). This signifies that their relationship is something unfinished, something that requires a further step. It also sounds tragic that the two worlds do not really match even though "[h]umans and aliens [are] so alike" (*ibid.*). If the two parties overcome their problem of being "out of sync", there is the possibility of co-existence. Yet, Ellen Kershaw evidently ignores the fact that the Aleutians are about to become rulers of Earth.

Apart from the alien-humanoid dichotomy, there is another antithesis that generates an ambiguous portrayal of the aliens: they are simultaneously perceived as 'savages' and 'superbeings'. Basically, the Aleutians share several characteristics with a subject race. Throughout the novel, they are frequently referred to as "baboons" (*WQ*, pp. 97, 111, 115, 170; *NW*, pp. 15, 33). On the one hand, this is due to their outward appearance: they have dark eyes,

---

[341] Joseph Conrad, *Heart of Darkness & Other Stories*, pp. 63f.

wide nostrils and claws (cf. *WQ*, pp. 54, 170). On the other hand, they seem to be in between Nature and culture, just like anthropoid apes that resemble man in many ways: "The Aleutians were like animals, animals who had attained civilization still possessing and developing all their animal traits" (*PC*, pp. 16f.). This depiction characterizes the Aleutians as 'savages' or the 'primitive race' in colonial encounters.[342] Furthermore, they sing, make music and dance in the evenings (cf. *NW*, p. 29). The aliens also spend the nights as a group. They nap and chat in the hall of their accommodation, and it would be unusual for them to seek privacy (cf. *ibid.*). In fact, pastime activities such as singing and dancing, as well as the big number of 'family members' living together under one roof, are stereotypical characteristics associated with so-called 'primitive' cultures. Another trait that reminds the reader of 'savages' is the Aleutians' fear of the "deadworld": "[T]hings that are intrinsically not alive – like electrons, photons, the image in a mirror or on a screen, they consider uncanny…."[343] For instance, they avoid human communication technology since the lifeless images on the computer screens are like "a blasphemy, an offence against reason and religion" (*PC*, p. 37) to them, which might recall the 'taboo religion' of exotic peoples depicted in travel and adventure literature such as Herman Melville's *Typee: A Peep at Polynesian Life* (1846) – albeit the idea of a 'taboo religion' seems to be a cliché.

Some people, however, perceive the Aleutians as 'angelic superbeings', i.e. a superior race (cf. *WQ*, pp. 99, 175; *PC*, p. 159). On the one hand, the aliens actually do 'miraculous' deeds on Earth. First, their biotechnology gives them a godlike quality: "They were the lords of life" (*PC*, p. 37). Second, the Aleutians suppress the Gender Wars on Earth since their "influence kept the reformers and the traditionalists – the 'Women' and the 'Men' –

---

[342] For example, Charles Darwin likens the natives of Tierra del Fuego to animals, and John Lubbock compares 'savages' in general to fearful antelopes. Cf. Charles Darwin, *The Voyage of the Beagle. Journal of Researches into the Natural History and Geology of the Countries Visited during the Voyage of HMS Beagle round the World, under the Command of Captain Fitz Roy, RN.*, p. 204, and John Lubbock, *Pre-Historic Times as Illustrated by Ancient Remains and the Manners and Customs of Modern Savages*, p. 595.

[343] Gwyneth Jones, "Aliens in the Fourth Dimension," 207.

living in reasonable harmony" (*NW*, p. 24). Therefore, even though Earth has not transformed into a utopia after the arrival of the aliens, they mitigate violence. Unfortunately, it is never revealed in what way they achieve that. On the other hand, though, their superior status is based on numerous misconceptions produced by the fact that the people see the Aleutians 'through human eyes'. Perhaps they even assume superpowers when confronted with alien intelligence. For example, people think that the Aleutians are mind-reading telepaths (cf. *NW*, p. 57). This idea develops in popular imagination since the Aleutians communicate in their Common Tongue, "the silent language of their expression and gesture" (*NW*, p. 10). What is more, some think the Aleutians are immortal, an idea triggered by the aliens' concept of reincarnation. In fact, the Aleutians believe in the reincarnation of the personality, i.e. individuals are reborn and "taught to 'become themselves' psychologically by intense study of records of 'their' previous lives" (*WQ*, p. 259). Consequently, the aliens are not immortal in the way that they do not die.

The Aleutians are not the saviours of man, either. Johnny Guglioli, who suffers from HQ (a virus much like HIV), is sure that Clavel can heal him and end his miserable isolation in quarantine, whereas the alien believes that Johnny is in love with 'her'. What follows is a rape scenario, or a "ludicrous social error":

> The alien didn't know what he meant, or didn't care. It descended on him. He tried to scream. He could not. [...] Stark horror! This was how it was always going to end. The faith so close to fear, wonder so close to terror, betrayed him utterly: stripped him, robbed him and flung him out, meaningless, into a bursting vacuum. (*WQ*, pp. 193f.)

This incident, which becomes legendary in the Aleutian records, is generated through misconceptions of the Other. Clavel is perceived as some sort of miracle healer, either comparable to the witch doctors in 'primitive cultures' or like a magical or divine creature. Furthermore, sexual intercourse between man and alien is a transgression of boundaries between Self and Other, which is similar to concepts of racial miscegenation.

In science fiction, sexual intercourse between humans and aliens is a popular topic that ranges from serious problem awareness and criticism of sexual prejudices in our society to pornographic science fiction with either cheesy erotic contents or images that link sexuality with violence and disgust.[344] The question arises how Gwyneth Jones' novels evaluate miscegenation. Basically, the transgression of boundaries between Self and Other is depicted as positive from the point of view of the alien (Clavel loves Johnny) and as negative from Johnny's side. This is due to the fact that Johnny is a rape victim, i.e. the alien takes the dominant position and enforces sexual intercourse. Johnny is the inferior, passive human, much like the traditional subject races. Moreover, he perceives the incident as repulsive and even as dangerous since he feels infested with alien wanderers: "The bugs. They were all over me" (*WQ*, p. 199). Passing on microorganisms might allude to sexually transmitted infections such as AIDS, chlamydia or syphilis. As a consequence, we receive the impression that miscegenation can only be produced by a terrible misunderstanding and should be avoided. In contrast to the human point of view, the alien accepts and desires the 'fusion' of Self and Other. Clavel seems to believe that there is the possibility for man and alien to become lovers. On a more abstract level, Clavel might see a chance for peaceful co-existence of man and aliens on Earth.

Another misunderstanding that makes the aliens appear superior to man concerns faster-than-light (ftl) travel. When Johnny interviews Clavel about the home planet of the Aleutians, the alien is "evasive" in 'her' answers (*WQ*, p. 69). Finally, Clavel states that "[n]o one could possibly see it [the planet] from here" (*ibid.*). Therefore, Johnny deduces that the Aleutians must have travelled through space faster than light, which implies that their intelligence and technology are far advanced: "It was a truism that the aliens who landed, whoever they were, *had to be superior*. Or else we'd be visiting them" (*ibid.*, italics by G. Jones). In fact, advanced alien intelligence and 'miraculous' technology serve as tools of superior-

344 Cf. John Clute and Peter Nicholls (eds.), *The Encyclopedia of Science Fiction*, s.v. 'sex'.

ity and dominance. Braemer Wilson (one of the members of the resistance movement "White Queen"), however, understands that the Aleutians manipulate the people on Earth, just like in historical encounters between the 'civilized' Europeans and the 'savages'. The former lured and impressed the latter with technical gadgets such as firearms and thereby constructed authority. Accordingly, the Aleutians are considered superior as long as the humans believe the aliens can travel ftl. Nevertheless, Clavel offers no proof and Braemer is sceptic. If the Aliens did not travel to Earth from a faraway planet, the question is where the landing parties come from. Braemer has her own theory about the origin of the Aleutians, and it proves to be true in the course of the trilogy: the aliens inhabit a multigenerational spaceship located somewhere near Earth (cf. *ibid.*). This idea recalls Brian Aldiss' *Non-Stop* (cf. chapter 3.2) and, with Aldiss' novel in mind, the Aleutians might be considered 'primitive' peoples incarcerated in their ship. Thus, Braemer's theory evokes a shift of status: as the Aleutians do not possess any ftl travel devices, they are not necessarily superior to mankind. However, few people on Earth share Braemer's theory; they take it for granted that the aliens have developed highly advanced methods of transport (cf. *WQ*, p. 69).

To sum up, the depiction of the Aleutians is ambiguous: they resemble humans while they are simultaneously Other, and they are considered 'savages' and 'superbeings' at the same time. To a certain extent, the latter trait derives from misconceptions. Basically, the aliens in Jones' novels are "baboons in imperial robes" (cf. *NW*, p. 214; *PC*, p. 53), a trope that suggests a blend of colonizer and colonized. As the author explains in her essay, the Aleutians are equipped with "the characteristics, all the supposed deficiencies, that Europeans came to see in their subject races in darkest Africa and the mysterious East […]."[345] This time, however, the subject race is about to take over Earth.

The prerequisites of colonial rule that I have described so far, i.e. the desire to explore unknown territories, settlement in the invaded area and a somewhat superior position over the indigenous population, characterize what might be called the pre-colonization

[345] Gwyneth Jones, "Aliens in the Fourth Dimension," 203.

period. At this stage of the plot, the ambiguous relationship between humans and aliens leads to uncertainty: mankind oscillates between revolt against alien authority and deliberate submission. The people split into Aleutian-lovers and anti-Aleutians. As a next step, Aleutian colonial rule must be introduced and consolidated, which requires further aspects: the superiority of the aliens must be fully accepted, and the Aleutians need to maintain their dominant position on Earth.

In order to establish power, the Aleutians mock honesty and benevolence. In a video message to human officials, they stage a 'second first encounter' and stand in front of the camera naked (cf. *WQ*, p. 143). As the Aleutians have come to Earth for economic reasons, we can assume that they try to manipulate mankind again. Eventually, the revelation of the 'naked truth' is successful; the politicians trust them and everybody believes in "[o]ne world" (*WQ*, p. 145). What follows this rather ridiculous scene is that the aliens become some sort of pop stars; they go on tours around the world and people celebrate them:

> The baboon faces were everywhere [...]. Since they'd decided against blowing the world away they'd become fantastically famous. They were more respected than the chairman of Du Pont, more popular than the most adored Balkan royalty. A startling number of global tvsponders not only believed that earth would be under alien rule within five years, but also felt this was a good thing. Negotiations over a modified version of the famous 'real estate deal' continued. The visitors were staying. (*WQ*, p. 170)

The reader also learns that many people send them presents (cf. *WQ*, p. 181) and, above all, that the Aleutians visit the Queen of England (cf. *WQ*, p. 64). Thus, the aliens finally consolidate their superior status by gaining trust and admiration. The people on Earth actually want them to stay and rule the planet. Since the Aleutians pretend benevolence but do not improve the living-conditions for man, the *Aleutians* trilogy has been called a revisionist version of Arthur C. Clarke' *Childhood's End* (cf. chapter 2.1).[346]

Naturally, a colonizer that resembles the colonized in so many ways has to maintain the dominant position. Hence, the struggle for superiority is generated through similarities, not differences. The *alter ego* of the Aleutians is the resistance group, "White Queen", that gives the first novel its title. Actually, the White Queen is a character in *Through the Looking-Glass, and What Alice Found There* (1871) by Lewis Carroll (Charles Lutwidge Dodgson, 1832-1898). The White Queen in Carroll's work lives backwards in time,[347] and we can assume that the insurgents would like to go back in time as well, i.e. live before the arrival of the aliens. In Jones' trilogy, the resistance group started off as avatars in a virtual fantasy game and has developed into a real movement (cf. *WQ*, p. 220). Braemer Wilson is one of their founding members. Their aim is to debunk the Aleutians and, thereby, to destroy their status as 'superbeings'. They intend to "convince the world that there was something bad, dirty, evil lurking up there at Uji" (*WQ*, p. 159). First of all, Braemer steals an alien wanderer. Research shows that the Aleutians resemble man, as I have elaborated on before (cf. *WQ*, pp. 178f.). Moreover, White Queen are sure that the aliens live in a spaceship near Earth and decide to sabotage it. According to their plan, this would undermine the 'angelic' connotation of the Aleutians (cf. *WQ*, p. 280). Hence, Braemer convinces Johnny to accompany her to the so-called "Aleutian shipworld" (*NW*, p. 9), and the couple travels by Peenemünde Buonarotti's ftl device. After having landed in the shipworld, Braemer tries to destroy its source of energy, and the deed is made public through video recordings (cf. *WQ*, pp. 287ff.). Sabotage of the infrastructure built by the colonizer also happened in colonial history, of course. For example in India, Ireland and Egypt, guerrillas selected railways and telegraph systems as targets for anti-British attacks.

---

[346] Cf. Sherryl Vint, "Double Identity: Interpellation in Gwyneth Jones's Aleutian Trilogy," 424n20.

[347] Cf. Lewis Carroll, *Alice's Adventures in Wonderland &Through the Looking-Glass and What Alice Found There*, illustrated by John Tenniel, with an Afterword by Anna South (New York, NY: Barnes & Noble, 2004), p. 193.

It is debatable if the sabotage act of White Queen mitigates the Aleutians' superiority over mankind. On the one hand, it threatens their dominant position since human beings find out that the aliens are not the ones that have developed ftl travel – a major feature of their 'miraculous' technology. In fact, this means of transport was invented on Earth. Additionally, the aliens execute Johnny for having exposed them to the media (cf. *WQ*, pp. 300f.), which is a rather harsh punishment and which does not imply any benevolence. Yet, on the other hand, the Aleutians still have many admirers on Earth. The government is on their side, too (cf. *WQ*, p. 289). Among the general public, many start imitating the Aleutians, a theme that is treated in *North Wind* and *Phoenix Café*. To conclude, human resistance is not depicted as noble and entirely positive in Jones' trilogy and, more importantly, it does not deprive the aliens of their superior status. This is a major difference to other works of alien-encounter science fiction. Finally, we learn that the attack in the shipworld impairs the reputation of White Queen. Braemer eventually leaves the group and, at the age of sixty-six, she dies of lung cancer in a hospital in England (cf. *WQ*, p. 303).

One hundred years after the first contact, the Aleutians have permanently settled on Earth, as the reader learns in *North Wind*. What is striking is that the aliens do not exercise power or exploit mankind despite their role as colonizers. Instead, they have established eleven trading posts on the planet (cf. *NW*, p. 9). One of them is in "Mykini", or Mycenae, in Greece. The locals have been relocated to make space for the Aleutian city which is separated from the world around "under a hemisphere of antibiotic and carbon-strengthened glass" (*NW*, p. 26). By choosing Mycenae as one of their trading posts, the Aleutians take over a major site of human history and culture. The Mycenaean culture was one of the first advanced civilizations on the Greek mainland. Around 1600 BC, Mycenae dominated large parts of southern Greece, and the military stronghold displayed immense wealth. In addition, the Lion Gate of the citadel is considered the oldest monumental structures in Europe, and various Greek legends are set in the city.[348] Furthermore, it becomes evident that the Aleutians live like rich peo-

[348] For photographs and more information on Mycenae, see http://www.britannica.com/ EBchecked/topic/400227/Mycenae (2011-08-26).

ple in the trading post. Together with their servants, they dwell in an elegant hotel (cf. *NW*, p. 29).

The behaviour of the Aleutians generates an ambiguous relationship with human beings. Some are hostile towards the aliens, others admire and imitate them in a way that an alienation from their original culture takes place. The local soldiers in Mycenae are against the Aleutian settlement for various reasons: the natives have lost their homes due to the relocation programmes, there is no contact, let alone communication, between the aliens and their neighbours (cf. *NW*, p. 20) and the people harshly criticize the Aleutian terraforming plans (the aliens make use of their "heavy-duty rock-munching microbes to level the peaks of the Himalaya ranges, thereby bringing refreshment to the climate of the subcontinent", *NW*, p. 24). Thus, the Aleutians cause tension and distrust. The local soldiers eventually destroy the trading post; they burn down the hotel and kill the aliens. Only one of them, Bella, and the human interpreter, Sidney Carton,[349] can escape (cf. *NW*, pp. 42ff.).

On a global scale, anti-Aleutian feelings manifest themselves in the "Great Quarantine": North and South America, called the "USSA" (United Socialist States of America) in the trilogy, are entirely closed to alien settlements:

> Americans had torn up their undersea cables, set a defence shield around their coasts, jammed satellite signals and refused to recognize the existence of the alien-ruled world. Presumably there was some covert human contact, since such barriers are never totally impermeable, but the Aleutians had been completely shut out. (*PC*, p. 36)

The Great Quarantine splits the planet in halves, one half under alien control and the other half independent from the extraterrestri-

[349] In Charles Dickens' *A Tale of Two Cities* (1859), Sydney Carton is a drunkard who wastes his life until he meets Lucie Manette. He then promises to change in order to make her happy. Cf. Charles Dickens, *A Tale of Two Cities*, edited with an introduction and notes by Richard Maxwell (London *et al.*: Penguin Books, 2003). In *North Wind*, Sid saves Bella and falls in love with her.

als. What is more, the Americas are socialist (cf. *ibid.*), i.e. their economic system "calls for public rather than private ownership or control of property and natural resources."[350] This is a contrast to the Aleutian doctrine. The aliens are traders who have established settlements for economic purposes. Hence, they do not work for the good of the community but trade for their own profit. The USSA consider themselves further developed than the rest of the world, which results in a ban of Aleutian influence.

There are, however, people who have a high regard for the Aleutians. In fact, they admire them in a way that they have become estranged from human culture. Those human beings who imitate the aliens are referred to as "halfcastes" (*NW*, p. 18) or "looty-lovers" (*NW*, p. 87). The term 'halfcastes' clearly has a racist overtone, albeit the halfcastes in Jones' trilogy "are a cultural rather than biological miscegenation."[351] Generally speaking, they attempt to leave their human physique and culture behind in order to be similar to the Aleutians. For instance, they have their noses and genitalia removed surgically, and they study records – or TV programmes – to find their own identity (cf. *NW*, p. 18). Just like Sidney Carton, his wife and children are halfcastes. In the novel, their depiction evokes pity and a lack of comprehension. Basically, the family consists of freaks, and their "stupid *muddle*" (*ibid.*, italics by G. Jones) of human and alien culture appears ridiculous to the reader. The halfcastes are like a joke, i.e. not to be taken seriously.

Since they escape clear-cut categories such as male/female or human/alien, the looty-lovers frequently become victims of discrimination and violence. Sherryl Vint argues that the establishment of boundaries between Self and Other is crucial for a sub-

---

[350] http://www.britannica.com/EBchecked/topic/551569/socialism (2011-08-26).

[351] Sherryl Vint, "Double Identity: Interpellation in Gwyneth Jones's Aleutian Trilogy," 407. Incidentally, the trilogy also features characters that are products of biological miscegenation: in *North Wind*, Bella is an Aleutian engineered from human tissue (cf. *NW*, p. 241) and Catherine in *Phoenix Café* is the reincarnation of the alien Clavel. The Aleutian embryo was re-engineered as a human female and implanted into the womb of a woman (cf. *PC*, p. 212). It is striking that these hybrid creatures are the protagonists of the novels. This might be due to the idea that the reader can sympathize with aliens and humans alike when the story centres around a 'neutral' being.

ject's identity formation and for the acceptance of the subject in society:

> Those subjects that occupy a border space between categories (be they categories of race, gender or sexuality) are not "really" subjects at all because they do not occupy *culturally intelligible* subject positions. In order to maintain coherence, the subject must disavow any continuity between itself and its constructed others, those subjects that represent the boundary of the subject's definition. The subject's "belief" that this boundary is necessary to its existence is what underlies the anxiety and aggression that can emerge when this boundary is challenged by the existence of subjects who don't "fit" into a predefined category.[352]

Thus, by imitating the aliens, the halfcastes are in between their culture and the one of the Other. This implies that those who do not accept them deprive them of their status of self-determined subjects. Their opponents, the "purebreds", persecute and burn the halfcastes in the streets (cf. *NW*, p. 85). These hate crimes recall racist violence, i.e. the halfcastes take the roles of Blacks in the USA, for example. Without the aliens, the halfcastes would lose their sense in life. In this case, being a looty-lover seems to be a futuristic religion, comparable to a sect. Consequently, the halfcastes have been alienated from their original beliefs under the influence of the extraterrestrial colonizers.

The imitation of the colonial power by its subject race is the *sujet* of Homi Bhabha's essay "Of Mimicry and Man: The Ambivalence of Colonial Discourse" (1984).[353] 'Mimicry' signifies 'copying' or 'closely imitating'. In a colonial context, the subject race imitates the colonial power. Incidentally, the process of 'going native' would then be the inversion of colonial mimicry. In his essay, Bhabha holds that a colonial subject can never fully resem-

---

[352] *Ibid.*, italics by S. Vint.

[353] Homi Bhabha, "Of Mimicry and Man: The Ambivalence of Colonial Discourse," in: *October. Discipleship: A Special Issue on Psychoanalysis* 28 (1984): 125-133.

ble the colonizer despite the efforts to copy the latter, i.e. there is a crucial difference between "being English and being Anglicized".[354] Therefore, the colonizer and its colonial subjects are "almost the same, *but not quite*."[355] Subsequently, Bhabha points out the ambiguous effects of colonial mimicry. On the one hand, the "mimic men" can easily be governed by the colonial power as they are educated by the latter. Examples are the "reformed" colonial subjects or "interpreters" in Thomas B. Macaulay's "Minute on Education" (1835): these "interpreters" are "a class of persons Indian in blood and colour, but English in tastes, in opinions, in morals and in intellect,"[356] and therefore considered "appropriate" colonial subjects. According to Bhabha, they can be found in literature as well, for instance in the works of Kipling, Forester, Orwell, Naipaul and Anderson.[357] On the other hand, though, these "authorized versions of otherness" are simultaneously "inappropriate" colonial subjects that threaten the colonial enterprise:

> The *menace* of colonial mimicry is its double vision which in disclosing the ambivalence of colonial discourse also disrupts its authority. And it is a *double* vision that is a result of what I've described as the partial representation/recognition of the colonial object. Grant's colonial as partial imitator, Macaulay's translator, Naipaul's colonial politician as play-actor, Decoud as the scene-setter of the *opéra bouffe* of the New World, these are the appropriate objects of a chain of command, authorized versions of otherness. But they are also, as I have shown, the figures of a doubling, the part-objects of a metonymy of colonial desire which alienates the modality and normality of those dominant discourses in which they emerge as 'inappropriate' colonial subjects.[358]

---

[354] *Ibid.*, 130.
[355] *Ibid.*, 127, italics by H. Bhabha.
[356] Thomas B. Macaulay, "Minute on Education," quoted in Bhabha (1984), 128.
[357] Cf. Homi Bhabha, "Of Mimicry and Man: The Ambivalence of Colonial Discourse," 128.
[358] *Ibid.*, 129, italics by H. Bhabha.

Since he talks about a "metonymy of colonial desire", Bhabha makes clear that the "double vision" is generated by the fact that the colonized mimic the colonizer incompletely or "in part."[359] They are split between reality and constructed reality (the replacement of reality by a product of desire). This leads to what Bhabha calls the "metonymies of presence",[360] i.e. the colonized take parts of the culture of the colonizer as the whole, which can be a "*menace*" to the colonizer in various ways. First, when the colonial subjects mimic only certain features of the colonizer, the hollowness of those features might be revealed. Moreover, the colonial subjects learn about the rights of the colonizer without being granted these rights to their full extent, which implies that, with reference to the colonizer, the colonized are almost the same but "not white."[361] This might eventually lead to resistance: "The ambivalence of mimicry – almost but not quite – suggests that the fetishized colonial culture is potentially and strategically an insurgent counter-appeal."[362] Hence, due to the "*double* vision" of mimicry, the colonial enterprise might be corrupted from within.

The halfcastes portrayed in the *Aleutians* trilogy can be called "mimic men" in Bhabha's sense of the term. With their sexless bodies and cleft lips, they are a mockery of the alien conquerors. Furthermore, due to their pseudo-religious practice of watching video-tapes, the halfcastes find their identities in the past, i.e. before the first contact, which is a contradiction. Thus, their customs' hollowness or lack of connection to reality is revealed. In addition, the "stupid *muddle*" (*NW*, p. 85, italics by G. Jones) of human and alien appears partial and incomplete. Even though the halfcastes imitate the aliens, they never have the same possibilities. For example, they are not hermaphrodites, and they are without any wanderers so that they cannot create anything from their body cells. Conversely, the depiction of the halfcastes has implications on the one of the colonizer: it demonstrates the meaningless codes of Aleutian culture, and it also shows a lack of care since the half-

---

[359] *Ibid.*, 131.
[360] *Ibid.*
[361] *Ibid.*, 132.
[362] *Ibid.*, 131.

castes are entirely dependent on the aliens, but the latter do not offer any tutelage or protection from hate crimes.

The fact that Gwyneth Jones as a white British author appropriates the concept of mimicry raises issues of British national identity. In fact, Jones text evokes the question whether British people also mimic another culture. With regard to mainstream culture and entertainment, the USA is pioneering, and many young British adore US-American singers and film stars. Some even try to imitate their looks and lifestyle. In addition, they spend their free time shopping American gadgets and in social networks such as Facebook. With her treatment of mimicry, Jones illustrates that personal and national identity are *in flux* and largely depend on the influence of other people or cultures on one's life. Through her depiction of rather foolish halfcastes, she warns us that uncritical imitating can make people appear ridiculous. However, mimicry in Britain seems to be a personal – not a political – phenomenon, and it thus differs tremendously from Bhabha's understanding of the term.

In 2338, i.e. two hundred years after the establishment of Aleutian trading posts and the split of the human population into Aleutian-lovers and anti-Aleutians, the changes on Earth are even more dramatic. Generally speaking, we receive the impression that living-conditions have changed for the worse. The countries and cities we know today do not exist anymore. Instead, people live in vast conurbations such as "Asaba" in West Africa (cf. *PC*, p. 163) or "Youro" in Europe, where *Phoenix Café* is set. We can assume that Earth is a post-national world. The mega-cities are managed by the Aleutian colonizers (cf. *PC*, pp. 29, 87). Moreover, even though the Aleutians mitigate gender violence, Reformers and Traditionalists are still "bitterly at odds" (*PC*, p.36) and there is the risk that a war breaks out again. As to the lifestyle of the people, we might speak of cultural imperialism or deculturation of the human species. The aliens hold that the development of mankind is a change for the better, though (cf. *PC*, p. 142).

Nevertheless, the alterations the Aleutians have brought to the planet actually have negative implications. In contrast to widespread future scenarios of overpopulation, the human species is slowly dying out due to the fertility decline that accompanies an adaptation to city life (cf. *ibid.*). Other reasons mentioned in the novel are organochlorines[363] and an "AIDS vaccine that made women allergic to being pregnant" (cf. *PC*, pp. 85f.). Furthermore, human religion and culture have degenerated. Churches or sects promote group suicide (cf. *PC*, p. 20), the abolition of sex and gender as markers of identity dehumanizes people (cf. *PC*, p. 159), drugs are easily accessible as they can be created virtually (cf. *PC*, p. 211), rich individuals have human sex toys (cf. *PC*, pp. 144, 241) and men escape into the virtual worlds of video games (cf. *PC*, pp. 122f., 236ff.). Consequently, long-term Aleutian domination is generally harmful for mankind.

The most obvious manifestation of bad living-conditions are "the hives, the packed tenements where the doomed [wait] to die – so many, so many" (*PC*, p. 15). The hives are slums shaped like termite nests, with insufficient water and energy supplies. The indoor streets are littered with "debris" and "foul liquid", and the "sanitation bacteria" are insufficient to keep the hives clean. The inhabitants of the hives are "beggars", "weed-cutters", "squatters" and "dull-eyed children" that pick through garbage for food. In addition, the rich "poison[ed] the land and everything that grew on it with the antifeedant genes that kept pests at bay", so that the crops of the poor do not grow (cf. *PC*, pp. 95-97). The situation in the hives makes the reader think of nineteenth-century poverty depicted in Friedrich Engels' *The Condition of the Working Class in England* (1845). In the chapter "The Great Towns", Engels carefully describes the so-called "rookeries" in the slums of major British cities, for instance London, Liverpool and Birmingham.[364] We can deduce that, under Aleutian rule, nothing is left from the former welfare states in Europe, and the aliens do not offer any solutions.

In contrast to the average population and the poor on Earth, the rich and the Aleutians live under much better conditions. This is expressed by their gardens – an antithesis to the city of humans. The gardens are walled places of virtual beauty or futuristic versions of the "*pristine wilderness*" (*PC*, p. 204, italics by G. Jones) that does not exist on the planet anymore:

---

[363] Organochlorines can be found in pesticides, for example.

[364] Cf. Friedrich Engels, *The Condition of the Working Class in England*. Edited with a Foreword by Victor Kiernan (London *et al.*: Penguin, 2005), p. 98.

> There was a sharp twittering of birdsong. The distant walls (the garden's physical dimensions were doubled, at least, by the artful use of virtual display screens) were bright with vividly coloured Aleutian creepers. Fruit trees stood in rows, bearing flowers and fruits together: apples and pears, apricots and peaches, the leaves, either dark or pale, showing the un-green of hybrid Aleutian genes. Butterfly wings flickered, birds darted. (*PC*, p. 42).

Interestingly, terrestrial and alien plants mix. It seems that the people have accepted the intrusion of alien elements into Nature, as they have accepted the alien conquerors. It is evident that the Aleutians live like rich people on Earth. They are aware of the problems of man but 'hide' from the world around them in their sealed enclaves. Thus, the colonizers are reluctant to take responsibility for the colonized, and mankind degenerates.

With regard to human resistance, *Phoenix Café* features the "renaissance", a counter-movement to those who accept the aliens and the changes they have brought to Earth. Their symbol is a painting by Leonardo da Vinci that shows a "symbolic birth [...] set among ruins" (*PC*, p. 79).[365] The aim of the renaissance is the return to a pre-contact world, i.e. they reject Aleutian lifestyle. For instance, the members walk instead of using live transport (cf. *PC*, p. 82), they wear man-made clothes called "native costume" (*PC*, p. 92), and they enjoy going to an 'old-Earth' food market (cf. *PC*, p. 82). As a result, it becomes obvious that they are nostalgic. What is equally important to them is the revival of human technology. One of their leaders, Lalith,[366] claims:

---

[365] In the novel, the nativity scene is described in the following way: "Renewal held in the disintegrating womb of the past, the sacred child surrounded by a chaos of broken columns, refractory camels, investigative journalists, topping palm trees, mad astrologers" (*PC*, p. 79). The painting might be Leonardo da Vinci's "Adorazione dei Magi" (1481).

[366] The name Lalith recalls Lilith, Adam's first wife who would not surrender to male domination. Equally, Lalith and her followers refuse to accept Aleutian domination. In science fiction, Octavia Butler draws upon Lilith's mythological qualities in *Lilith's Brood* (*Xenogenesis 1-3*, 2000), a collection of novels depict-

> Why have we given up our own past? We have become dependent on their [the Aleutians'] effortless biotechnology, their skills at altering our landscapes, at generating tailored hybrids so much superior to our original crops, animals and machines. But we had our own life sciences once. We can recover them. We can build *our own* customized world. (*PC*, p. 58, italics by G. Jones)

This implies that mankind does not need the Aleutians; humans will not surrender to them anymore if their only true advantage – biotechnology – becomes obsolete. Furthermore, Lalith makes clear that a shift in the attitude towards the Other has taken place: the aliens are not perceived as 'angelic superbeings' anymore (cf. *ibid.*). The venue of the renaissance is the Phoenix Café that gives the novel its title. The atmosphere of the café perfectly suits the nostalgic group: it is hidden between old houses and the tables are under the branches of a sycamore tree where "*musique naturelle*" (natural sounds) can be heard (cf. *PC*, pp. 88f.). In the café, the renaissance members discuss Aleutian affairs, muse about alternative social concepts (cf. *PC*, p. 157) and play video games (cf. *PC*, pp. 236ff.). In addition, they look for a scapegoat. Thus, one of their members, Misha Connelly, wins the trust of the hybrid creature, Catherine, and abuses her sexually (cf. *PC*, pp. 125ff., 164ff., 197).

Nevertheless, Catherine understands that the renaissance is not truly 'old-Earth'. Mankind cannot go back to its original state (i.e. before the arrival of the aliens), because the influence of the Other cannot simply be eradicated. Catherine's viewpoint bears parallels to Edward Said's analysis of cultural resistance in *Culture and Imperialism* (1993). Said holds that cultural domination is always accompanied by cultural resistance. Nonetheless, a certain amount of influence from another culture is natural: "Far from being unitary or monolithic or autonomous things, cultures actually assume more 'foreign' elements, alterities, differences, than they con-

---

ing genetically altered beings that are able to reunite different sexes and species on Earth. Cf. Octavia E. Butler, *Lilith's Brood* (New York, NY: Warner, 2000).

sciously exclude."[367] Equally, Catherine thinks that the lifestyle the renaissance advocates is new instead of old, "[n]ot a survival, but a birth" (*PC*, p. 228). On a more abstract level, this means that the colonized cannot deny the impact of the colonizer on society and culture; the latter unavoidably changes the former. Even though the subject race might be nostalgic for the past, it can never fully return to what it was like before the arrival of the Other. On the whole, the depiction of the renaissance is rather negative, just like the portrayal of the White Queen movement: the renaissance members use Catherine as a scapegoat for three hundred years of Aleutian domination and they are blind to the fact that they cannot go back to a long-lost past, a past they do not even know much about, as we assume. Here, Gwyneth Jones evidently criticizes cultural nostalgia: a solution to man's problems must be found in the present, not in the past.[368]

Another topic that is crucial with regard to Aleutian domination is the exploitation of the planet for the benefit of the invader. The conquerors are traders, but they have not yet found anything valuable to trade or exploit. Nevertheless, the situation changes with the second space race. As the saboteurs, Johnny Guglioli and Braemer Wilson, travel to the Aleutian mothership faster-than-light, the Aleutians learn that human beings have developed a unique device with which massive distances in space can be cov-

---

[367] Edward W. Said, *Culture and Imperialism*, p. 15.

[368] The renaissance in *Phoenix Café* is only a minority group. In his essay "Cultural Nostalgia: A Philosophical Critique of Appeals to the Past in Theories of Re-Making Africa" (2006), Moses Òkè demonstrates the dangers of cultural nostalgia as a mass movement. After having pinpointed the most important concepts that advocate a return to 'African roots' (Léopold Sédar Senghor's Négritude or Ahmed Sékou Touré's Re-Africanisation, among others), Òkè makes clear that going back in time is clearly counter-productive. For instance, he argues that traditional African institutions are unable to cope with complex issues of globalization, that a de-monetization is unrealistic, that communalism hinders progress, that traditionalist despots and dictators exploit their peoples for personal enrichment, *et cetera*. Yet, Òkè does not offer a solution to Africa's social and economic problems. As a starting point, he suggests that scholars "fashion out a genuinely African blueprint of social, political and economic life" that also takes foreign cultural influences into consideration. Cf. Moses Òkè, "Cultural Nostalgia: A Philosophical Critique of Appeals to the Past in Theories of Re-Making Africa," in: *Nordic Journal of African Studies* 15:3 (2006): 332-343.

ered without any means of transport. In fact, selling the technology would mean an enormous material gain for the aliens. The machine is called "Buonarotti Device", named after its inventor, Peenemünde Buonarotti (cf. *WQ*, p. 173). Getting hold of the technology would be a triumph for both man and aliens, and a quest – the main strand of narration in *North Wind* – begins. Key characters in the hunt for the Device are Bella, a hybrid creature that Clavel had built from Johnny's tissue (cf. *NW*, p. 241), and Clavel, who 'sacrifices' himself for a test of the Buonarotti Device: he travels to the Aleutian spaceship and returns dead (cf. *NW*, pp. 262ff.). Kumbva, an alien engineer, guards the Device on Earth.

The quest closely resembles treasure hunts in the romances of Empire, for instance the descent into the caves and temple of Kôr or into the Solomonian mines in Sir Henry Rider Haggard's works. Just like in the romances of Empire, the treasure in *North Wind* is fabulous, unique and incredibly precious. For humans and Aleutians alike, finding the treasure would not only be a material gain but also a basis for superiority. The question arises who deserves the Buonarotti Device: one of the natives on Earth invented it, but apparently only the alien invaders can use it. Haggard's *King Solomon's Mines* (1885) depicts a similar dilemma which is finally solved in favour of the European intruders. When Allan Quatermain and his band find the Solomonian treasure in a cave in southern Africa, the exploitation of the natives' land is generally presented as legitimate. Quatermain claims that the Europeans are the true owners of the treasure:

> There we stood and shrieked with laughter over the gems which were ours, which had been found for *us* thousands of years ago by the patient delvers in the great hole yonder, and stored for *us* by Solomon's long dead overseer [...]. *We* had got them; there before us were millions of pounds' worth of diamonds, and thousands of pounds' worth of gold and ivory, only waiting to be taken away.[369]

[369] Henry Rider Haggard, *King Solomon's Mines*, p. 173, italics by H. R. Haggard.

This might be interpreted as imperial theft. In the novel, though, various aspects eradicate the notion of stealing. First, the Europeans' goal is to leave the cave, not to take the treasure. Second, the narrator presents the act of stuffing the pockets with diamonds as rather 'natural' or 'instinctive', and the diamonds might also be seen as a compensation for the Europeans who restore order and peace among the 'savage' natives. Accordingly, the fact that ftl travel might be too dangerous for human beings justifies the idea that the Aleutians are the rightful owners of the Device. Above all, Clavel sacrifices himself in an experiment, which adds a spiritual dimension to the treasure. Consequently, the reader perceives the alien invaders as the winners of the second space race.

Two hundred years later, the legitimate ownership of the Buonarotti Device is still a political issue. Teams of human and alien scientists are strictly separated from each other for "security reasons" (*PC*, p. 133), and it becomes obvious that the Aleutians do not intend to share the technology with the people from Earth: "The Aleutians were not interested in the interplanetary travelogue. Their appetite for adventure was sated. They only wanted to use the device to get home; and sell it there" (*PC*, p. 133). In order to show respect, they surrender to a protocol they do not take seriously. In addition, their plan to steal the Buonarotti Device displays an awareness of their dominant position and maybe even arrogance; as they believe that only Aleutians can travel ftl, they consider themselves the owners of Peenemünde's invention. Generally speaking, Jones shows that structures of power and hierarchy are hidden behind ostensive equality, protocols and political agreements. Eventually, the renaissance members find a way to replicate the Device and thereby win the second space race. They actually travel to Earth-like planets while playing a computer game about a weapon conspiracy on the fictive Tracy Island (cf. *PC*, pp. 260ff.). Here, virtuality and reality blend. Ftl technology in the hands of man triggers the departure of the Aleutians: as the Device can be replicated, the treasure loses its significance for the aliens and they do not see a reason to stay on Earth (cf. *PC*, p. 283).

The last novel of the trilogy, *Phoenix Café*, treats the disengagement of the Aleutians from Earth and its inhabitants in 2338, i.e. three hundred years after the first contact. With regard to colonialism, the central topics of the novel are responsibility and guilt. Generally speaking, it is undeniable that the living-conditions on the planet have deteriorated under the rule of the Aleutians. Many blame the aliens. They claim that Earth is "trashed" (*PC*, p. 21) because the Aleutians have "[s]tolen it, played with it, broken it, thrown it on the dump [...]" (*PC*, p. 12). Thus, the aliens are likened to children: out of playfulness and naivety, they have destroyed the world of man and intend to leave it behind like a broken toy. This evokes the question to what extent the Aleutians are responsible for the decline of their colony. On the one hand, Aleutian rule has fuelled the problems on Earth. For instance, their terraforming methods have influenced the climate in a negative way so that farmland has become even scarcer (cf. *PC*, p. 82). In addition, they do not offer any solution to gender violence. Last but not least, the Aleutians have created self-distrust among the people: "*nothing in the world belongs to you* [human beings], *everything you do someone else can do better, you can never be first...*" (*PC*, p. 75, italics by G. Jones). This idea refers to the Aleutians' effortless biotechnology, and it implies that the people do not trust in their ability to solve problems anymore. In the future, they might remain a subject race that requires tutelage or paternalism.

Yet, on the other hand, the Aleutians are not fully responsible for the deterioration of the planet as it had already started before their landing: "The aliens had simply arrived, by chance, in time to witness the last acts of a long drama: tragic, fascinating, rich and rank and strange..." (*PC*, p. 160). Furthermore, resources are scarce due to war and overuse of farmland (cf. *PC*, p. 23) and the "old rivalries" between Reformers and Traditionalists are manmade; the Aleutians are not to blame for outbreaks of violence on Earth albeit the decrease of food, water and other resources aggravates aggression (cf. *PC*, p. 142). Hence, one of the Aleutians, Maitri, explains: "We must leave, and they must work out things for themselves. There's no sane alternative" (*PC*, p. 49). To conclude, the Aleutians have not created man's problems, but their rule has definitely accelerated the deterioration of Earth.

Before the departure of the aliens, both Aleutian and human characters speculate about the future of mankind. The scenarios they imagine differ crucially. Dr Bright, an Aleutian scientist who works on the Buonarotti Device, sees a positive future for Earth and its inhabitants:

> *[E]verything must happen.* [...] If the humans were to suffer now, no doubt they'd get their revenge some time in the lives to come. There is no lasting harm. It was beyond the [Aleutian] team's imagination to conceive otherwise. (*PC*, p. 143, italics by G. Jones)

Not only does the alien's belief in determinism disavow any responsibility, it also illustrates a feeling of optimism that appears blind to reality. In contrast to Dr Bright, Misha Connelly thinks that only few humans will survive in the long run since the lack of resources triggers war, and since humans have learnt new methods of producing mass-destruction weapons from the Aleutians:

> It's not being openly discussed [...]. There *will* be panic on the streets, there already is, but not over that. The idea that the human race may soon, literally, run out of food and water and *die* if we're left stuck on this rock, is beyond most people. [...] We'll probably squeeze through the crunch [...]. We'll lose a lot of genetic variance, but we'll come through. (*PC*, pp. 233f., italics by G. Jones)

Misha's view of the future is rather negative as he imagines that the human race will almost die out. It becomes obvious that Aleutians and humans have entirely different ways of thinking; after three hundred years of Aleutian presence on Earth, the two species are still "out of sync" (*WQ*, p. 309).

In Gwyneth Jones' trilogy, the fate of Earth after the departure of the aliens remains untold. In 2338, the Aleutians eventually leave the planet for good with the Buonarotti technology. They leave out of free will, which is a contrast to other works of alien invasion. We assume that they are aware of the fact that there is nothing to exploit and that Earth is about to collapse. Their departure is invisible and silent: "Somewhere far out in the dark, invisible above the city's atmosphere, the moon's three hundred year's companion had winked out of existence. Gone" (*PC*, p. 292). It seems that they 'sneak away' from the planet they have mismanaged for three hundred years, without taking any responsibility for the damages. To a certain extent, this recalls Britain's voluntary withdrawal from India in 1947 and from Africa in the 1960s: the colonial power saw itself unable to cope with the overwhelming pressure of nationalism and with social problems such as ethnic tensions and poverty. In Jones' work, the human population is cheerful: "People were trampling the fields, shouting, singing, letting off firearms" (*ibid.*). Liberated from their colonizer, they celebrate the future despite the problems that surround them.

Quite unusually, Gwyneth Jones treats postcolonial guilt in a way that she projects it on one of the novels' characters. Catherine, the protagonist of *Phoenix Café*, tries to make up for the shortcomings of the Aleutians and thereby embodies postcolonial guilt. Catherine is the reincarnation of Clavel as a human female (cf. *PC*, p. 212). Yet, despite her human body, she identifies herself with the Aleutians in a way that she takes personal responsibility for the colonization of Earth. Just like Catherine of Siena (1347-1380), Catherine works for a mission where she serves the sick and poor (cf. *PC*, p. 12). More importantly, Catherine becomes the victim of rape, a theme that informs the entire trilogy: Clavel rapes Johnny, the Aleutians figuratively rape Earth (cf. *NW*, pp. 237f.), Greek soldiers rape Maitri (cf. *NW*, p. 42) and Misha sexually abuses Catherine (cf. *PC*, pp. 125ff., 164ff., 197). What is striking is that Catherine deliberately acts as a victim: "The rape [of Johnny] continues. I can't stop it so I want to be raped too" (*PC*, 172). Catherine also thinks that the Aleutians leave man "with all [their] debts and [hers] unpaid" (*PC*, p. 231). This clearly expresses extreme feelings of guilt which transform into perverse sexuality and vulnerability during the rape scenes.

On a more abstract level, Catherine lets Misha 'colonize' her body as some sort of compensation for Aleutian rule. Rape is thus redemption of postcolonial guilt.[370] After the departure of the

[370] In colonial literature, there are various examples where European or white women are raped by native or Black men without incriminating them, probably out of a feeling of postcolonial guilt. Cf. E. M. Forster, *A Passage to India*, edited by Oliver Stallybrass, with an introduction by Pankaj Mishra (London *et al.*:

Aleutians, Catherine stays behind with the feeling that her 'mission' is fulfilled: "All debts paid, the long strain over" (*PC*, p. 296). The ending illustrates how selfish postcolonial guilt actually is: the colonizer feels 'absolved from sins', but postcolonial guilt does not provide any real benefits for the former subject race. In contrast to the Overlords in *Childhood's End* (cf. chapter 2.1), for example, the Aleutians are not man's saviours, and man does not expect a higher purpose or a better future. Humans will have to find their own solutions to the disastrous living-conditions on Earth.

To conclude, the *Aleutians* trilogy reflects various issues of colonial encounters in an original way. First, it demonstrates the introduction of Aleutian colonial rule: the aliens develop from private traders into colonizers of Earth. They are not involuntary colonizers, though, as they seek opportunities to make profit. Just like Europeans from the Renaissance onwards, they extend their networks for economic purposes, they settle in the invaded territory, and they gain a dominant position over the natives due to technology. However, Gwyneth Jones also breaks with the depiction of common prerequisites of colonial rule. The Aleutians are not portrayed as undoubtedly superior; they actually evade clear-cut categories. Instead, the Aleutians are simultaneously human and alien as well as 'superhuman' and atavistic, i.e. they share various characteristics with the subject races in history. A consolidation of Aleutian colonial rule is eventually achieved by pretending benevolence and honesty, and people celebrate the aliens like pop stars.

In addition, the trilogy illustrates the long-term development of Earth under alien influence. The population splits into anti-Aleutians and Aleutian-lovers. The latter transform into halfcastes or "mimic men" in Homi Bhabha's words. The degeneration of the

---

Penguin Classics, 2005); John M. Coetzee, *Disgrace* (London: Vintage, 2000); Paul Scott, *The Raj Quartet. Vol. One: The Jewel in the Crown. The Day of the Scorpion*, with an Introduction by Hilary Spurling (London *et al.*: Everyman's Library, 2007). For a detailed analysis of the treatment of rape in British colonial literature, see Nancy L. Paxton, *Writing under the Raj: Gender, Race, and Rape in the British Colonial Imagination, 1830-1947* (London *et al.*: Rutgers University Press, 1999).

planet manifests itself in a decline of the population and the deterioration of the living-conditions. Nonetheless, the Aleutians, who live in sealed enclaves like the rich, offer neither tutelage nor true solutions. What is more, resistance against Aleutian rule might have started as a noble idea, but the underlying ideology does not correspond to reality. Here, Jones criticizes cultural nostalgia. Finally, the Aleutians voluntarily leave Earth (like the British in India and Africa) since there is nothing to exploit on the planet. The aliens refuse to take responsibility for their subject race, so that the people have to find their own solutions to the problems on Earth. Catherine redeems postcolonial guilt through rape, which reveals the narcissistic notion of guilt since there are no benefits for the subject race. Thus, in the end, there is no real 'winner' – a difference to the romances of Empire – and the two worlds are still "out of sync".

Conclusion

I hope to have shown that all novels discussed draw back on various aspects of the British Empire, albeit each in its own way. All novels deal with concepts of dominance that are similar to British imperial strategies, with the alien Other, with technology as an agent of power and with human resistance. Thus, these features seem to be the essence of alien-encounter science fiction. With regard to the form of rule the extraterrestrial invaders establish on Earth, *The Interpreter*, *Timelike Infinity* and the *Aleutians* trilogy feature futuristic versions of trading companies: the aliens' sole target is making profit by extracting and processing the natural resources of Earth or by opening up new markets for their products. Trade is accompanied by the annexations of territories, by thorough organization and institutionalization of alien rule and by the exploitation of the local population. The procedures occasionally parallel the 'Scramble for Africa'. The Masters in the *Tripods* trilogy, however, do not aim for trade but for the complete and irrevocable takeover of the planet: they plan to change the atmosphere of Earth in order to adjust it to their biological requirements, a project that would bring about the end of the human race. The alien cities – the Masters' symbols of dominance – recall settler rule in the colonies, and the alien settlers transform humans into slaves and impose a new world order on man. The xenobaths in *The Kraken Wakes* also establish settlements on Earth, but they kill rather than control humans. If it was not for man's victory, settler rule might have followed the colonization of the deep sea.

In those texts that give accounts of benevolent alien invasions, i.e. *Childhood's End* and the *Andromeda* novels, the aliens dominate man by means of indirect rule and paternalism. Humans are depicted as self-destructive, as stuck in an evolutionary *cul-de-sac* or as 'children' that have to be taken care of. Thus, mankind as a whole does not only require but eventually benefits from alien tutelage. Simultaneously, though, the self-determination and independence of humans are strictly limited. This issue is treated particularly in *Non-Stop*, which is much more pessimistic than the previous texts since Aldiss questions and criticizes intervention into a 'less civilized' culture and refusal too take full responsibility for the consequences.

With regard to the portrayal of the alien Other, the novels can be grouped into works in which the boundaries between Self and Other are clear-cut and works that overcome this unambiguous distinction. In the first case, the extraterrestrials are technologically and intellectually superior to humans. Man is equipped with orientalist paradigms. This unfolds a reversal of John Rieder's "colonial gaze" (cf. Introduction): Western narrators become subjects of alien invaders, i.e. the latter look down upon former imperialist nations (and on the rest of mankind, of course). Some of them are evidently hostile. For instance, the Masters in the *Tripods* trilogy dehumanize people by turning them into slaves, and the xenobaths in *The Kraken Wakes* wipe out the majority of the population of Earth. In Wyndham's novel, the image of the alien Other is shaped by poems, mythology and dream scenes; man never sees a xenobath. In *Non-Stop*, the "colonial gaze" is not reversed: humans from Earth are still superior to the alien Others in the spaceship. By studying the 'savages', the scientists travel into man's own past and witness what they think is superstition, ignorance and cruelty. Interestingly, *Non-Stop* is the only novel that is narrated through the eyes of the Other only, and it becomes obvious that Aldiss – rather than denouncing stereotypical features of 'primitive' cultures – criticizes the arrogance and ruthlessness of the human manipulators. In contrast to that, the Overlords in *Childhood's End* and the aliens from the Andromeda Galaxy are depicted as idealized imperial rulers that parent man and advance human evolution. The immaterial Overmind is godlike; humans can only join it after having undergone tremendous changes. In general, the differences between Self and Other in colonial encounters are a crucial prerequisite for hierarchical structures.

The extraterrestrials in the remaining novels do not appear entirely alien, which implies that the boundaries between Self and Other dissolve. Apart from their physical features, the nuls in *The Interpreter* and the Qax in *Timelike Infinity* display an overwhelming number of similarities to human colonizers in history. They are driven by the striving for profit, by greed and by competition. What is more, they thoroughly organize the exploitation of subject planets by means of colonial infrastructure and jurisdiction. With these novels, the authors hold a mirror up to former imperialist nations; they object to arrogance towards the subject peoples, mismanagement, colonial crimes and reckless exploitation. The Aleutians and Andromeda or André respectively are not unmistakably Other, either. Their humanoid nature opens up the possibility of miscegenation and Andromeda is even considered a human woman in the end. More importantly, though, the Aleutians as "baboons in imperial robes" (cf. *NW*, p. 214; *PC*, p. 53) are not undoubtedly superior to man. They are 'savages' and 'superbeings' at the same time, which has severe implications on politics and cultures on Earth. In general, those texts that are narrated from the point of view of the Self and that of the Other (*The Interpreter*, *Childhood's End*, the *Aleutians* trilogy) offer more complex images of rulers and subjects.

In all the novels discussed, science and technology are pillars of interstellar empires. The most important issues are space-travel devices (colonialism would be impossible without mobility) and military technology which enables the invaders to conquer planets. For example, they use armed spaceships, sea-tanks, stereosonic weapons and tripods with mechanical tentacles and guns. The benevolent aliens do not invade the planets with brute force, but they punish what they consider morally incorrect behaviour with the help of technology: the Overlords inflict pain on people and switch off the sun, and the aliens from Andromeda make scientists develop life-threatening enzymes and bacteria. In addition, just like the benevolent extraterrestrials, the nuls and the Masters create means of surveillance and manipulation, of which the Capping of humans is definitely the most extreme form (Capped people are deprived of their free will and individuality). In order to ensure their superior position, the Masters and the Qax ban human science on Earth.

With regard to terraforming, some extraterrestrial colonizers alter the climate of Earth, for instance the Aleutians and the xenobaths. The Masters' plan to change the atmosphere would end all life on the planet, but they are eventually stopped from carrying it out. Further examples of futuristic science are alien cells that can produce things (cf. the *Aleutians* trilogy and *Timelike Infinity*), a supercomputer than instructs scientists in the creation of life (cf. the *Andromeda* novels), a television receiver that shows the past (cf. *Childhood's End*) and time travel (cf. *Timelike Infinity*). On the whole, scientific and technological achievements guarantee the hegemonic position of the imperial ruler. Much like Europe from the Renaissance onwards, the extraterrestrials represent science and reason, which makes them appear powerful and advanced; science and technology are thus indicators of their 'high level of civilization'. In contrast, mankind seems to be 'primitive', especially when human industry and innovation are destroyed.

Just like in colonial history, individuals and resistance movements in alien-encounter science fiction fight for the freedom of the subject race and, in most works, mankind finally defeats the invaders from outer space (although there are two exceptions: *The Interpreter* and *Childhood's End*). Two resistance movements are successful. The Free Men in the *Tripods* trilogy pave the way for the infiltration and sabotage of the alien cities, and White Queen in Gwyneth Jones' eponymous novel destroy the myth that surrounds the 'angelic superbeings'. Their common strategy is victory over the aliens by means of accumulating information, wit and courage. In contrast, the actions of four resistance movements fail. The insurgents in *The Interpreter* are nostalgic and rather unorganized guerrillas, the Friends of Wigner in *Timelike Infinity* appear blinded by their philosophy, and both the renaissance in *Phoenix Café* and the Freedom League in *Childhood's End* remain minority groups without any support from the general public. Accordingly, these movements cannot be considered serious opponents.

Nonetheless, some of the novels analyzed do not only feature resistance movements but they also portray individual heroes that try to liberate the entire human species. For instance, the teenagers in the *Tripods* trilogy develop into spies and saboteurs, the interpreters in Aldiss' novel manage to reveal colonial crimes on Earth, and Jim Bolder destroys the planet of the Qax. Unfortunately, he remains a shadow. Furthermore, the alien protagonists in *Non-Stop* discover the truth about their world (the spaceship) and their relation to human beings from Earth. In general, these individuals are considered honourable and brave, so that the reader sympathizes with them. Likewise, the scientists who enter into some sort of competition with the intellectually and technologically superior extraterrestrials by developing more powerful weapons (cf. *The Kraken Wakes*) or by manipulating alien tools (cf. the *Andromeda* novels) are regarded as heroes.

In the majority of works discussed, liberation implies that humans regain their freedom and their territories, and that the oppressors are either killed or withdraw voluntarily like the British in India or Africa. To the reader, this sort of ending appears justified, i.e. he or she feels that humans deserve freedom and happiness after having experienced exploitation, slavery and genocide. Nevertheless, freedom is only a temporary state in the *Tripods* trilogy in which national resentments and power struggles comparable to the ones in India, South Africa or Vietnam re-emerge. Imperial domination or tutelage can also be depicted as a recurrent motif in history, an idea that implies inevitability and the impossibility of ultimate liberation from alien rule, as in *Timelike Infinity*, for example. This illustrates that the state of freedom is something precious that must not be taken for granted and should be protected for as long as possible.

Man almost always wins over the aliens; few novels, however, treat the decolonization of Earth. In *The Kraken Wakes*, the *Tripods* trilogy and the *Andromeda* novels, humans restore pre-colonial conditions on Earth: they rebuild their living-space, recover lost knowledge and live self-determined lives. In contrast, there is no clear-cut separation from the former colonizers in the *Aleutians* trilogy. *Phoenix Café* ends with the departure of the extraterrestrials but, after three hundred years of alien rule, virtually every human lives like an Aleutian and the reader assumes that trade and space tourism will continue. Basically, Earth has undergone a process of deculturation so that a return to pre-colonial conditions appears virtually impossible. The dependence on the former ruler bears parallels to contemporary neo-imperialist relations. Four novels do not mention decolonization at all. In *Non-Stop* and *Timelike Infinity*, the fate of the former subject race remains untold; in *Childhood's End*, Earth is entirely annihilated, and in *The Interpreter*, mankind is not liberated from the alien overlords and unable to govern itself.

Just like the decolonization of Earth, postimperial or postcolonial guilt is a subject matter that is not apparent in all novels. In general, postimperial or postcolonial guilt manifests itself in various forms, depending on the role of man, or more precisely of Western society, in the novels. One possibility in alien-encounter science fiction is that the latter assumes the role of the native in colonial history (cf. the *Tripods*, *The Interpreter*). After having been colonized by extraterrestrials, human beings undergo experiences of exploitation and genocide and, simultaneously, recall encounters of the past. Thus, they acknowledge guilt, which is depicted as a process that eventually leads to some sort of 'redemption' or 'absolution' from their nation's former sins. When the alien invaders are overpowered, society is free to make a new start. In some texts, however, human beings are portrayed as colonial subjects and tools of alien imperialism at the same time. For instance in *Timelike Infinity*, the human protagonists admit to the fact that European history provided object lessons of conquest and destruction. In this case, they feel shame – as a consequence of guilt – but are denied redemption. Typical characters that serve as agents of dominance are scientists and quasi-religious followers of the aliens. They see a beneficial purpose behind the invasion and therefore assist in the colonization of their home planet (cf. most of the scientists in the *Andromeda* novels and the so-called "half-castes" in the *Aleutians* trilogy). When the exploitative nature of the rulers is revealed, they seem to oscillate between the belief in a good cause and feelings of guilt. Taking full responsibility for what the invaders do to the planet and its inhabitants must be unbearable for them.

Some works, however, do not deal with postimperial or postcolonial guilt at all. The aliens are the evil Others – an assumption that establishes man's innocence. This juxtaposition appears to come 'naturally' in *The Kraken Wakes*, for example. Consequently, victory over the invaders through superior fire power is portrayed as desirable and glorious. Similarly, no guilt is expressed whenever man – as the 'native' – seems to require assistance and tutelage. A major reason for this is the self-destructive potential of humanity (cf. *Childhood's End*).

To sum up, narratives that feature aliens are not only about aliens – they provide the opportunity to discuss political and ethical issues by projecting human history and behavior on different beings. Interestingly, they blend colonial and postcolonial issues. Even in the novels published right after the decline of the Empire, when hardly anybody talked about postcolonialism, the authors did not shun dealing with their nation's imperial past and successfully wove historical facts into the fabrics of their fiction. It becomes evident that the Empire was and still is a vital background for British alien-encounter science fiction.

Bibliography

Primary Texts

Aldiss, Brian W. *Hothouse.* With an Introduction by Neil Gaiman and a New Afterword by Brian Aldiss. London *et al.*: Penguin Classics, 2008.

——. *Non-Stop*. London: Orion, 2000.

——. *The Helliconia Trilogy. The Classic Epic Trilogy in One Volume*. New York, NY: Voyager, 1996.

——. *The Interpreter*. London: Four Square Books, 1967.

Asimov, Isaac, Martin Harry Greenberg and Charles G. Waugh (eds). *Last Man on Earth*. New York, NY: Fawcett, ²1985.

Ballantyne, Robert Michael. *The Coral Island*. Ware: Wordsworth Classics, 1993.

Ballard, J. G. *The Drowned World*. London: Orion, ³2001.

Baxter, Stephen. *Coalescent: A Novel (Destiny's Children Book One)*. New York, NY: Del Rey, 2004.

——. *Exultant (Destiny's Children Book Two)*. New York, NY: Gollancz, 2004.

——. *The Time Ships. An Astonishing Quantum Voyage to the Far Future*. New York, NY: Eos, 2000.

——. *Timelike Infinity*. London: Voyager, 1997.

——. *Transcendent (Destiny's Children Book Three)*. New York, NY: Gollancz, 2005.

——. *Vacuum Diagrams. Stories of the Xeelee Sequence*. New York, NY: Eos, 2001.

——. *Xeelee: An Omnibus*. With an Introduction by Paul McAuley. London: Gollancz, 2010.

Bradbury, Ray. *The Martian Chronicles*. New York, NY: Simon & Schuster, 2012.

Brunner, John. *Age of Miracles*. London: Sidgwick & Jackson, 1973.

Butler, Octavia E. *Lilith's Brood*. New York, NY: Warner, 2000.

——. *Dawn (Xenogenesis)*. London: Gollancz, 1988.

Campbell, John W. Jr. *Who Goes There?* Cutchogue, NY: Buccaneer Books, 1991.

Carr, Terry Gene. *The Light at the End of the Universe*. Palm Springs, FL: Pyramid, 1976.

Carroll, Lewis. *Alice's Adventures in Wonderland & Through the Looking-Glass and What Alice Found There*. Illustrated by John Tenniel. With an Afterword by Anna South. New York, NY: Barnes & Noble, 2004.

Christopher, John. *The City of Gold and Lead*. New York, NY *et al.*: Puffin Books, 1984.

——. *The Pool of Fire*. New York, NY: Aladdin Paperbacks, ^{2}1988.

——. *The White Mountains*. New York, NY *et al.*: Simon Pulse, 2003.

——. *When the Tripods Came*. New York, NY *et al.*: Simon Pulse, 2003.

Clarke, Arthur C. *Childhood's End*. New York, NY *et al.*: Random House, 1990.

——. *Childhood's End*. New York, NY: Del Rey Impact, 2001.

——. *The City and the Stars*. London: Gollancz, ^{3}2003.

——. *The Space Trilogy: Islands in the Sky, The Sands of Mars, Earthlight*. London: Gollancz, 2001.

Coetzee, John M. *Disgrace*. London: Vintage, 2000.

Conrad, Joseph. *Heart of Darkness & Other Stories*. Ware: Wordsworth Classics, 1999.

Constantine, Storm. *Hermetech*. Stafford, UK: Immanion Press, Revised Edition 2004.

Darwin, Charles. *The Descent of Man, and Selection in Relation to Sex*. London *et al.*: Penguin Classics, 2004.

——. *The Voyage of the Beagle. Journal of Researches into the Natural History and Geology of the Countries Visited during the Voyage of HMS Beagle round the World, under the Command of Captain Fitz Roy, RN.* Edited by Tom Griffith. With an Introduction by David Amigoni. Ware: Wordsworth Classics, 1997.

Defoe, Daniel. *The Life and Adventures of Robinson Crusoe,* Edited by Angus Ross. London *et al.*: Penguin Books, 1965.

Dick, Philip K. *Do Androids Dream of Electric Sheep?*. New York, NY: Del Rey, 1996.

Dickens, Charles. *A Tale of Two Cities*. Edited with an Introduction and Notes by Richard Maxwell. London *et al.*: Penguin Books, 2003.

——. *Hard Times*. London *et al.*: Penguin Popular Classics, 1994.

Engels, Friedrich. *The Condition of the Working Class in England*. Edited with a Foreword by Victor Kiernan. London *et al.*: Penguin, 2005.

Forster, Edward M. *The Machine Stops*. London *et al.*: Penguin Classics, 2011.

——. *A Passage to India*. Edited by Oliver Stallybrass. With an Introduction by Pankaj Mishra. London *et al.*: Penguin Classics, 2005.

Friel, Brian. *Translations*. London and Boston, MA: Faber & Faber, 1980.

Haggard, Henry Rider. *King Solomon's Mines*. Oxford *et al.*: Oxford University Press, 2008.

——. *She*. London *et al.*: Penguin Classics, 2001.

Heinlein, Robert A. *Farmer in the Sky*. Introduction by William H. Patterson Jr. Riverdale, NY: Baen, 2008.

——. *Orphans of the Sky*. London: Gollancz, 1963.

——. *The Puppet Masters*. New York, NY: Del Rey, Reissue 1986.

Hoyle, Fred and John Elliot. *A for Andromeda*. London: Souvenir Press, 2011.

——. *Andromeda Breakthrough*. London: Corgi Books, 1966.

Hoyle, Fred. *Ossian's Ride*. Portsmouth, NH *et al.*: Heinemann, 1959.

Huxley, Aldous. *Brave New World*. New York, NY: HarperCollins, 2004.

Jefferies, Richard. *After London; or Wild England*. Cirencester: Echo Library, 2005.

Jones, Gwyneth. *North Wind*. London: Vista, 1998.

——. *Phoenix Café*. London: Vista, 1998.

——. *The Buonarotti Quartet*. Seattle, WA: Aqueduct Press, 2009.

——. *The Universe of Things*. Seattle, WA: Aqueduct Press, 2011.

——. *White Queen*. London: VGSF, 1992.

King, Stephen. *Dreamcatcher*. New York, NY: Scribner, 2001.

Le Guin, Ursula K. *Always Coming Home*. Berkeley and Los Angeles, CA: University of California Press, 2001.

——. *The Left Hand of Darkness*. London: Hachette Digital, 1969.

Lovecraft, Howard Phillips. *The Call of Cthulhu and Other Weird Stories*. London *et al.*: Penguin Books, 1999.

Lubbock, John. *Pre-Historic Times as Illustrated by Ancient Remains and the Manners and Customs of Modern Savages*. London: Williams and Norgate, [3]1872.

Matheson, Richard. *I am Legend*. London: Millennium, 1999.

Melville, Herman. *Omoo. A Narrative of Adventures in the South Seas*. New London *et al.*: Penguin, 2007.

——. *Typee. A Peep at Polynesian Life*. London *et al.*: Penguin, 1996.

——. *Moby Dick; or, The Whale*. Ware: Wordsworth Classics, 1993.

Miller, Walter M. *A Canticle for Leibowitz*. London: Gollancz, 2001.

Rousseau, Jean-Jacques. *Discourse on the Origin of Inequality*. Translated by Franklin Philip. Oxford *et al.*: Oxford University Press, 1994.

Scott, Paul. *The Raj Quartet. Vol. One: The Jewel in the Crown. The Day of the Scorpion*. With an Introduction by Hilary Spurling. London *et al.*: Everyman's Library, 2007.

Shelley, Mary. *Frankenstein or, The Modern Prometheus*. London *et al.*: Penguin Popular Classics, 1994.

——. *Frankenstein; or, the Modern Prometheus*. Edited by D. L. MacDonald and Kathleen Scherf. Orchard Park, NY: Broadview, [2]1999.

——. *The Last Man*. With Introduction and Notes by Pamela Bickley. Ware: Wordsworth Classics, 2004.

Shelley, Percy Bysshe. *Percy Bysshe Shelley, Poetical Works*. Edited by Thomas Hutchinson. Oxford *et al.*: Oxford University Press, [2]1970.

Stapledon, Olaf. *Last and First Man*. London: Gollancz, [4]2003.

Stevenson, Robert Louis. *The Beach of Falesá*. Hoboken, NJ: Melville House Publishing, 2005.

Verne, Jules. *Twenty Thousand Leagues under the Sea*. Translated and Foreword by Mendor T. Brunetti. New York, NY: Signet Classic, 1969.

Vonnegut, Kurt. *Cat's Cradle*. New York, NY: Dell, 1963.

Watts, Peter. *Starfish*. New York, NY: Tor, 1999.

Wells, Herbert G. *The First Men in the Moon*. Rockville, MD: Arc Manor, 2008.

——. *The Island of Doctor Moreau*. New York, NY: Bantam Classic, [2]2005.

——. *The Time Machine*. London: Phoenix, 2004.

——. *The War of the Worlds*. New York, NY: Barnes and Noble Classics, 2004.

Wyndham, John. *The Day of the Triffids*. New York, NY: The Modern Library, 2003.

——. *The Kraken Wakes*. London *et al.*: Penguin Books, 2008.

——. *The Midwich Cuckoos*. London *et al.*: Penguin, 1960.

Films and TV Series

2012. Dir. Roland Emmerich. USA: Columbia Pictures *et al.*, 2009.

Alien³. Dir. David Fincher. USA: Twentieth Century Fox, 1992.

Alien. Dir. Ridley Scott. UK: Twentieth Century Fox, 1979.

Alien: Resurrection. Dir. Jean-Pierre Jeunet. USA: Twentieth Century Fox, 1997.

Aliens. Dir. James Cameron. UK and USA: Twentieth Century Fox, 1986.

Armageddon. Dir. Michael Bay. USA: Touchstone Pictures *et al.*, 1998.

Artificial Intelligence: AI. Dir. Steven Spielberg. USA: Warner Bros. Pictures, 2001.

Blade Runner. Dir. Ridley Scott. USA, Hong Kong, UK: Warner Bros. Pictures, 1982.

Cargo. Dir. Ivan Engler and Ralph Etter. Switzerland: Atlantis Pictures, 2009.

Cast Away. Dir. Robert Zemeckis. USA: Twentieth Century Fox *et al.*, 2000.

Close Encounters of the Third Kind. Dir. Steven Spielberg. USA: Sony Pictures Home Entertainment, 1977.

Communion. Dir. Philippe Mora. UK and USA: Allied Vision, 1989.

Contact. Dir. Robert Zemeckis. USA: Warner Bros. Pictures 1997.

Deep Impact. Dir. Mimi Leder. USA: Paramount Pictures *et al.*, 1998.

District 9. Dir. Neill Blomkamp. USA: Tristar Pictures, 2009.

Fire in the Sky. Dir. Robert Lieberman. USA: Paramount Pictures, 1993.

I am Legend. Dir. Francis Lawrence. USA: Warner Bros. Pictures, 2007.

I, Robot. Dir. Alex Proyas. USA and Germany: Twentieth Century Fox *et al.*, 2004.

Intruders. Dir. Dan Curtis. USA: Dan Curtis Productions, 1992.

Mad Max. Dir. George Miller. Australia: Kennedy Miller Productions *et al.*, 1979.

Matrix. Dir. Andy and Lana Wachowski. USA and Australia: Warner Bros. Pictures *et al.*, 1999.

Matrix Reloaded Dir. Andy and Lana Wachowski. USA and Australia: Warner Bros. Pictures *et al.*, 2003.

Matrix Revolutions. Dir. Andy and Lana Wachowski. USA and Australia: Warner Bros. Pictures *et al.*, 2003.

Monsters. Dir. Gareth Edwards. UK: Vertigo Films, 2010.

Prometheus. Dir. Ridley Scott. USA and UK: Twentieth Century Fox *et al.*, 2012.

Puppet Masters. Dir. Stuart Orme. USA: Hollywood Pictures, 1995.

Quatermass 2. US Title: *Enemy from Space*. Dir. Val Guest. UK: Hammer Film Productions, 1957.

Resident Evil. Dir. Paul W. S. Anderson. USA: Constantin Film Productions *et al.*, 2002.

Signs. Dir. M. Night Shyamalan. USA: Touchstone Pictures, 2002.

Survivors. Creat. Terry Nation. UK: British Broadcasting Corporation (BBC), 1975-1977.
The Terminator. Dir. James Cameron. USA and UK: Hemdale Film *et al.*, 1984.
Terminator 2: Judgement Day. Dir. James Cameron. USA and France: Carolco Pictures *et al.*, 1991.
Terminator 3: Rise of the Machines. Dir. Jonathan Mostow. USA, UK and Germany: C-2 Pictures *et al.*, 2003.
Terminator Salvation. Dir. McG. USA, UK, Germany and Italy: The Halcyon Company *et al.*, 2009.
The Day after Tomorrow Dir. Roland Emmerich. USA: Twentieth Century Fox *et al.*, 2004.
The Day the Earth Stood Still. Dir. Scott Derrickson. USA: Twentieth Century Fox, 2008.
The Last Man on Earth. Dir. Ubaldo Ragona. Italy and USA: Produzioni di Regina, 1964.
The Tripods. Dir. Graham Theakston, Christopher Barry and Bob Blagden. UK: British Broadcasting Corporation (BBC), 1984-1985.

Computer and Console Games

Dawn of War. THQ, 2004.
Dawn of War II. THQ, 2009.
Half-Life. Valve, 1998.
Half-Life 2. Valve, 2004.
Halo. Bungie, 2002-2009.
James Cameron's Avatar: The Game. Ubisoft Lightstorm Entertainment, 2009.
StarCraft. Blizzard Entertainment, 1998.

Secondary Sources

Adas, Michael. *Machines as the Measure of Man. Science, Technology, and Ideologies of Western Dominance*. Ithaca and London: Cornell University Press, 1998.

Aldiss, Brian W. and David Wingrove. *Trillion Years Spree: The History of Science Fiction*. London: Gollancz, 1986.

Aldiss, Brian W. *Billion Years Spree: The True History of Science Fiction*. London: Weidenfeld & Nicolson, 1973.

———. *Bury My Heart at W.H. Smith's: A Writing Life*. London: Hodder & Stoughton, 1990.

———. *The Detached Retina: Aspects of SF and Fantasy*. Syracuse, NY: Syracuse University Press, 1995.

———. *The Twinkling of an Eye or My Life as an Englishman*. London: Warner Books, ^{2}1999.

Aldiss, Margaret and Boden Clarke. *The Work of Brian W. Aldiss: An Annotated Bibliography and Guide. Bibliographies of Modern Authors, No 9*. San Bernardino, CA: Borgo Press, 1992.

Arnold, David. *The New Cambridge History of India. Science, Technology and Medicine in Colonial India, Vol. 3*. Cambridge *et al.*: Cambridge University Press, 2000.

Ashcroft, Bill and Pal Ahluwalia. *Edward Said*. London and New York, NY: Routledge, ^{2}2001.

Ashcroft, Bill, Gareth Griffiths and Helen Tiffin. *Post-Colonial Studies. The Key Concepts*. London and New York, NY: Routledge, ^{2}2007.

Bailey, K. V. "Masters, Slaves, and Rebels: Dystopia as Defined and Defied by John Christopher." In: *Science Fiction for Young Readers*. Edited by C.W. Sullivan. Westport *et al.*: Greenwood Press, 1993. 97-112.

Barr, Marleen S. "Fantastic Language/Political Reporting: The Postcolonial Science Fiction Illocutionary Force Is with Us." In: Raja, Masood Ashraf, Jason W. Ellis and Swaralipi Nandi (eds.). *The Postnational Fantasy: Essays on Postcolonialism, Cosmopolitics and Science Fiction*. Jefferson, NC: McFarland, 2011. 188-210.

Baudrillard, Jean. *Simulacra and Simulation (Body: In Theory, Histories)*. Translated by Sheila Glaser. Ann Arbour, MI: University of Michigan Press, 1994.

Beatie, Bruce A. "Arthur C. Clarke and the Alien Encounter: The Background of *Childhood's End*." In: *Extrapolation* 30:1 (1989): 53-69.

Bell, Duncan S. A. "Dissolving Distance: Technology, Space, and Empire in British Political Thought, 1770-1900." In: *The Journal of Modern History* 77:3 (2005): 523-562.

Bhabha, Homi. "Of Mimicry and Man: The Ambivalence of Colonial Discourse." In: *October. Discipleship: A Special Issue on Psychoanalysis* 28 (1984): 125-133.

——. *The Location of Culture*. London: Routledge, 1994.

Blackford, Russell. "Technological Meliorism and the Posthuman Vision: Arthur C. Clarke and the Ultimate Future of Intelligence." In: *The New York Review of Science Fiction* 14:3 (2001): 10-12.

Bould, Mark. "Gwyneth Jones: An Introduction." In: *FEMSPEC: An Interdisciplinary Feminist Journal Dedicated to Critical and Creative Work in the Realms of Science Fiction, Fantasy, Magical Realism, Surrealism, Myth, Folklore, and Other Supernatural Genres* 5:1 (2004): 190-196.

Buruma, Ian and Avishai Margalit. *Occidentalism: A Short History of Anti-Westernism*. London: Atlantic Books, 2004.

——. *Occidentalism: The West in the Eyes of its Enemies*. New York, NY: Penguin, 2004.

Candelaria, Matthew. "The Overlord's Burden: The Source of Sorrow in *Childhood's End*." In: *Ariel* 33:1 (2002): 37-58.

Carrier James G. (ed.). *Occidentalism: Images of the West*. Oxford *et al.*: Oxford University Press, 1995.

Carter, Mia, and Barbara Harlow (eds.). *Archives of Empire. Vol. 2: The Scramble for Africa*. Durham, NC, and London: Duke University Press, 2003.

Chambers, Claire. "Postcolonial Science Fiction: Amitav Ghosh's *The Calcutta Chromosome*." In: *Journal of Commonwealth Literature* 38.1 (2003): 57-72.

Childs, Peter, Jean Jacques Weber and Patrick William. *Post-Colonial Theory and Literatures. African, Caribbean and South Asian*. Trier: WVT, 2006.

Clute, John and Peter Nicholls (eds.). *The Encyclopedia of Science Fiction*. London: Orbit, ²1999.

Collings, Michael R. *Brian W. Aldiss. Starmont Reader's Guide 28*. Mercer Island, WA: Starmont House, 1986.

Combee, Jerry. "Rousseau's Noble Savage and European Self-Consciousness." In: *Modern Age* 17:2 (1973): 173-182.

Crispin, Edmund. *Best Science Fiction Stories*. London: Faber & Faber, 1957.

Crosby, Alfred. *Ecological Imperialism: The Biological Expansion of Europe, 900-1900*. Cambridge *et al.*: Cambridge University Press, 1986.

Csicsery-Ronay, Istvan. "Science Fiction and Empire." In: *Science Fiction Studies* 30:2 (2003): 231-245.

———. "The Lost Child: Notes on *White Queen*." In: *FEMSPEC: An Interdisciplinary Feminist Journal Dedicated to Critical and Creative Work in the Realms of Science Fiction, Fantasy, Magical Realism, Surrealism, Myth, Folklore, and Other Supernatural Genres* 5:1 (2004): 234-253.

Dale, Peter A. *In Pursuit of a Scientific Culture: Science, Art, and Society in the Victorian Age*. Madison, WI: University of Wisconsin Press, 1989.

Dillon, Grace L. "Miindiwag and Indigenous Diaspora: Eden Robinson's and Celu Amberstone's Forays into 'Postcolonial' Science Fiction and Fantasy." In: *Extrapolation: A Journal of Science Fiction and Fantasy* 48.2 (2007): 219-243.

Dinello, Daniel. *Technophobia! Science Fiction Visions of Posthuman Technology*. Austin, TX: University of Texas Press, 2005.

Faulkner, John. "Remembering Fred Hoyle." Text of an After-Dinner Speech. In: *Astrophysics and Space Science* 285 (2003): 593-608.

Ferguson, Niall. *Colossus: The Price of America's Empire*. New York, NY: Penguin Press, 2004.

——. *Empire: The Rise and Demise of the British World Order and the Lessons for Global Power*. New York, NY: Basic Books, 2004.

Fiamengo, Janice. “Postcolonial Guilt in Margaret Atwood’s *Surfacing*.” In: *American Review of Canadian Studies* 29:1 (1999): 141-163.

Förster, Stig, Wolfgang J. Mommsen and Ronald E. Robinson. *Bismarck, Europe, and Africa: The Berlin Africa Conference 1884–1885 and the Onset of Partition*. Oxford *et al.*: Oxford University Press, 1989.

Foucault, Michel. *Discipline and Punish: The Birth of the Prison*. New York, NY: Vintage Books, ²1995.

Freedman, Carl. “Hail Mary: On the Author of *Frankenstein* and the Origins of Science Fiction.” In: *Science Fiction Studies* 29:2 (2002): 253-264.

Gaylard, Gerald. “Postcolonial Science Fiction: *The Desert Planet*.” In: *Science Fiction, Imperialism and the Third World: Essays on Postcolonial Literature and Film*. Edited by Ericka and Reema Sarwal. Jefferson, NC: McFarland, 2010. 21-36.

Geraths, Armin and Kurt Herget (eds.). *Viktorianische Lyrik: Englisch – Deutsch*. Stuttgart: Reclam, 1985.

Gibbs, Philip. *The Romance of Empire*. London: Hutchinson, 1924.

Gillooly, Eileen (ed.). *Rudyard Kipling*. New York, NY: Sterling Publishing, 2000.

Grainville, Jean-Baptiste Cousin de. *The Last Man, or Omegarus and Syderia*. Translated by I. F. Clarke and M. Clarke. Introduction and Critical Materials by I. F. Clarke. Middleton, CT: Wesleyan University Press, Reprint 2003.

Greenland, Colin. *The Entropy Exhibition: Michael Moorcock and the UK “New Wave” in Science Fiction*. London: Routledge & Kegan Paul, 1983.

Hammond, Andrew. “‘The Twilight of Utopia’: British Dystopian Fiction and the Cold War.” In: *Modern Language Review* 106 (2011): 622-681.

Harper, John. *The Sea-Side and Aquarium or Anecdote and Gossip on Marine Zoology*. Edinburgh: William P. Nimmo, 1858.

Harrison, Mark. "Science and the British Empire." In: *Isis* 96:1 (2005): 56-63.

Hearn, Markus. "Viewing Notes." In: *A for Andromeda*. UK: BBC, 2006.

Hiller, Susan (ed.). *The Myth of Primitivism. Perspectives on Art*. London and New York, NY: Routledge, 1991.

Hollow, John. *Against the Night, the Stars. The Fiction of Arthur C. Clarke*. London *et al.*: Ohio University Press, 1983.

Holt, Terence. "The Bomb and the Baby Boom." In: *Tri Quarterly* 80 (1990): 206-220.

Hopkinson, Nalo and Uppinder Mehan (eds.). *So Long Been Dreaming: Postcolonial Science Fiction and Fantasy*. Vancouver, B.C.: Arsenal Pulp Press, 2004.

Hunter, I.Q. (ed.). *British Science Fiction Cinema*. London and New York, NY: Routledge, 1999.

Hurley, Kelly. *The Gothic Body. Sexuality, Materialism, and Degeneration at the* Fin de Siècle. Cambridge *et al.*: Cambridge University Press, 1996.

James, Edward. "Yellow, black, metal and tentacled: the race question in American science fiction." In: *Science fiction, social conflict and war*. Edited by Philip John Davies. Manchester and New York, NY: Manchester University Press, 1990. 26-49.

Jameson, Frederic. "Generic Discontinuities in SF: Brian Aldiss' *Starship*." In: *Science Fiction Studies* 1:2 (1973): 57-68.

———. "Shifting Contexts of Science-Fiction Theory." In: *Science Fiction Studies* 14:2 (1987): 241-247.

———. "Towards a New Awareness of Genre." In: *Science Fiction Studies* 9:3 (1982): 322-324.

Jensen, Derrick and George Draffan. *Welcome to the Machine: Science, Surveillance, and the Culture of Control*. White River Junction, VT: Chelsea Green Publishing, 2004.

Jones, Gwyneth. "Aliens in the Fourth Dimension." In: *Speaking Science Fiction. Dialogues and Interpretations*. Edited by Andy Sawyer. Liverpool: Liverpool University Press, 2000. 201-213.

Jones, Langdon (ed.). *The New SF: An Original Anthology of Modern Speculative Fiction*. London: Hutchinson, 1969.

Jung, Carl G. *Archetypes and the Collective Unconscious. The Collected Works of C. G. Jung Vol 1, Pt 1*. Princeton *et al.*: Princeton University Press, 1969.

Knight, David. *The Age of Science: The Scientific World-View in the Nineteenth Century*. New York, NY: Blackwell, 1986.

Lal, Deepak. *In Defense of Empires*. Washington, DC: American Enterprise Institute for Public Policy Research, 2002.

——. *In Praise of Empires: Globalization and Order*. New York, NY: Palgrave Macmillan, 2004.

Langer, Jessica. *Postcolonialism and Science Fiction*. Basingstoke: Palgrave Macmillan, 2012.

Langford, David. *War in 2080: the Future of Military Technology*. London: Sphere, 1979.

Lightman, Bernard (ed.). *Victorian Science in Context*. Chicago and London: University of Chicago Press, 1997.

Lombroso, Cesare. *Criminal Man*. London and Durham, NC: Duke University Press, 2006.

Mahanti, Subodh. "Fred Hoyle: The Most Versatile Physicist of the 20th Century." In: *Dream 2047* 11 (2008): 34-30.

Malmgren, Carl D. "Self and Other in SF: Alien Encounters." In: *Science Fiction Studies* 20:1 (1993): 15-33.

Matikkala, Mira. *Empire and Imperial Ambition: Liberty, Englishness and Anti-Imperialism in Late-Victorian Britain. Library of Victorian Studies. Vol. 4*. London *et al.*: I. B. Tauris, 2011.

McAleer, Neil. *Arthur C. Clarke, The Authorized Biography*. Chicago, IL: Contemporary Books, 1992.

McCarthy, Conor. *The Cambridge Introduction to Edward Said*. Cambridge *et al.*: Cambridge University Press, 2010.

McGrath, Martin. "Against Utopia: Arthur C. Clarke and the Heterotopian Impulse." In: *Vector* 267 (2011): 8-14.

McKelvey, Maureen D. *Evolutionary Innovations. The Business of Biotechnology*. Oxford *et al.*: Oxford University Press, 1996.

Morgan, Cheryl. "Women SF Writers: An Endangered Species?" In: *Vector* 269 (2012): 4-6.

Moskowitz, Sam. *Seekers of Tomorrow. Masters of Modern Science Fiction*. Westport, CT: Hyperion Press, ^{2}1974.

Nagl, Manfred. *Science Fiction. Ein Segment populärer Kultur im Medien- und Produktverband*. Tübingen: Narr, 1981.

Newsinger, John. "Rebellion and Power in the Juvenile Science Fiction of John Christopher." In: *The Science Fiction Foundation* 47 (1989): 46-54.

Nordau, Max. *Degeneration*. Lincoln and London: University of Nebraska Press, 1993.

Òkè, Moses. "Cultural Nostalgia: A Philosophical Critique of Appeals to the Past in Theories of Re-Making Africa." In: *Nordic Journal of African Studies* 15:3 (2006): 332-343.

Pabst, Eckhard. "Das Monster als genrekonstituierende Größe im Horrorfilm." In: *Enzykopädie des Phantastischen Films. Vol. 3*. Edited by Norbert Stresau and Heinrich Wimmer. Meitingen: Corian, 1986-1998. 1-18.

Pakenham, Thomas. *The Scramble for Africa: White Man's Conquest of the Dark Continent from 1876 to 1912*. London: Abacus, 1991.

Paxton, Nancy L. *Writing under the Raj*: *Gender, Race, and Rape in the British Colonial Imagination, 1830-1947*. London *et al.*: Rutgers University Press, 1999.

Pearson, Wendy Gay. "Postcolonialism/s, Gender/s, Sexuality/ies and the Legacy of *The Left Hand of Darkness*: Gwyneth Jones's Aleutians Talk Back." In: *The Yearbook of English Studies* 37:2, Science Fiction (2007): 182-196.

Pixley, Andrew. "Viewing Notes." In: *The Andromeda Anthology: A for Andromeda & The Andromeda Breakthrough. 3 DVD Box Set*. UK: 2 Entertain Video, 2006.

Priest, Christopher. "British Science Fiction." In: *Science Fiction: A Critical Guide*. Edited by Patrick Parrinder. London: Longman, 1979. 187-202.

Reid, Robin Anne. *Arthur C. Clarke: A Critical Compendium*. Westport, CT: Greenwood Press, 1997.

Rieder, John. *Colonialism and the Emergence of Science Fiction*. Middleton, CT: Wesleyan University Press, 2008.

Roberts, Adam. "On Science Fiction Music." In: *Vector* 269 (2012): 22-27.

Rubiés, Joan-Pau. "Foundation Forum: The Logic of Time Travel." In: *Foundation* 69 (1997): 80-85.

Said, Edward W. *Culture and Imperialism*. London: Vintage, 1994.

——. *Orientalism*. New York, NY: Vintage, 1979.

Samuelson, David Norman. *Arthur C. Clarke: A Primary and Secondary Bibliography*. Boston, MA: G.K. Hall, 1984.

——. *Studies in the Contemporary American and British Science Fiction Novel.* Los Angeles, CA: University Microfilms International, 1979.

Sawyer, Andy. "'A Stiff Upper Lip and a Trembling Lower One': John Wyndham on Screen." In: *British Science Fiction Cinema*. Edited by I.Q. Hunter. London and New York, NY: Routledge, 1999. 75-87.

Slemon, Stephen. "The Scramble for Postcolonialism." In: *De-Scribing Empire. Post-Colonialism and Textuality*. Edited by Chris Tiffin and Alan Lawson. London: Routledge, 1994. 15-32.

Smith, Eric D. *Globalization, Utopia and Postcolonial Science Fiction: New Maps of Hope*. Basingstoke: Palgrave Macmillan, 2012.

Spinrad, Norman (ed.). *The New Tomorrows*. New York, NY: Belmont, 1971.

Stableford, Brian. *Scientific Romance in Britain 1890-1950*. New York, NY: St Martin's Press, 1985.

——. *The Dictionary of Science Fiction Places*. New York, NY: Wonderland, 1999.

Stephensen-Payne, Phil. *Brian Wilson Aldiss, a Man for All Seasons: A Working Bibliography. Galactic Central Bibliographies for the Avid Reader. Vol. 26*. San Bernardino, CA: Borgo Press, 1992.

Stockwell, Peter. *The Poetics of Science Fiction*. London *et al.*: Pearson, 2000.

Stott, Rebecca. "Through a Glass Darkly: Aquarium Colonies and Nineteenth-Century Narratives of Marine Monstrosity." In: *Gothic Studies* 2/3 (2000): 305-327.

Suvin, Darko. *Metamorphoses of Science Fiction. On the Poetics and History of a Literary Genre*. London and New Haven, CT: Yale University Press, 1979.

Sykes, Tom. "Ideascape: How the British New Wave of Science Fiction Addressed the Social, Political, and Intellectual Themes of the 1960s and 1970s." In: *Foundation* 39:110 (2010): 73-79.

Thrall, James H. "Postcolonial Science Fiction? Science, Religion and the Transformation of Genre in Amitav Ghosh's *The Calcutta Chromosome*." In: *Literature & Theology: An International Journal of Religion, Theory, and Culture* 23.3 (2009): 289-302.

Todorov, Tzvetan. *The Conquest of America. The Question of the Other*. Translated by Richard Howard. New York, NY: Harper & Row, 1984.

Trompf, Garry W. *The Idea of Historical Recurrence in Western Thought: From Antiquity to the Reformation*. Los Angeles, CA, *et al.*: University of California Press, 1979.

Valdez Moses, Michael, Lucy Valerie Graham, John Marx *et al.* "*District 9*: A Roundtable." In: *Safundi: The Journal of South African and American Studies* 11:1-2 (2010): 155-175.

Venn, Couze. *Occidentalism: Modernity and Subjectivity*. London *et al.*: SAGE Publications, 2000.

Vint, Sherryl. "Double Identity: Interpellation in Gwyneth Jones's Aleutian Trilogy." In: *Science Fiction Studies* 28:3 (2001): 399-425.

———. "Why Have There Been No Great Women Scientists? Gender and Genetics in Gwyneth Jones's Life." In: *New York Review of Science Fiction* 22:2 (2009): 1, 8-13.

Walsh, Claire. "From 'Capping' to Intercision: Metaphors/Metonyms of Mind Control in the Young Adult Fiction of John Christopher and Philip Pullman." In: *Language and Literature* 12 (2003): 233-251.

Internet Sources

http://public.wsu.edu/~brians/world_civ/worldcivreader/world_civ_reader_2/kipling.html (2012-05-10).

http://www.guardian.co.uk/books/audio/2012/jan/06/books-podcast-science-fiction-now-tomorrow (2012-06-27).

http://www.yume.co.uk/british-science-fiction-cinema (2012-06-27).

http://www.sf-foundation.org/publications/essays/reid.html (2012-04-06).

http://www.edwardsaid.org/?q=node/1 (2012-03-11).

http://www.britannica.com (2012-03-25).

http://www.poemhunter.com/poem/last-man-the/ (2012-05-11).

http://classiclit.about.com/ library/bl-etexts/eapoe/bl-eapoe-conversation.htm (2012-05-11).

http://www.online-literature.com/wellshg/17/ (2012-05-11).

http://www.victorianweb.org/authors/carlyle/signs/signs1.html (2012-03-31).

http://www.independent.co.uk/news/blair-issues-apology-for-irish-potato-famine-1253790.html (2012-04-05).

http://news.bbc.co.uk/2/hi/uk_news/6492291.stm (2012-04-05).

http://www.telegraph.co.uk/news/politics/david-cameron/8430899/David-Cameron-Britain-caused-many-of-the-worlds-problems.html (2012-04-05).

http://www.guardian.co.uk/books/2011/oct/19/end-myths-britains-imperial-past (2012-04-05).

http://www.postcolonialweb.org/poldiscourse/bibl.html (2012-07-05).

http://www.independent.co.uk/news/world/africa/mau-mau-torture-files-were-guilty-secret-2281456.html (2011-06-07).

http://www.stephen-baxter.com/articles.html#nazis (2011-10-05).

http://www.stephen-baxter.com/articles.html#xeelee (2011-11-21).

http://www.stephen-baxter.com/author.html (2011-10-05).

http://www.plosmedicine.org/article/info:doi/10.1371/journal.pmed.0020097 (2011-10-09).

http://www.cienciayreligion.org/articulos/pdfs/how_science_discovered_god.pdf (2011-10-31).

http://www.telegraph.co.uk/news/worldnews/africaandindianocean/uganda/7139493/Ugandans-sue-Britain-over-colonial-era-crimes.html (2011-06-07).

http://www.bbc.co.uk/history/british/victorians/indian_rebellion_01.shtml (2011-06-07).

http://www.undergroundkent.co.uk/maunsell_towers.htm (2012-05-09).

http://bartleby.com (2010-05-10).

http://www.constellation-guide.com/constellation-list/carina-constellation/ (2012-05-23).

http://www.britannica.com/EBchecked/topic/24105/Andromeda-Galaxy (2011-12-28).

http://planetary.org/explore/topics/search_for_life/seti/alien_signal.html (2011-12-28).

http://www.britannica.com/EBchecked/topic/564427/steady-state-theory (2012-05-28).

https://faculty.washington.edu/ellingsn/MntgCnbl.pdf (2011-03-27).

http://stars.astro.illinois.edu/sow/procyon.html (2011-03-13).

http://www.britannica.com/EBchecked/topic/416988/noble-savage (2011-03-22).

http://spectrum.library.concordia.ca/1011/ (2012-06-17).

http://nineplanets.org/jupiter.html (2012-06-17).

http://www.britannica.com/EBchecked/topic/400227/Mycenae (2011-08-26).

http://www.britannica.com/EBchecked/topic/551569/socialism (2011-08-26).

http://www.nuforc.org/ (2011-09-03).

http://www.merriam-webster.com/dictionary/deculturation (2011-09-06).

http://www.seti.org/page.aspx?pid=584 (2011-09-20).

The Oxford English Dictionary. 2nd ed. 1989. *OED Online*. Oxford University Press. 4 Apr. 2000, http://dictionary.oed.com/cgi (2010/05/01).